College at 13:

Young, Gifted, and Purposeful

by Razel Solow, Ph.D.
and
Celeste Rhodes, Ph.D.

Great Potential Press ™

College at 13: Young, Gifted, and Purposeful

Edited by: Jennifer Ault
Interior design: The Printed Page
Cover design: Hutchison-Frey

Published by Great Potential Press, Inc.
7025 E. 1ˢᵗ Avenue, Suite 5
Scottsdale, AZ 85251

Printed and bound in the United States of America using partially recycled paper.

Great Potential Press and associated logos are trademarks and/or registered trademarks of Great Potential Press, Inc.

16 15 14 13 12   5 4 3 2 1

At the time of this book's publication, all facts and figures cited are the most current available. All telephone numbers, addresses, and website URLs are accurate and active; all publications, organizations, websites, and other resources exist as described in this book; and all have been verified as of the time this book went to press. The author(s) and Great Potential Press make no warranty or guarantee concerning the information and materials given out by organizations or content found at websites, and we are not responsible for any changes that occur after this book's publication. If you find an error or believe that a resource listed here is not as described, please contact Great Potential Press.

Library of Congress Cataloging-in-Publication Data
Solow, Razel, 1954-
  College at 13 : young, gifted, and purposeful / by Razel Solow, Ph.D., and Celeste Rhodes, Ph.D.
    pages cm
  ISBN 978-0-910707-10-7
  1. Gifted girls--Virginia--Staunton--Case studies. 2. Program for the Exceptionally Gifted (Mary Baldwin College)--Case studies. I. Rhodes, Celeste, 1944-2008. II. Title. III. Title: College at thirteen.
  LC3995.S83S65 2012
  371.95082--dc23
                    2012003487

Advance Praise

This is a book about inspiration. I ... *lives of 14 women who were given (and accepted) an opportunity to develop not only their talents, but their lives based on their readiness. The book also gives a "face" to the robust research on acceleration and the extensive benefits of acceleration for students who are ready and motivated. I was on an evaluation team that visited the PEG program in its early years. I met many of the young girls in the program and saw first-hand the enthusiasm of being freed from an educational system that could not keep pace with their minds and hearts. I also met Celeste Rhodes. This book is a fitting tribute to her vision and caring about all the young women in her care. College at age 13 is clearly not for the majority of teen girls and boys, but for those who are ready, it is not so much a radical acceleration as a radical fit.*

~ Nicholas Colangelo, Ph.D., Myron and Jacqueline Blank Professor of Gifted Education and Director of the Belin-Blank Center, co-author of *A Nation Deceived: How Schools Hold Back America's Brightest Students*

Razel Solow and Celeste Rhodes spent nearly a decade studying 14 remarkable young women to provide readers with three-dimensional understanding of what it's like to grow through adolescence with a hunger for academic challenge and for peers who can join them in exploring complex issues—and in giggling and eating pizza. Educators, parents, and young people are the beneficiaries of the narratives and insights gathered in this book.

~ Carol Ann Tomlinson, Ed.D., William Clay Parrish, Jr., Professor, University of Virginia

This compelling and beautifully written book provides insight into the power of an early college experience in contributing to the talent development of an amazing group of young women. Their success as young adults supports the choice they made to enter college early, but this book also probes the factors and experiences before college that made this the right choice for them. What we learn about the roles their personalities, motivation, values, maturity, school experiences, and family support, as well as the nurturing environment provided by PEG, all played in making this experience successful and will help readers evaluate whether early college entrance is the right choice for the gifted students in their lives.

~Linda Brody, Ed.D., Director, Study of Exceptional Talent, Center for Talented Youth, Johns Hopkins University

Dedication

*To Celeste Rhodes, Ph.D., wife, mother, grandmother,
professor, dancer, gifted woman, friend, and colleague.
And to the 14 women who shared information about their lives
with us to make this study of gifted young women possible.*

Table of Contents

Part V. Case Studies of Five PEG Women   153

Acknowledgments

In January 2004, my good friend Dr. Celeste Rhodes asked me to take over her research study on gifted girls, as her cancer recurrence was seriously affecting her stamina. I worked with Celeste through her brave battle until her death in May 2008. Her selfless, loving, and intelligent spirit buoyed me throughout this project. I owe my greatest thanks to her, and I miss her very much.

Celeste's family was incredibly kind and helpful. Carl Larsen, Celeste's husband, welcomed me to their home for working weekends. Adam Stein and Marcy McDougall Stein, Celeste's son and daughter-in-law, supported all of my efforts. Marcy had worked with Celeste professionally and thus was able to fill in a number of knowledge gaps.

Although Emma Branch started as Celeste's graduate assistant, she stayed on and became my research assistant. She played a vital role in the organization and analysis of our survey data, compiling records, maintaining contact with the study participants, presenting early results at national conferences, and providing key information. A quintessential professional, she did every task efficiently and with good humor.

The 14 young women who started this research study with Celeste graciously finished it with me. I thank Julia, Rachel, Georgia, Darcy, Ruby, Nikita, Kristen, May, and Liz (all pseudonyms) for their generosity in sharing their rich ideas and memorable words about their purposeful lives. Special thanks go to the five women who invited me to look at and listen more deeply to their lives: Madison,

Lucy, Jessica, Claire, and Nina. I also thank parents and mentors who answered questionnaires, providing additional insights.

Lydia Petersson, Director of Sponsored Programs and Undergraduate Research at Mary Baldwin College, gave me invaluable guidance and feedback. She was my indefatigable link to the college. The staff at the Program for the Exceptionally Gifted (PEG) was also very helpful. Thank you to past directors Christine Garrison, Judith Shuey, and Elizabeth O'Connell and present director Stephanie Ferguson for their cooperation. I thank Dr. Pamela Fox, President of Mary Baldwin College, for making this study possible through her leadership.

The Malone Family Foundation provided a grant for Celeste's initial research and then gave me an additional grant to write this book. I thank them for their patience and assistance over the many years of this endeavor. Cathie Wlaschin, Director of the Malone Family Foundation, encouraged me throughout this extended process and always expressed faith in its completion.

President Jennifer Raab, Provost Vita Rabinowitz, and Special Assistant to the President Nicole Vartanian have my gratitude for supporting the final writing and editing of this book when I became Director of the Center for Gifted Studies and Education at Hunter College (CUNY) in New York City.

I thank Janet Gore and James Webb, my Great Potential Press publishers and editors. They mentored me and were extremely thoughtful as my life changed considerably during the course of the writing. Their wise feedback helped shape the book. I also thank Jen Ault for her patient and careful editing.

Thank you to my dear friends Penny Wolfson and Erin Halleran for their feedback and friendship. My mother Bayla Solow, my sister Debbie Ginsberg, and my brothers Barry, Harold, and Pinchas Solow and their families cheered me on through this project, for which I am most grateful. Dr. Carolyn Callahan and Dr. Carol Tomlinson at the University of Virginia, where both Celeste and I earned our Ph.D.s in Educational Psychology (Gifted), were responsible for our engagement and excitement in our study of gifted children and gifted education.

To my husband Joel Trugman and to my two children Noah and Dena Trugman, thank you for your unwavering support and great sense of humor as I locked myself away for hours at a time to work. Of course you mean the world to me.

~ Dr. Razel Solow

On behalf of Celeste, I thank her family: Carl Larsen, Marcy, Adam, Thomas, Joseph, and Julia Stein, Jason and Jake Stein and Nancy Engebretson, David Stein, Shana Larsen and her son Matthew Dougherty, for their love, devotion, and encouragement. Celeste greatly cherished her sister Naomi Rhodes and her brother and sister-in-law Samuel Rhodes and Hiroko Yajima Rhodes, as well as their daughters Harumi and Amy (and her husband Dan Froehlich). They all inspired and sustained her. Sadly, there is no way that I can reproduce the profound feelings that Celeste would have expressed.

Although I do not know all of the names of Celeste's wonderful, caring colleagues at Mary Baldwin College (and especially at PEG), I know that she would have wanted to thank each of them for their many personal and professional kindnesses in her career. President Cynthia Tyson deserves the greatest credit for establishing PEG at Mary Baldwin. Because of PEG, more than 500 girls have found a "safe harbor" for their intellectual dreams, and without it, this research study could not have been conducted.

I know Celeste would want to join me in thanking the Malone Family Foundation, especially Tracy Lord and Director Cathie Wlaschin, for their belief in her ability to discover important aspects of gifted girls' healthy development and its relationship to purpose.

The deep connection that Celeste felt toward the graduates during her 16-year tenure as Assistant Director, Director, and Executive Director of PEG was apparent in every conversation we had about her experience at Mary Baldwin. Of course, she was most grateful to the women whose lives fill this book. She immensely respected and cared for each one.

~ Dr. Razel Solow on behalf of Dr. Celeste Rhodes

Foreword by Rita Dove

Imagine you are 14 years old all over again. You're a girl, and you've been raised to believe that you can become anything you desire as long as you study diligently and apply yourself. You're curious and enthusiastic about all that life has to offer; you want to learn more, do more, be more—to fly to the moon and discover a cure for cancer, all in an afternoon. Yet when you turn on the television, you see intellectuals portrayed as awkward, socially inept nerds. When you page through a magazine or walk through a shopping mall, the vacant gaze of the fashion model seems to whisper, "Just shut up and look beautiful, and doors will open."

Even at school, it's hard to reconcile your dreams with the peer pressures all around you. Other kids accuse you of ruining the curve, so you downplay every A you get so as not to appear arrogant; you might even get a B every now and then, trying to fit in. And if you belong to a minority, you have the extra stress of the exhortation to be "a credit to your race" (or to your family or your ancestors) while classmates demand that you show how "cool" you are.

And now high school awaits, where the main topics of conversation are boys and cheerleading, clothes and cars. What can you do? Dumb down? Get a purple Mohawk? Pierce your nose or navel? Transfer to a boarding school and hope it'll be different there? Or just keep on applying yourself and hope you fit in somehow, somewhere?

Those were the options I had when I was growing up, and none of them seemed attractive. I stuck it out in the public school system, found refuge in high school AP classes, and thwarted the kids who called me *Brainiac* by joining the majorette squad. I came out okay, but I remember always feeling a little out of place, vaguely ashamed without knowing why. Back then, there was nothing like the Program for the Exceptionally Gifted, which allows girls to attend college early anywhere in the nation.

In early 1997, my husband and I were surprised when a letter came in the mail, addressed to our daughter, inviting her for an interview at Mary Baldwin College. This college, with its all-female student body, was only 50 miles from us in the Shenandoah Valley, on the other side of the Blue Ridge Mountains. I knew it was a small liberal arts college in Staunton, Virginia, but I couldn't imagine what this had to do with my daughter. She was in eighth grade, doing just fine, thank you. I tossed the envelope onto the pile of bulk mail.

Yes, I confess: I opened my daughter's mail—by accident (really!); I had seen the return address, assumed it was for me (I teach at the University of Virginia), and slit it open along with the others. Then I looked down at the envelope, suddenly feeling guilty, saw it was addressed to Aviva, and only Aviva had the right to throw it away.

After reading the letter, my daughter started to smile. "This is crazy," she said. "How can anyone just skip high school?" Then a thoughtful pause. "And I want to go to my prom." But the smile never left her face, and before long she had hatched a tentative plan to go "check out the place" and treat the interview as a practice run for possibly joining the PEG program after a year of high school.

My husband and I had never thought of our daughter as "Exceptionally Gifted," although by sixth grade she had been identified as such by Johns Hopkins University's Center for Talented Youth, doing the testing in collaboration with our public school district. She didn't walk around the house solving complex mathematical equations in her head or spouting gobbets of Shakespeare, nor was she socially maladjusted, painfully shy, or uncomfortably earnest—common misperceptions of a gifted child. And even though she got all A's in middle school and never seemed bored with her classes, she had a solid core of friends and would play as hard as anyone in rollerblading, horseback riding, or in gluing on whiskers and fur for the school choir's production of *Cats*. Geeky? Not our kid. How could anyone who watched *Xena the Warrior Princess* religiously every week be considered a geek?

We saw the spark in her eyes, so we helped her fill out the papers, signed the parental release, and, when the time came, drove her over the mountain to Mary Baldwin College, where she was interviewed and spent the night in the PEG dormitory. I'll never forget the sight of her the next morning; she was literally transfigured with excitement: They had watched *Who's Afraid of Virginia Woolf* with Richard Burton and Elizabeth Taylor, played CDs by They Might Be Giants, and discussed Kant over cheese pizza. Who said Wittgenstein and Care Bears couldn't coexist?

A few months later, Aviva—our 14-year-old "baby"—became a PEG. She spent four exciting, challenging, wonderful years at Mary Baldwin College, graduated with honors at the age of 18, then moved on to graduate school. By the time her secondary school peers were entering their junior year in college, she had already earned an M.A. and was working toward her Ph.D. "The best decision I ever made," she says, reflecting on that spring day in 1997 when she abandoned her high school prom in favor of leapfrogging into her future. And that smile, that "Yes I can" expression, still brightens her face.

Who can define intelligence? Not just sparks-and-fireworks smarts, but the reasoning kind of brilliance that lasts, the supple imaginative force we recognize in people like Emily Dickinson, Thomas Edison, Albert Einstein, Susan Sontag, Madame Curie, and Margaret Mead. It is vexing to admit how elusive a quality it can be. The slew of tests aimed at measuring intelligence is a testimonial to our desperation.

The education system stands just as good a chance of letting a gifted child fall through the cracks as a delinquent one. Boredom can be a powerful catalyst for pranks and, further down the line, underachievement, even juvenile delinquency. So how can we nurture the outsized brain in its tiny package, an adolescent parcel of firing hormones and emotional quagmires, growing rapidly in size if not in emotional patience?

For more than two decades now there has been a place for these talented young women. The Program for the Exceptionally Gifted is the only formal program in the country that allows students (albeit only girls) to skip two to four years of secondary education while providing them with a social support system.

The 13- to 16-year-olds accepted into this unique setting have demonstrated, through outstanding academic records, as well as SAT scores most high school seniors would drool over, their ability to take on the high academic demands of a university curriculum. They attend regular college courses alongside traditionally aged students and participate in campus life as fully as their age and the law allow. For the first two years, they live among themselves in a special dormitory with a 24-hour staff of advisors and counselors. This way, they are challenged academically without having to suffer the social isolation so common among prodigies who advance out of their peer group.

Although these young women are called PEGs, they are nothing like the proverbial round peg in a square hole. They may be dazzling intellectually, but they are also vivacious and fun-loving young women, equally at ease with their brains and their bodies, bubbling over with a love of life and all its mysteries. When I look at them, I am reminded of a Persian proverb: *Go and wake up your luck.*

Thanks to this remarkable program, these PEGs are drilling their own holes.

~ Rita Dove
Former Poet Laureate of the United States

Preface

When my daughter was five years old, I took her to see an IMAX film about the rainforest. The narrator spoke about the endangered woods and ecosystem while beautiful jungle images of the Amazon filled the screen. Dena was smart, but I wondered how much she was really grasping. Suddenly, a tree in the film was felled, and Dena began sobbing. Within seconds, I knew that the implications of that scene had deeply pained her. My daughter had always felt things intensely, but her grieving at this scene really took me aback. As I tried to comfort her, I realized that she cared about the world to her very core.

Dena is not the only bright, sensitive child to have felt bereft at injustice or loss. You probably know children who have seen homeless people on the street and are so moved that they are determined to help them. Profound empathy is not simply a desire to help; it is a need. Such remarkable children are so strongly driven to alleviate suffering that they cannot rest until they act.

Sensitive gifted children often come to an awareness of the world's problems earlier than most of their age peers. With their advanced comprehension, intensity of feeling, and early moral reasoning, they often strive to resolve big societal problems that are far beyond their capacity to change. Parents who are attuned to their children's needs often try to help them channel that energy into something age-appropriate that will somehow make a difference, if only on a small scale—perhaps by giving canned food or warm clothing to a shelter, for instance. These acts are the first that many gifted children will take on the road to self-discovery and self-fulfillment as they learn more advanced ways to solve the problems that affect them so deeply—as they discover *purpose*.

This book explores the lives of 14 girls who were driven with this kind of altruism. These young women all skipped two to four years of high school to attend the Program for the Exceptionally Gifted (PEG), an early college entrance program at Mary Baldwin College in Staunton, Virginia. Here, we examine their experiences. Besides looking back at their lives and the influence of their parents before they entered PEG, we also describe and analyze their experiences while at college and following graduation. Readers will watch these young women grow and thrive as they gain a knowledge base and self-knowledge, as they challenge themselves and discover their strengths and weaknesses. Most rewarding, we have found through this study that as adults, these women are still focused on bettering communities locally, regionally, nationally, and globally. They are living meaningful lives of purpose and are grateful for the opportunity to have participated in the early college entrance program.

We hope that you will find this book provocative and useful and that you will find some valuable ideas for "preventive care" within these pages. Rather than waiting for obstacles to appear, parents and their children may read about daunting issues in advance and be prepared with various coping strategies so that the children may thrive. A key point for bright children to understand is that there is no one correct way to self-actualize or make a significant difference in the world. Determining one's truest values, beliefs, and passions and then acting on them are important components of healthy development.

For parents whose bright children have not been labeled *gifted* or *talented*, this book may provide you with knowledge about how to encourage your child to live with purpose. Perhaps you have a smart child who would like to make a positive impact on the world. Or you may have a highly empathetic child who truly suffers when others do. Or you simply may want to raise your child to act with kindness toward others as she matures. Reading about these remarkable young women illuminates how they maintained their commitment to volunteerism and concern for the larger society at the same time as they developed their own career paths.

Adult women who have felt a strong pull toward serving humanity may also benefit from this book. Some of the young women featured here have coped with matters that may be familiar to your own life story. Learning how these young women resolved problems, became self-aware, and kept on the path of purpose can help all readers reflect on their own direction and decisions.

Educators may be interested in the results of the qualitative research described in this book because it examines the optimal development factors in these early college entrance students. Some of the findings may sound familiar (i.e., they reinforce previous research), but we hope that following the arcs of the study participants' lives and discovering the steps they took along the way will give you additional insight into how to help gifted youth reach their full potential.

In Her Own Words: Dr. Celeste Rhodes

Dr. Celeste Rhodes battled bravely against cancer as she helped to write this book. She died in May 2008, maintaining her incredible optimism, kindness, and courage until the end. Prior to her death, she had written part of this Preface, which follows.

As a child, I had the good fortune to grow up in a family that was immersed in the arts. My mother, Martha Ephraim, was intellectually gifted and was skipped through many years in the New York City school system. She graduated from Hunter College, Phi Beta Kappa, when she was only 18. Growing up, I heard many stories about my mother's academic achievements from my grandmother, Julia Ephraim. We lived right next door to my grandparents in a suburb of New York City. I also heard from my mother about her struggles in adjusting to college peers who were at least four years older than she was. In addition to her intellectual accomplishments, my mother was a musician who taught her three children how to read music and play the piano.

My father, Bernard Rhodes, was passionate about classical music; he was a watercolorist by avocation and a businessman by vocation. My grandfather, Harry Ephraim, was a talented jeweler who painted in oils during his early retirement years and later wrote family memoirs, poems, and stories to entertain his two children, five grandchildren, and five great-grandchildren.

My older brother, Samuel Rhodes, was a young person with a profound love of music, baseball, and the New York City subway system. I witnessed the respect he received from his family and music teachers, as well as the social rejection he endured through his elementary school years. Later, at the High School of Music and Art, my brother enjoyed the company of other serious young musicians and felt accepted by a group of these peers.

My mother's and brother's experiences as highly gifted young people who endured social isolation at various points in their young lives left an indelible impression on me. Later, as an advocate for gifted young people, I realized that my passionate commitment to and deep appreciation for gifted individuals stemmed from those early experiences of my gifted mother and my talented brother.

I had a strong need as a young person to find my own creative voice. Modern dance became my way of artistic expression, beginning in mid-adolescence. I ended up completing a Bachelor of Science and Master's in Dance Education, which prepared me to teach on the college level.

In the early 1970s, my husband and I moved our family to central Pennsylvania so that I could teach dance at Lock Haven University and he could write full time while being a stay-at-home-dad for our three sons, David, 10, Adam, eight, Jason, eight, and our daughter Shana, 12.

During our 11 years in Pennsylvania, I became active for the advancement of women by being a co-founder of the Clinton County Women's Center (which continues to help women today). As chairperson of the Women as Agents of Change Committee for AAUW, I worked hard to empower women who were victims of domestic violence. In addition to chairing the board of directors for CCWC, I also worked as a volunteer in the women's center answering the hotline and providing referral services for local women.

After my three sons were identified as gifted, I became an active parent advocate for them and later for all gifted children in Pennsylvania by starting the Keystone Central Affiliate Group of the Pennsylvania Association for Gifted Education (PAGE). In the early 1980s, I rose to the position of Vice President of PAGE and was the co-chair of the PAGE committee for teacher certification in gifted education.

Although I enjoyed teaching dance to physical education majors at Lock Haven University, I soon realized that my true interest was in supporting gifted children. After receiving a brochure announcing the formation of the Program for the Exceptionally Gifted at Mary Baldwin College, I called the director and asked if she might be interested in someone with my background for the assistant director position. She encouraged me to apply, and I was eventually selected as the PEG Assistant Director, responsible for the residential component of PEG.

In the summer of 1985, my husband and I moved to Staunton, Virginia, to begin a new phase in our lives. I was excited to be a part of this innovative program for highly gifted adolescent girls. By being open to my various passions, I had found a position that brought them all together.

I am the kind of person who always wants to know why. The need to understand and then help solve problems has me on a life-long journey to support the healthy growth of gifted young women. I believe that my curiosity and my need for personal expression and meaning have guided me in finding an integrated purpose in my life. The journey began with dance, choreography, and teaching dance, moved to advocate for the advancement of women, and finally resulted in providing and directing an early college program for gifted girls.

In Her Own Words: Dr. Razel Solow

Much like Celeste, I came to the field of gifted education mostly as a sister and as a parent. I have four loving siblings, including an extremely intelligent older brother. Watching his struggles with traditional schooling and seeing how difficult it was for my parents to meet his needs affected me deeply. I also have two children who were identified as intellectually gifted in preschool. My son had a relatively even-keeled disposition as a young child (just like his father). My daughter was more intense, much as I had been growing up.

I took my first course in gifted education at the University of Virginia to learn how to be a better parent, and I continued my education so that I might serve other families of gifted children with guidance and support. I also wanted to contribute to the educational system. Getting a Ph.D. in the field of gifted education helped me become a better mother because I learned how to deal with my children's intellectual, social, and emotional needs. I also learned how to respond to them more constructively. My hope is that this book will shed some light on the intellectual, social, and emotional needs of gifted children as they grow into productive, resilient, caring adults.

Introduction

PEG: A Brief History

Mary Baldwin College (MBC) is a small liberal arts women's college in Staunton, Virginia. In the early to mid-1980s, college President Dr. Cynthia Tyson received a number of requests from young girls who wished to start college three to four years early. Mary Baldwin is a small, single-sex college; it was an ideal place for a special on-campus program that would meet these girls' need for accelerated curriculum. Dr. Tyson decided to act.

In 1984, the college received a grant from the Jessie Ball duPont Educational, Religious, and Charitable Foundation for the development and implementation of an early college residential program for gifted high school-age females, and the Program for the Exceptionally Gifted (PEG)[1] was born. It was the first—and remains the only—college that offers a full-time residential early college entrance program for gifted girls in the United States. Most girls enter PEG after eighth or ninth grade; a few enter after tenth. Typically, they graduate from college when other teenagers are graduating from high school.

The first director of the PEG program was Dr. Christine N. Garrison. The college hired Dr. Celeste Rhodes as PEG Assistant Director in 1985. Dr. Rhodes became Associate Director in 1986, Director in 1989, and Executive Director from 1998 to 2001.

In developing the program, Mary Baldwin's administration defined *exceptionally gifted* as those who are capable of skipping several high school grades. PEG admissions personnel considered IQ and other standardized test scores alone too narrow a measure of intelligence for proper assessment. Instead, they used a number of criteria to select the students who would most likely benefit from and succeed in the program.

The PEG admissions staff required candidates to answer essay questions that demonstrated the applicants' advanced thinking and writing abilities. They also looked for outstanding academic achievement in middle and/or high school records. In personal interviews, the PEG staff evaluated the applicants for social and emotional qualities that they considered essential to college success. In addition, they searched for girls with a powerful love of learning. They gave preference to candidates with internal rather than external motivation (e.g., parents who pushed their daughters to apply) because they knew that only the girls who were self-motivated would succeed.

Dr. Tyson and her team put considerable thought into the program's design. They realized that inviting 13- to 15-year-olds into a student population of 18- to 22-year olds raised issues of both academic transition and social and emotional adjustment. There were other concerns as well: How well would the young girls manage the freedom and demands of college life? What effect might homesickness have on them as they left the security of their families and entered an unknown community? What support would they need to stay and succeed at the college?

When the program began, it looked somewhat different from its present form. Whereas the charter class contained only 11 students, the program today serves more than 70 students who come from across the country and from abroad. Initially, students were required to take certain core subjects like English at a local high school. As time went on, the college concluded that this transitional program was unnecessary. Subsequently, all incoming students take a full load of freshman courses as soon as they arrive.

The admissions process also evolved. At first, administrators focused more on academic prowess and evidence of school success than on social and emotional maturity. Later, they became adept at selecting girls who were both socially and emotionally prepared to handle the enormous responsibility and independence of college life.

The PEG Study

In 2001, the Malone Family Foundation gave the program a large endowment to fund scholarships and also offered Dr. Rhodes (by then the program's director) a grant to study some of the PEG graduates to evaluate the effects of early college entrance on their growth. Had it helped or hindered the PEGs'[2] academic, social, or emotional development? Dr. Rhodes and her team were eager to determine whether these younger girls were able to compete on a level playing field with the older students. How would the graduates evaluate their experiences? Had the program been worthwhile? After working with a few PEG administrators, Dr. Rhodes created a list of 20 women whom she invited to participate in her study. Fourteen accepted the invitation.

Dr. Rhodes initiated the research by distributing a pilot study to all PEG graduates to determine some relevant questions. Next, she sent questionnaires to the 14 young women who had accepted. In addition, she read and reviewed school transcripts, early documentation of the girls' applications to the programs, and parent and mentor questionnaires. Meanwhile, another survey went out to graduates in 2002 and 2003. All of these sources of information were used to compile data on the lives of these young women.

Between 2003 and 2004, the 14 gifted women in the PEG study answered surveys and an in-depth questionnaire that focused on their childhood, adolescence, and adulthood. They wrote about the impact of PEG on their development, and they described their philosophy of life and the people who'd had a major influence on them. It should be noted that, since the last data were gathered in 2005, it is possible or even likely that some of the participants' opinions have changed.

In January 2004, Dr. Rhodes, who was battling a recurrence of cancer, asked Dr. Solow to become chief investigator and take over the study as Director of PEG Research. Dr. Solow analyzed the data, presented findings at conferences, and then received a new Malone grant to write this book. Although Dr. Rhodes's health was compromised, she continued to discuss findings with Dr. Solow. Having served as a PEG administrator for 16 years, Dr. Rhodes's assumptions and biases may have colored the research somewhat, but it also gave her unique insight into the data. She could compare the study participants to other PEG students and to traditionally aged Mary Baldwin undergraduates. Her longitudinal perspective about the women's exceptionalities gave context to their comments. Her concepts were an integral part of the ideas presented in this book.

As an independent researcher, Dr. Solow brought a more objective perspective to the PEG study. Although she lacked prolonged, real-life knowledge of the women, she developed a good picture of their lives through analysis of their application files, newspaper articles, personal essays, parent and mentor questionnaire statements, supplemental interviews, and documents, as well as through extended conversations with Dr. Rhodes. She also had personal interactive experiences with five of the women. Sadly, Dr. Rhodes did not live to see the publication of this book, but the information contained within its pages is the result of the combined efforts and balancing viewpoints of both Dr. Rhodes and Dr. Solow. Their findings and conclusions will serve to illuminate the development of purpose so apparent in the PEG study women's lives.[3]

The PEG Mission and Goals

Despite many changes since its inception, PEG continues to honor its original mission—to support the full talent development and personal growth of gifted girls. Initially a five-year high school/ college combination, PEG is now a four-year college program. It offers support, enrichment, and structure in an age-appropriate setting. Administration and staff provide full-time supervision for the first two years and extracurricular activities for all four years. Starting as freshmen, PEG students enroll in regular college courses with traditionally aged students and participate actively in campus life.[4]

Besides providing accelerated academics, PEG promotes independent living during college and after graduation. At first, administrators create leadership and communication objectives for the students. The young teenagers get better at setting and meeting their own goals by attending interpersonal sessions, presentations by academic role models, and weekly small-group meetings with resident advisors who provide feedback. Community service is a priority so that students will generously focus outward as they seriously focus inward.[5]

Mary Baldwin College is also home to the Virginia Women's Institute for Leadership (VWIL), which "is the nation's premier leadership program for young women. It is unlike any other U.S. military academy for women.... Its comprehensive program builds tomorrow's leaders in military and civilian service."[6] Although not focused on the military, PEG adopted VWIL's commitment to leadership. One of PEG's specific goals is to shape lives of purpose by preparing young women to contribute generously to society.

The Purpose of This Book

This book tells the story of 14 exceptionally gifted young women who started college early, graduated successfully, and gave back to society by sharing their talents and abilities through their work and volunteerism. These girls entered the Program for the Exceptionally Gifted between the ages of 13 and 16 because they enjoyed challenge and wanted to accelerate their learning. With staff guidance, the young women became fully participating members of the student body. As campus leaders and innovators, they increased the vibrancy of Mary Baldwin College. As young adults, they have all contributed meaningfully both to their professions and to their communities.

What motivated these PEG study women to act for the good of others? Why did they care so deeply, and how can other bright, motivated girls benefit from their experience? The stories of these women exemplify positive psychology—the study of what makes people strong, empathetic, resilient, and fulfilled.[7] Their commitment to purposes greater than themselves and their strength in overcoming obstacles provide insights about the healthy intellectual, social, and emotional growth of gifted women.

The intent of this book is to demonstrate what Drs. Rhodes and Solow learned from these exceptionally gifted young women who have dedicated themselves to creating lives of purpose. All names of individuals, institutions, organizations, and publications, with the exception of Mary Baldwin College, PEG, director Christine Garrison, Dr. Rhodes, and Dr. Solow, have been changed to protect the study participants' and others' privacy.

Part I of this book presents details about the women in the study, as well as a conceptual framework for the research findings.

Parts II, III, and IV focus primarily on the findings of the first phase of the study (years 2001-2004). Influences that helped produce the academic, professional, and personal successes of these young women may contribute new and useful perspectives to the field of gifted education, as well as to the positive psychology literature. The findings reinforce some earlier research and some speculative ideas in the gifted education field and will help parents, schools, and communities understand how to better encourage the growth of their talented and eager children and adolescents. Parents may find the information helpful when deciding whether early college entrance is a good option for their child, schools may better appreciate the importance of providing challenge to very bright students, and communities may learn to value highly talented young people.

Part V looks more closely at five of the women who agreed to participate in a follow-up study during 2005. Hours of interviews, time spent together in their environments, and searches of documents that date back to their PEG admissions applications offered

Dr. Solow a deeper understanding of the dynamics of these dedicated and complex young women's development. Their life lessons will resonate with all girls and young women who want to change the world, whether through small, local efforts or large, global ones.

Part I

Exceptionally Gifted Students and PEG

CHAPTER 1

Misconceptions about Gifted Students and Acceleration

Acceleration and Early Entrance

School acceleration, especially the form of acceleration called "grade skipping," has always been, and continues to be, a controversial issue. Some educators support this type of acceleration when a child is quite capable and eager to move ahead more quickly. Others argue against it, insisting that students will miss critical knowledge and "normal" peer friendships, depriving them of important academic and social growth. They fear that students will incur large gaps in their knowledge.

However, when school consistently fails to meet their needs, exceptionally gifted children feel enormous frustration and discouragement.[1] These children may endure more social and emotional trials than their moderately gifted classmates because their age peers frequently reject them. With intellectual interests and comprehension so far from the norm, they often struggle to find true friends who can appreciate their talents and understand their interests.

There is a risk that exceptional students who are stuck in unchallenging classrooms every year may become confused about their identity and their place in the world. Researcher Miraca Gross writes, "To protect themselves from peer rejection, highly gifted children can become masters of camouflage...concealing and shielding their developing identity behind a more acceptable facade." When a gifted child hides behind a mask, she risks creating a "false identity with which the [she] herself feels uncomfortable."[2] Because she has not fully accepted herself, her ability to achieve may be greatly impaired. Peers who don't accept gifted students' true selves, as well as the lack of academic growth that such gifted children often experience, may lead to stultified individuals who lose their sense of purpose.[3]

Radical acceleration and early college entrance offset some of the problems that young gifted and talented adolescents face in secondary school. In college, they can interact more comfortably with a true peer group based on similar abilities and interests.[4] Challenging academic opportunities add to their self-esteem as they meet high expectations.[5] In a study of the University of Washington Early Entrance Program, girls felt that peer, faculty, and staff support enabled them to "expand their sense of self."[6] They also felt greater self-confidence and more accepted for their love of learning and ideas. Researchers found that the girls' environment offered "a rare combination of acceptance and encouragement at a critical age," which researchers thought could "help to inoculate them against less-supportive work environments as they grew older."[7] This book confirms these findings.

Misconceptions about Gifted Students

False assumptions about gifted children and young adults may lead to unrealistic expectations about their achievement and personal growth. They also may result in gifted children being denied the academic challenge that they need in order to learn how to push themselves and meet challenge with courage and resilience. Many misconceptions exist about gifted children and adolescents that create stumbling blocks for those who wish to help these children attain the academic rigor they require. Here are four of them.

Misconception 1: Exceptionally gifted young adults should be superstars. They are gifted only if they produce extraordinary work at a young age.

None of the 14 PEG study women are "superstars" in their disciplines, yet all are high achievers, and most are quite successful in their fields. One is a doctor of international medicine, another is an outstanding social activist, and two are award-winning poets, among other admirable professions and avocations. To be a "superstar" in a discipline, a person must enormously exceed the normal range of performance. Psychologist Ellen Winner distinguishes between individuals who fundamentally change their fields (i.e., creators) and those who become innovative problem solvers. Winner warns that "we should never expect a prodigy to go on to become a creator. The ones who do…are the exceptions, not the rule."[8]

Expecting all highly gifted children to become extraordinary producers early in their lives also assumes that there is a unity to growth and development in all fields. Half of the PEG study graduates were arts and humanities majors, and the other half majored in math, science, and technology. Whether any of them might eventually become renowned will take varying periods of time and might not become evident until later in their lives.[9]

Misconception 2: Most gifted children who radically accelerate through school will become emotionally unstable and will miss the opportunity for normal adolescent development and fun.

Most of the women in the study accelerated radically, entering college at ages 13 to 15. Three entered college at age 16. Yet all were as emotionally stable as most college students and had time to enjoy life. They participated in clubs and activities and often held leadership roles in various campus organizations. They integrated well into campus life and gained the respect of older students.

Problems for highly gifted children often stem from being placed in classrooms without intellectual peers or appropriately differentiated instruction. Spending most of their time with children whose interests, senses of humor, and perspectives differ radically from their own may cause highly gifted students to feel alone and isolated from chronological peers. In settings where others like them understand how they think and perform at the same level, gifted children often are freer to reveal their thoughts and emotions—their real selves. The PEG study women described feeling, for the first time, "normal" and truly accepted when they entered the program. Emotionally safer, they more readily opened up to others, made friends, and participated in co-curricular activities.

The authors of *A Nation Deceived: How Schools Hold Back America's Brightest Students*[10] provide evidence that many highly capable students should be allowed to test out of grade-level curriculum and move on to more demanding material. These bright students need to be able to progress continually in their learning rather than spend their class time waiting for other students to catch up to them. This report concludes that, when managed correctly, acceleration does not lead to irreparable learning gaps or social and psychological troubles.

As for fun and a social life, everyone defines *fun* differently. *In Lives of Promise: What Becomes of High School Valedictorians*, educational researcher Karen Arnold describes Matthew, one of the more intellectual of the Illinois valedictorians interviewed for her 14-year study. When Matthew was asked whether he had spent enough time having fun in college, he asked what that meant. "To me, it's fun to read; it's fun to learn," he said.[11] Similarly, most of the PEG study women said that getting the chance to learn to their hearts' content far outweighed any "fun" that they might have missed at high school proms or football games. Like Matthew, who also played college football, they made time for fun in areas that most interested them.

The prediction that children who go to college early will necessarily become social misfits assumes that they will experience a much older, alien environment. The girls in the PEG program were in a protected and nurturing environment. Because there was a cohort of same-aged teenagers, these young freshmen were not isolated. Instead, they lived with 40 to 50 other female PEG students in a special residence hall for two years, where they received social and emotional guidance from counselors and mentors who had been trained to work with young gifted females. Among the young women who were both their intellectual and their age peers, the

PEGs socialized well. Many formed lifelong friendships and stayed in touch with friends from around the world. They also made friends with traditionally aged students.

Misconception 3: Gifted children who enter college at a young age likely will be unsuccessful in their adult work and relationships.

People who believe this misconception greatly underestimate the maturity and competence of gifted young adults. By enrolling in college as teenagers, many of the PEG women entered graduate or professional school as young as 17 or 18 years of age. They negotiated relationships with older graduate students. Some even taught older undergraduates, who didn't realize the young age of their graduate teaching assistants.

PEGs also effectively made their way in the work world. At 18, May Crane entered the highly competitive art dealership world and assumed huge responsibility from the outset. Nikita Escher, a software engineer at age 20, became the team leader of a major project at her world-renowned company, successfully directing the work of men much older than she was—mostly in their forties and fifties. Relatively quickly, these women became comfortable in their business and leadership roles.

Misconception 4: Exceptionally gifted girls face no real barriers in their schooling or careers.

In the past, researchers determined that gifted girls faced numerous social and emotional barriers to understanding and using their remarkable potential. Gifted girls often had difficulty relating to their peers when they did not share the same interests and priorities. The perceived conflict between being intellectual and being popular led some girls to hide their abilities to gain popularity. When mixed with encouragement for achievement, traditional messages about femininity, dating, and popularity confused some gifted girls and eroded their self-confidence. Lack of guidance and support, fear of failure, and even fear of success made some girls avoid challenging academic areas. They sometimes signed up for algebra and geometry, but not for the more difficult physics and calculus classes.[12]

Some of these issues persist. Most schools in the U.S. today do not challenge highly gifted girls adequately, and when their academic needs are unmet, these students suffer from frustration and boredom.[13] Culturally diverse girls are still under-represented in gifted programs nationwide, which leads to widespread underachievement.[14]

In recent years, there have been signs of positive change. One study found that girls in gifted programs were participating actively and doing their best in school. Only a small percentage worried about popularity when expressing their opinions.[15] Bright young women now outnumber men in most professional schools, except for engineering, computer science, and the physical sciences (e.g., physics, astronomy, chemistry).[16]

Women are getting ahead in education, but there are other problems. Too often, gifted girls who eventually want to have a family may think they can do everything at once but fail to plan realistically for the successful balance of work and personal life.[17] Today, women are leaving their professions far earlier and more often than men, while others shift away from demanding professions despite having advanced degrees.[18] Women in business still face major career obstacles as they get lost in the "labyrinth of leadership."[19] Gifted girls do not have it easy.

Misconceptions like the ones outlined here can seriously impede the academic, intellectual, and social progress that gifted girls can make in programs like PEG, which in turn hinders their ability to succeed in graduate studies, the world of work, and in their personal lives. When students are given appropriate levels of challenge in an environment that includes others like them, the benefits can be enormous, both to themselves and to society as well. It is only by providing our intellectually advanced students with an equally advanced curriculum (which in some cases may mean skipping an entire grade—or even skipping high school altogether) that we allow them to stretch their minds and develop their talents to their fullest.

Social Responsibilities of the Gifted

In a book about purpose, we must ask: What are the societal responsibilities, if any, of intellectually gifted people? In the early 1990s, Israeli educator Raphi Amran lamented the lack of discussion about gifted students' civic responsibilities: "I say this not just because society needs their talents but also because gifted children, like all children, need to hear such expectations for their own character development."[20]

Psychologist Ellen Winner argues for an economic quid pro quo. She believes that resources given to gifted children should be repaid by serving society. "If our schools are to provide specialized education for the most able, then the most able must also learn to give back to the society that grants them extra resources."[21] Although Winner approves of gifted children developing their talents for their own psychological health and productivity, she also wants them to use their talents for community service.

Yet why should gifted children have to "pay back" society any more than other children for having received an appropriate education? Talented children do not owe their service to society solely because the school system has met their academic needs. They should contribute to society, like all children, because they are caring human beings who are citizens in a community. If the economic model is used solely with gifted children, when will their obligation to society end, and what modes of service are acceptable?

If educators explore "giving back to society" with gifted children in a moral context, they may better succeed in creating the desire for service. Exploring one's moral obligation to society could be incorporated into a continuing conversation about social responsibility in gifted programs at all grade levels. The object would be to encourage students to consider how they could help build a stronger society; it would not be to induce guilt or create undue pressure. Gifted children in this kind of environment might reflect more seriously about ways to develop character based largely on a profound sense of responsibility to others.[22]

Many of the women in the PEG study demonstrated a sense of justice far earlier than their childhood peers. Like many gifted children, they were idealistic. None of the PEG graduates in the study had an elementary or secondary school-based moral education that focused on giving back to society. Instead, almost all of the study women had adopted their values of service from their parents and other key adults. In addition, their college—Mary Baldwin—encouraged their search for purpose by promoting women as leaders.

Search for Meaning and Purpose

Viktor Frankl, the Austrian psychiatrist credited as one of the forerunners of positive psychology, wrote *Man's Search for Meaning* in 1946, following his years in two different Nazi concentration camps. Frankl believed that at the core of a person's being is a need to find meaning and that a person can live meaningfully in the most horrific, depraved circumstances—even in a concentration camp. He believed that men and women feel happiness as a by-product of finding meaning in life. "Happiness cannot be pursued; it must ensue," he said.[23] Acting humanely toward others makes their lives meaningful.

All of the young women in the PEG study expressed a long-lasting and widespread intent to "accomplish something that is at once meaningful to the self and of consequence to the world beyond the self."[24] These women were clearly living with purpose that was outer-directed with actions intended to promote the betterment of society. Their profound desire to act with kindness, decency, and respect, to make a positive mark on the world, and to help effect change gave their lives meaning. Although the women sometimes changed their purposes and the ways in which they contributed to their communities, they always maintained their desire to serve.[25]

Many of the study women could not remember having a specific life purpose when they entered PEG in early to mid-adolescence. As the PEGs grew older, finished college, and started working in their professions, however, they developed clearer goals and direction. They were typical of most college students who "may take years of experience and reflection"[26] to identify a life purpose.

The PEG study alumnae energetically pursued their goals. By choosing difficult tasks, they increased their self-knowledge, understanding, and growth and achieved at even higher levels. Those successes helped them to further their reach and feel more confident of their abilities. As young people develop, their "purposes need not be highly specific, nor must commitment be absolute."[27] Students need only enough clarity about their direction to plan their next destination, even if they cannot map out their entire journey. Although the PEG study women could speak about their immediate purposes and long-standing values, they did not always know exactly where they were heading. Instead, they relied on their sense of rightness to determine which actions would best suit their life purposes.

Some critics say that gifted education, particularly if it involves major acceleration, turns students into elitist adults. The PEG research demonstrates the opposite. The young alumnae in the study were grateful for academic challenge and personal guidance. They energetically developed their abilities and, as young adults, dedicated their efforts to a world of need.

CHAPTER 2

Fourteen PEG Women:
Then and Now

In a book about women who have lived lives of purpose and whose stories others can learn from, it is essential that the reader get to know the individual women who participated in the PEG study. This chapter is an introduction to these remarkable women.

To select participants for the PEG study, Dr. Rhodes and two other PEG administrators teamed up to find alumnae who had demonstrated a sense of purpose as young girls while at Mary Baldwin College. Selection criteria included undergraduate academic success and leadership potential or accomplishment.[1] The research questions included: *What has become of these women of promise? If they have built a sense of purpose and are committed to serving others, then what contributed to that development? If they have not, then what stopped them?*

The committee selected 20 PEG graduates to participate in the study; 14 accepted. These women had each excelled as young college students. As Table 1 indicates, all of the study participants graduated cum laude, magna cum laude, or summa cum laude, with most earning additional awards for their outstanding scholarship and leadership as undergraduates.

Although these women entered college as young teenagers, they participated fully in college life. Remarkable in both spirit and accomplishment, all 14 young women achieved at high levels academically, participated in extracurricular activities enthusiastically, and nurtured one other socially and emotionally. The caring community at Mary Baldwin helped them gain psychological strength to prepare for the outside world. Each of these girls developed an orientation toward service and social responsibility while leading a meaningful life in college.

At the time of the study, the women were in their twenties and thirties and had been out of college from seven to 14 years. Their careers were in law, medicine, academics, journalism, business, art, education, government consultation, engineering, and the military. Their civic involvements included social justice, literacy, urban culture, rural poverty, mentoring, community building, legal advocacy, and global health. Some of their personal priorities, such as maintaining romantic relationships, staying close to family and friends, keeping fit, and saving time for fun, claimed much of their limited time, yet these women still maintained their allegiance to the welfare of others.

What can we learn from these women? How did their early college experience affect who they became? What influence did their families have on them? What lessons did they learn from each other and from their mentors? What values did they cherish? By tracing the PEG women's perspectives, behaviors, and choices, perhaps we can help others create rewarding, purposeful lives.

Table 1: Study Alumnae Information

Pseudonym (Ethnicity)	Current Job/Future Plans	Undergraduate Majors	Graduate Degrees	Age upon Entering PEG[‡]	Graduation Date
Claire Hagan (Caucasian)	Biology professor	B.A., Biology[†] (M)	Ph.D., Biology	14	1990
Darcy Maddox (Caucasian)	Military intelligence analyst	B.A., History,[†] International Relations[†] (C)	M.S., Strategic Intelligence	13	1997
Georgia Sullivan (Caucasian)	Senior analyst/environmental disaster	B.A., Mathematics[†] (C)	M.S., Accounting	13	1992
Jessica Holmes (African American)	Former economics journalist; teaching college; plans to attend international business school	B.A., Economics (C)	M.A., Economics; working on Ph.D.	13	1995
Julia Hix (Caucasian)	Secondary school biology teacher	B.A., Biology (C)	M.S., Medical Genetics	14	1989
Kristen Edwards (Caucasian)	Associate at a consulting firm	B.A., History[†] (M)	M.A., International Economics and International Relations	16	1997
Liz Bennett (Caucasian)	Criminal defense lawyer	B.A., Political Science,[†] History[†] (S)	J.D., Law	14	1998
Lucy Jacobs (Caucasian)	Published poet	B.A., English[†] (M)	M.A., English Literature, M.F.A., Poetry; working on doctorate in English and Education	15	1989
Madison Kennedy (Caucasian)	International medicine, medical resident	B.S., Biology (C)	Working on M.D.	16	1999
May Crane (Asian)	Art dealer	B.A., Art History/ Art Management (C)	M.A., Liberal Studies	14	1993
Nikita Escher (Caucasian)	Software engineer	B.S., Mathematics (C)	M.S.E., Software Engineering	14	1999
Nina Carpenter (Caucasian)	Woodworking shop owner, art center director	B.A., Art[†] (M)	Considering applying for a Master's in the peace and justice field	15	1995
Rachel Sinclair (African American)	Information systems; plans to attend graduate school	B.S., Biology (C)	Applying for a Master's in Organizational Psychology	16	1999
Ruby Kelp (Caucasian)	Published, award-winning poet; family business	B.A., Political Science[†] (C)	M.F.A., Poetry	14	1991

[†] Graduated with distinction in major: C=cum laude, M=magna cum laude, S=summa cum laude

[‡] Four of the girls—Claire, Darcy, Georgia, and Madison—had birthdays within a few days of the start date of the program. Readers should keep in mind that these girls were making decisions about early college entrance at an even younger age than that listed in the table.

The PEG Women

Dr. Celeste Rhodes was a director of PEG for 16 years. Here, she has provided brief reminiscences that capture the special spirit of each teenager when she was in PEG. Dr. Rhodes's descriptions (in italics) include impressions of the girls' personalities from their early college days and a few facts about their lives at the time of the study. Short biographies of these women, which follow Dr. Rhodes's remembrances, reflect their lives as of the last collection of data. The girls' extreme youth makes the honors listed in these brief biographies all the more notable. Subsequent chapters further illuminate each woman's complexity and exceptionality.

Claire Hagan

Claire was a highly sensitive girl who hated to think ill of anyone, especially those whom she most cherished. She had a delicate, sweet face with an equally pleasant disposition. Although loved deeply by her family, Claire kept her personal struggles private. A gentle soul who was kind and loving to all of her friends, she worked very hard to develop her musical and sports talent. First violinist in the Mozart Ensemble, she was also on the college varsity volleyball team, where she received the college's scholar-athlete award for two consecutive years. For her academic and leadership achievements, Claire was inducted into the honor societies Phi Beta Kappa and Omicron Delta Kappa.

Claire entered PEG at age 14 and was 31 years old at the time of the study. Her parents divorced after she graduated from MBC. Although she suffered from an autoimmune disorder, at the time of the study, she was happily married and wanted to have children. She was a biology professor at a small liberal arts college, where she focused on the quality of her teaching and also cared deeply about building community on campus.

Darcy Maddox

A powerhouse of energy and personality, Darcy stood about five feet tall and was muscular. She had a wonderful sense of humor, which she shared daily at her campus job. A natural leader, Darcy was not afraid to assume challenges. She always had a positive perspective and would not let others affect her disposition. As president of the Mary Baldwin College Honor Scholar's Society, she received the MBC President's Award for leadership during her junior year. As a senior, she was inducted into Phi Beta Kappa and received double distinction in her history and international relations majors.

Darcy was 24 at the time of the study, having entered PEG at the age of 13. After graduating from PEG, she entered the military. Because she was too young to enroll in officer training, she became an enlisted soldier, rising in rank at every opportunity. She served with the military for seven years. At the time of the study, Darcy had just ended her engagement with her fiancé and was considering new directions for her career.

Georgia Sullivan

A remarkably tall and slender freshman at age 13, Georgia looked and acted much older. She was a warm and concerned friend to both PEG and traditionally aged Mary Baldwin students. Arriving at PEG with an unusual sense of her potential, Georgia displayed amazing self-confidence for her young age. She balanced those strengths with sensitivity to others, which made her an exceptional student leader. As a sophomore, she received the PEG Merit and Leadership Award, given to the most outstanding student in her class. She undertook her academic program with focused energy and sought to develop her logical thinking skills by majoring in math. She earned "Distinction in Mathematics" at MBC because of a superlative senior thesis.

Georgia entered PEG at age 13 and was 28 at the time of the study. She graduated as a math major and earned her M.S. in accounting at a large state university. She then went on to work as an environmental consultant for 11 years. As a senior analyst, she helped to reduce the impact of natural and technological disasters through program management for the federal government. Although she was considering entering a Ph.D. program, Georgia decided to seek career counseling before pursuing her doctorate.

Jessica Holmes

Jessica's quiet personality balanced her obvious gifts of vitality, intelligence, athleticism, and beauty. As an economics and mathematics major, she was a teaching assistant and math tutor. Jessica received the scholar-athlete award as a member of the lacrosse team and was a member of the House President's Council. A Phi Beta Kappa inductee, she was also an active African American member of the campus organization Minority Women in Unity. Elected to the MBC Judicial Board, she made disciplinary decisions concerning all students. The PEG Merit and Leadership Award and membership in Omicron Delta Kappa honored her numerous contributions on campus. For her Master's at an extremely prestigious university, Jessica was named a special scholar—a rare honor—and received a scholarship.

Jessica, who entered PEG when she was 13, was 26 when she was interviewed for the study and was in her first year of a doctoral program at a highly competitive international business school abroad. An economics major at PEG, she received her M.A. in economics from a renowned graduate school. Between her Master's and Ph.D. programs, she reported for a prestigious business magazine and then taught college economics for a year. At the time of the study, Jessica was in a romantic relationship with a fellow graduate student.

Julia Hix

Julia's small physical presence gave no clue to the large size of her heart. Sensitive and reserved, she maintained a balanced perspective on her goals and interests. Others' expectations did not sway her because she was motivated by her own beliefs. Although she struggled in some social situations initially, she soon developed good interpersonal skills. As a Junior Olympian and as a church altar person, Julia shared her passions with people. She also sewed numerous costumes for the MBC theatre. A member of Beta Beta Beta, the Biology Honor Society, she received the Charter Fellowship Award for Leadership and was inducted into Omicron Delta Kappa. Every top medical genetics graduate program to which she applied accepted Julia and offered her full scholarships.

Julia entered PEG at 14. Age 28 at the time of the study, she taught seventh-grade science and general and AP biology at a private day school. She earned an M.S. in medical genetics and worked for several years as a research specialist in pediatric cardiology at a major medical institution. She also taught biology part-time and coached college fencing. Julia co-authored a dozen research papers in biology, taught young children swimming at the YMCA, and fenced nationally.

Kristen Edwards

A warm, personable, and resourceful young woman, Kristen arrived at PEG wanting to use her time meaningfully. She became good friends with all types of students. Vice president of the MBC Scholar and Omicron Delta Kappa honor societies, Kristen received the Emerging Leader Award. An MBC varsity swimmer, she was elected team captain and given the college's scholar-athlete award. Kristen volunteered locally with emotionally handicapped children and was an

MBC tutor, a docent at the Woodrow Wilson Museum, and a member of the college literary magazine's editorial board. She reached the finals in the grueling competition for the Rhodes scholarship.

Kristen entered PEG at 16 and was 26 at the time of the study. She received a Master's degree from a competitive international relations department. Although she was working as a consultant, she was looking for job opportunities abroad. Recently engaged, she wanted to make a smooth transition to marriage, which she knew would require mutual career sacrifice with her husband. More interested in the characteristics of a career than in the specifics, Kristen hoped to find a position that would eventually allow her to raise a family.

Liz Bennett

Thoughtful, caring, intelligent, and quiet, Liz was a young woman of great inner strength. Although reserved and soft-spoken, she was not afraid to speak out on important issues. Her energetic leadership was evident in organizations like the Volunteer Action Council, as well as the Status of Women and the Educational Support Self-Study committees. A student government senator and Student Honor Council member, Liz was an editorial staff member of the MBC literary magazine and a columnist for the newspaper. Achieving the highest grade point average in her class, she was also a Class Marshall, an Honor Scholar, a recipient of the PEG Merit and Leadership Award, and a PEG Academic Achievement Scholar. Liz graduated with double distinctions in history and political science and was a member of both Phi Beta Kappa and Omicron Delta Kappa.

Liz entered PEG at age 14. Ten years later, at the time of the study, she worked as an attorney specializing in criminal law and was involved primarily in court-appointed cases of abuse, neglect, child support, and dependency. At 24, she was the youngest person to serve as the secretary of her county bar association. She was also training for a marathon and volunteered as a literacy tutor and as a manager for a nonprofit civic organization. She had an active personal life with many good friends.

Lucy Jacobs

A physically and personally strong person, Lucy was tested by life at a very young age. While her manner was quiet, she related to people with sincerity and interest. She became a leader early in her freshman year when she was elected president of the PEG class. She made important contributions to campus life by tutoring in the writing center, playing sports, being a student senator, and acting as a PEG peer advisor. Deeply reflective, caring, and disciplined, Lucy took life very seriously. During the summer of her freshman year, she led her team in the Biking Odyssey for the American Youth Foundation. In her sophomore year, she received the PEG Merit and Leadership Award, and as a rising senior, she attended a prestigious foreign university. Lucy graduated Phi Beta Kappa as an English literature major.

Lucy entered PEG at age 15. At 33, she was a second-year graduate student in a joint doctoral program in English and Education at a major university. She planned to focus her research on composition pedagogy. It took Lucy six years after graduation to decide whether to pursue a Ph.D. in English and Education or an M.D. During that time, she worked as a bookstore manager, taught writing to undergraduates, and won awards for her poetry. At the time of the study, she was in a solid romantic relationship with her partner.

Madison Kennedy

Madison was one of the more expressive and fun-loving students, charming everyone she met. As a freshman and sophomore, she brought engaging social skills to her on-

campus jobs. Faculty, staff, and all types of MBC students greatly enjoyed her. In addition to being socially adept, she was also a focused student, passionately dedicated to learning. Majoring in biology, Madison also had minors in chemistry and religion. She was a member of the MBC Honor Scholars and Phi Beta Kappa. Her bubbly personality, coupled with her interest in making a difference in the world, made her a positive person to have in any setting.

Madison came to PEG at age 16. At the age of 24, she was in a first-year pediatric residency in the U.S. after having completed her training abroad in international medicine. As a medical student, she had spent about two years moving from country to country among a great variety of hospital settings to fulfill her requirements.

May Crane

During her early PEG years, May's shyness was expressed by the way she wore her hair. Her side part made her silky black hair fall forward, hiding half of her face as though to protect her private thoughts. When her curiosity was sparked, however, she would slowly move the hair away and reveal her large dark eyes peeking out to assess the situation with her characteristic wit. May's quirky perspective was evident in her ironic and wry sense of humor. She befriended unusual PEG students and adults; they piqued her interest and empathy. Her faculty advisor said that her writing in her dual majors of art history and art management was comparable to graduate-level work. By the time May graduated, her hairstyle had not changed, but her manner reflected a new level of self-confidence.

May had entered PEG at age 14. At 28, she was an independent art dealer who worked and lived in a major city. Her love of art had begun as a young child and was encouraged and sustained by her mother and her aunt. After entering the city's art scene at

18, she earned an M.A. in liberal studies at a private metropolitan university. At the time of the study, she was living happily with her boyfriend in their city condominium.

Nikita Escher

Nikita was a quiet, modest person with a subtle sense of humor and a caring disposition. She majored in mathematics and minored in computer information science. Everyone respected her academic self-discipline. Active in a local youth group, Nikita also played for the MBC softball team. The Youth Leadership Institute and the Staunton Chamber of Commerce gave her leadership awards. She tutored young PEG students in math, computer science, and study skills, offering them both life perspective and reassurance. Because of her maturity, the PEG staff chose Nikita to represent her class on an important student panel for two years. A Phi Beta Kappa graduate, Nikita received the Honor Scholar Award and the Taylor scholarship in mathematics. Kind and compassionate, she was a gracious presence during her undergraduate years.

Nikita entered PEG at age 14 and went on to earn an M.A. in software engineering. At 20, she worked as an engineer for an international corporation. She liked her job because it helped U.S. security and safety. Every year, she visited her old middle school to act as a mentor to girls by encouraging them to take higher-level math and science classes. Nikita was in a fulfilling relationship with her boyfriend at the time of the study.

Nina Carpenter

Nina emanated kindness. Her inner and outer beauty attracted the more mature and inventive PEG students. Bringing disparate groups together for fun events, she led others with refinement and originality. She developed an original art project for local community children that focused on the creative process. Most of her professors considered her to be highly innovative and productive. She related well to peers and adults but also enjoyed solitude. As she walked briskly and alone to classes, her willowy frame moved gracefully, and she smiled with delight. Recipient of the PEG Merit and Leadership Award, Nina also won a prestigious award as an exemplary student with the best plan for a senior research project.

Nina enrolled in PEG at age 15, majoring in art. At 24, she owned a woodworking shop and was the director of an art center in a small town. Before starting her own business, she had apprenticed with a carpentry mentor for many years. As an artist, she also sculpted pieces and designed furniture. At the time of the study, Nina was in a fulfilling relationship with her boyfriend.

Rachel Sinclair

Rachel entered PEG as a hidden gem waiting to let her quiet intensity shine. Soon afterward, she displayed her deep and reflective thinking as she wrote remarkably and shared her ideas more openly in class. An excellent academic role model for students, she was chosen for the PEG Merit and Leadership Award and for the Honor Scholars Outstanding Achievement Award. Besides engaging in both on- and off-campus activities and having a job, Rachel received a minority student summer scholarship to fund her senior year biology research. By the time she graduated, her individuality, intelligence, and grace were apparent, and she knew how to use her strengths to effect change.

Rachel, who had entered PEG at age 16, was 25 years old at the time of the study and was applying to graduate school in organizational psychology. Once she completed her M.A., she planned to enter a Ph.D. program. As an employee of a major retail food store for five years, Rachel loved the communication and organizational aspects of creating change within companies.

Ruby Kelp

During her PEG admissions interview, Ruby exuded a sense of inner stability and strength. Humorous and respectful, she was elected by her peers to represent them on the PEG Judicial Board. As board chairperson the following year, she meted out fair and consistent justice for students in conflict. The MBC Young Democrats elected Ruby vice president during her sophomore year. Concurrently, she joined the Amnesty International college chapter and eventually became its co-chair. An editorial board member of the MBC literary magazine, Ruby also tutored community elementary and high school students. The Benn Award in Creative Writing celebrated her remarkable literary promise. Ruby graduated from MBC with distinction in political science.

Ruby entered PEG at age 14. At 30, she had worked with her mother for seven years in a family business that sold recycled goods. After five years of teaching college English part-time, she decided to switch her focus back to writing, which was her passion. An award- and prize-winning poet, she earned an M.F.A. in poetry. Ruby was married and was building a home with her husband at the time of the study.

As these mini-biographies and brief reminiscences attest, the PEG study women achieved much more than good grades by graduation. Between 17 and 19 years old when they received their diplomas, it didn't take them long to catapult into their professional areas of interest in the real world, eager to make a difference.

Part II

Life Before PEG

CHAPTER 3

The Importance of Parental Support

Enrolling in a residential college as a young teenager was a big decision for the PEG study women. They had to choose between safely staying home with their families and friends and embarking on an independent journey to the Program for the Exceptionally Gifted at Mary Baldwin College. Once they set foot on campus, they entered an adult world that expected them to study seriously; manage their time, work, and emotions; participate in extracurricular activities; and make new friends. How did these girls have the courage to change their lives so drastically and begin to live independently? Part of the answer lay with their strong families.

Family relationships, communication styles, decision-making processes, work ethics, and attitudes all contributed to these women's healthy development. Through a balance of encouragement and expectations, the parents created homes where challenge was welcomed because it fosters personal growth. Mothers and fathers conveyed to their children the importance of discovering their interests and of working to achieve their self-created goals. They wanted their daughters to know their own minds and have enough strength of character to venture out into the world in search of their purpose. They set the stage for these young women to develop fully and also to care deeply about the well-being of others.

The Holding Environment

The PEG students who contributed meaningfully to the college community generally came from families that provided nurturance for growth within a "holding environment"—that is, a place where the girls could grow with guidance and support but still develop their individual identities separate from those of their parents. "Rather than focusing on giftedness as an end in itself and using the gifted identity of their children as a means of self-gratification or self-justification," Dr. Rhodes explained, "these parents appeared to hold a deep appreciation for the 'gift of life' and focused on gift-edness as a means to the end of living a meaningful life."[1] These parents modeled interdependence with their desire to contribute significantly to their communities as a form of gratitude. Having received much, they wanted to give back generously.

Psychologist Robert Kegan's model of development describes the human growth process as reconciling people's needs for both independence and community. It is a three-part process of "hold-ing on," "letting go," and "remaining in place."[2] Most of the PEG study women emerged from homes where this process occurred healthily so that they could later contribute to others outside of their families. As the girls grew up, most of the parents were responsive to their daughters' intellectual abilities, personal qualities, and need for independence. These parents wanted their children to be happy, and they trusted them to find the most satisfying paths for themselves with a minimal amount of interference.

Holding On

Unconditional love and acceptance are clearly conveyed to children whose parents know how to "hold on," yet who freely meet their daughters' needs as they affirm their individuality. Parents who are effective "pay careful attention to, respect, and support the development of their child's unique interests and abilities,"[3] which may involve substantial parental sacrifice. These parents demonstrate their love constructively, which allows their children to grow and develop in the supportive environment necessary for them to experiment with different facets of their identity as they explore who they are and what is important to them.

Letting Go

Parents with a firm sense of self also know how to let go. By offering honest advice based on their life experiences, parents can help optimize their daughters' growth. "By providing boundaries and expectations, and by modeling active listening and productive communication skills, parents can offer the adult perspective that young people need to get through their immediate experience and anticipate or learn from the consequences of their actions."[4] Parents who ultimately can let their children go on to live their own lives according to their own principles realize how important it is for children to learn about delayed gratification and the importance of earning rewards. With such tacit knowledge, their children are more likely to be successful as adults because they have learned the foundation of independence.

Remaining in Place

Remaining in place means that parents accept their children's rejection but do not reject the children themselves. It occurs "when parents understand the need for the adolescent to differentiate from them; and when parents maintain family continuity so their adolescent can return later as an independent person who chooses to reintegrate with the family on a more adult level."[5] These parents recognize their children's need to distance themselves emotionally (and sometimes physically) from the family to achieve independence. They also respect their daughters' privacy so that the girls can develop new friendships and relationships smoothly.

Encouragement and Expectations

It may be surprising to some people to know that very few parents of these successful gifted women pushed their daughters. Recognizing their children's talents and energy, most of the PEG study women's parents had a "Go for it!" attitude. Non-prescriptive in tone but engaged in dialogue and guidance with their daughters at crucial times, the majority of the parents achieved a strong balance of encouraging, supporting, and guiding their children.

The study parents expressed general expectations for their daughters, including the belief that they should do the best that they could in their given circumstances, find their strongest interests and pursue them, take responsibility for their actions, and seek life fulfillment. However, most of them did not force or push their daughters in any predetermined direction. Instead, they provided a foundation for the women's healthy social, emotional, intellectual, and moral development by cultivating their daughters' autonomy, critical thinking, and decision-making skills. Given freedom as children to pursue their interests, the PEG study women were able to explore authentically their own values, interests, and goals as they got older.

Nikita Escher, a young engineer at an international corporation, expressed gratitude for her parents' faith in her ability to find happiness. She felt that they did not have any specific expectations for her beyond her own satisfaction and fulfillment, and their message was consistent into her adulthood. "I think all that my parents hope for me in my life is that I am happy," she said. Of course, her family didn't expect her to leave home at age 14. Despite their surprise at their daughter's intention to go college at such a young age, Mr. and Mrs. Escher "let go." Nikita stated, "Regardless of their shock, my immediate family has always been fabulous because they only want the best things for me. They keep any other aspirations that they have to themselves." Involved freely in her own pursuit of happiness, Nikita felt lucky to have so much encouragement without pressure to fulfill her parents' dreams instead of her own.

Nikita's parents were supportive of her other intellectual pursuits as well. While she was in junior high school, Nikita wanted to attend an advanced summer math course at Johns Hopkins University run by the Center for Talented Youth (CTY). Students taking the course are required to take the SAT, a test designed for high school juniors and seniors as a college entrance exam. Nikita's parents completely supported her desire to take the test to qualify and, later, to take the course. They helped her to get information about the program, sign up for the SAT, and study for the test.

"I remember being so nervous the morning of the test," Nikita said. "I asked myself why I was trying to take this hard test so early and doubted my ability to do well. My mom drove me that morning, and she made a special donut stop and reminded me that there was no pressure. If I didn't do very well, then there was no shame because it was years before most students would take the test. She helped me to relax, and I felt calm and capable when I went into the test. I am sure that I did better simply because I was able to concentrate on the material instead of feeling insecure." Nikita's mother made her daughter's well-being paramount, which helped Nikita to feel more confident. That confidence allowed Nikita to perform her best on the difficult exam.

In Nikita's home, decision making was a thoughtful parent-child interaction. Not only did Mr. and Mrs. Escher create a setting of peace and seriousness when Nikita was thinking about entering PEG, but they also conveyed that they valued her independence of mind. When PEG accepted Nikita, her parents sat down with her away from distractions so that they could talk. They explained to her that they could afford to send her to college, and they wanted to discuss her options and what she wanted. "They made it very clear that they were proud of me no matter what I decided but that the decision to go had to be my own."

Nikita's parents took the steps necessary for clear and open communication with their daughter. They demonstrated their profound trust in Nikita to make important choices as a young adolescent and to follow through with her commitments. They had a good sense of their daughter's competence. They conveyed their belief in her ability to work independently and to be responsible far away from their immediate influence. Perhaps most importantly, they supported her need to determine what she wanted from life by expressing their love for her—independent of her choices.

Genuinely grateful for her parents' willingness to allow her to choose early college entrance, as an adult, Nikita recognized how well her mother and father had understood her as a child. Mr. and Mrs. Escher appreciated that their daughter's motivation was tied to her need to make decisions for herself. "They knew that I would only do well if it was something that I really wanted to do." Her parents' understanding and support were unconditional and made her feel "so blessed because I know from experience that many other children are not so lucky. They feel pressured to do what their parents expect and often become bitter and unhappy and then have to make a new start."

The constellation of family members who encouraged the PEG women included mothers, fathers, grandparents, aunts, uncles, brothers, sisters, and step- and half-relatives. The women whose families did not offer as much support managed to thrive by getting the encouragement and experiences that they needed elsewhere in their lives, such as through teachers, neighbors, or friends. No matter where it came from, the support and nurturance of significant adults were instrumental in helping the PEG women succeed.

The Importance of Living One's Own Dream

When college students expend energy rejecting parental goals to determine their own aspirations, they have less emotional energy to focus on the needs of others. Claire Hagan, a PEG student who is now a biology professor, echoed Nikita's observation about the importance of independence of thought and self-directedness. In her classes, Claire saw "so many biology students who would rather be somewhere else because they don't have the interest in it or the aptitude for it—they're there mostly because their parents want them to be doctors or nurses or vets."

It is likely that the same scenario plays out in pre-law, business, and other fields of study. "College is difficult enough," Claire remarked. "Dealing with parental pressure is too much on top of everything else!" The dual perspectives of having been a student without parental pressure and then working as a professor who saw students suffer from their parents' expectations of them made Claire even more grateful for her parents' hands-off policy, both before and after she entered PEG at age 14. She knew that her parents then, and now, "just want me to be happy." Being able to please herself according to her standards helped Claire build an emotional foundation of satisfaction, from which she could better reach out to others.

In a longitudinal study of 81 Illinois valedictorians, Karen Arnold comes to a similar conclusion.[6] Arnold states that in high school, the valedictorians were initially focused on achieving for others—primarily their parents and teachers. While many of them remained anchored by "hard work, purpose, and desire" as they entered college, others struggled with determining their own life course, even into adulthood. At age 30, Meg (one of the Illinois study participants) finally realized that by being super-responsible all through high school and college, she had concentrated so hard on what others wanted of her that she had failed to determine what she really wanted from life. With this new insight, she left her teaching position and retrained as a physical therapist. The PEG study women, who felt supported by their parents to pursue their own interests from childhood through adulthood, held a firm conviction that they could ascertain and fulfill their own aspirations.

General Academic Expectations

While most of the PEG study women's families did not insist on their daughters following particular paths of learning or professions, the parents did hold high academic expectations in general. Lucy Jacobs, a published poet and doctoral candidate in English, said that her mother, who had always encouraged her studies, was the one who noticed the PEG program and encouraged Lucy to apply. "She encouraged me primarily by responding so enthusiastically to my academic successes. She also always made it very clear to me that I could do or be anything I wanted to be, without gender restrictions." While still in elementary school, Lucy realized that her mother had higher expectations for her future than some of her teachers did.

Ruby Kelp described the way her family encouraged her academically. Ruby got a library card when she was very young, and her mother took her and her brother to the library weekly to get as many books as they wanted. "My family encouraged my academic abilities by expecting me to take them seriously and use them as best I could. They were supportive when I wanted to enter writing contests or academic fairs. My extended family (aunts, uncles, grandparents) also contributed books, praise, interest in my activities, and high expectations (though not oppressively)." Education was not a "means to make a living," but was rather "always valued as an end in itself. It was made clear to me that being educated (formally or otherwise) was valuable and made a person powerful and important."

Freedom of learning for its own sake and the guidance to study with focus and energy allowed Ruby to later follow some of her literary dreams. The discipline that she had developed early in life translated into her ability to keep to a regular writing schedule and produce award-winning poetry.

Math and Science Guidance

The PEG study participants' parents wanted their daughters to have as many future career opportunities as possible. Realizing that one of the barriers that keeps gifted girls from reaching their full career potential is that they often do not receive the guidance they need to enter math and science fields, some PEG study parents strongly encouraged their daughters to gain advanced proficiency in those disciplines. Unhampered by ignorance, their children would be prepared to open as many doors as they desired and thus have a greater chance of finding their passions.

Madison Kennedy, a student of international medicine, credited her parents with helping her through her math travails. "I was never very good at math in grade school," she said, but when she began learning multiplication in the third grade, the situation became worse. Her first quiz scores were dismal. "But my mom and dad didn't yell at me or punish me for it. Instead, they spent hours with me every night going over and over the times tables until I knew them by heart and even better." From then on, Madison had perfect scores on every multiplication quiz she took that year.

By maintaining their belief that Madison could succeed and by sitting with her nightly to ensure mastery, her parents displayed behavior that reassured their daughter and also taught her the process of studying. Madison knew that she would succeed with her parents beside her, and her improved math skills eventually allowed her to pursue medicine.

As an adopted child, Madison felt her parents' expressions of support intensely. "My mom and dad believed that if you had children, then you had to be willing to do whatever it took for that child to succeed. You loved them unconditionally regardless of their successes or failures." The Kennedys taught Madison to recognize that her failures and successes belonged to both the parents and the child. "They gave me a sense of security and along the way, taught me self-discipline, honesty, and compassion."

Mr. and Mrs. Kennedy taught Madison to work diligently on her school tasks with persistence and perseverance, and their compassion as they helped her to tackle obstacles was an early example of how people could help each other. As a physician years later, Madison transferred those lessons of diligence to her work and the lessons of caring to her patients.

Long before Jessica Holmes became a journalist for a major business magazine and a college economics instructor, her mother knew how important it was for women to study math and science. In addition to encouraging her children to study what they wanted, Mrs. Holmes insisted that her three daughters learn math and science as well. As an engineer, Jessica's mother realized that "strong skills in math and science, whether you used them or not, were extremely important for women to develop and that they gave you a lot more career options (in general)—and career options that are more financially lucrative."

When Jessica wanted to take both French and Spanish in junior high school, her parents made her a deal. They said that she could study both languages as long as she skipped a year in math. "Skipping a grade in math was definitely academically challenging, but I could do it. And so I think that was a good lesson in reasonable expectations in math," Jessica said. Mr. and Mrs. Holmes persuaded Jessica to take courses that they thought were critical to her success. By standing their ground and insisting that their daughter become appropriately prepared for her future, the Holmes parents could then "let go" of Jessica when she enrolled in college.

Later, as a 13-year-old college student, Jessica said that her parents "weren't too into grades. But I think that's also because they knew that I would do what was important to me." Jessica noted that if she had been failing in college, then her parents might have been more concerned with her grades. But in her first two years, she was getting "decent grades. My last couple of years, I had great grades. But it was because I was pursuing my interests." Jessica's mother and father gave her the opportunity both as a child and as an early college student to explore areas that appealed to her. Arnold's valedictorian study, mentioned earlier, shows that students who choose courses based on their intellectual interests, rather than because they are required on a career-striving path, tend to get the highest grades.

Reflecting on all three sisters' achievements, Jessica imagined that people incorrectly assumed that her parents must have been highly directive people. The sisters "definitely have minds of our own, but I think our parents really did a good job of developing our interests and providing encouragement." Like Nikita's parents, Mr. and Mrs. Holmes provided guidance at critical times in Jessica's learning, but they did so within the context of her own objectives and with the aim of Jessica ultimately achieving self-fulfillment.

As she approached adolescence, a time when many children rebel against their parents, Jessica was willing to listen to—and take—her mother's advice. She understood that her mother wanted to create future opportunities for her by insisting on studying advanced math in junior high school. Because her parents were able to establish the clear message that they wanted their daughters to be independent and to follow their own interests, and because they maintained open communication about important decision making with their children, Jessica was comfortable enough to accept her parent's guidance.

When Support Is Limited

Not every PEG study girl was lucky enough to have parents as supportive of their daughters' interests. Liz Bennett's parents thought they knew what was best for her, even when she had other ideas. By the time she applied for PEG, Liz was not getting along well with her mother and father. As a young teenager, she wanted to move far away from their influence.

Since she was the youngest child in the family with two older brothers, Liz's parents put most of their attention on the boys. From an early age, Liz learned to fend for herself. "I was a very independent, self-directed child. I used to wash my own clothes; I got myself up for school, made my own breakfast, did a lot of things for myself—even did my homework without really being told." As she became competent in performing chores and learning skills, Liz developed a strong sense of autonomy. "If I asked them for anything or if I wanted to do anything, they would sign the permission slip, but other than that, I was pretty much free to do what I pleased."

When her older brothers left for college, the parent-child conflict intensified. Liz was in seventh grade. "My mother wanted to start molding me and telling me the things I needed to do." However, Liz had "been living life my own way since second grade. I didn't really need somebody telling me how to do things, although I guess every teenager feels that way to a certain extent." She felt her mother's control and criticism acutely.

Liz's parents "did not really take a lot of note concerning my academic ability." When the Program for the Exceptionally Gifted contacted her about applying to the early college entrance program, her parents "were really shocked. They said, 'Wow, you could do that?'" Liz assured her parents that she could and promptly filled out the application. At first, Mrs. Bennett did not want Liz to attend PEG. Mr. Bennett was the one who supported Liz's wish. "My father said, 'We can't not let her have this chance. She has to go.'" Mrs. Bennett eventually agreed to the plan.

It is important to note that the decision to apply to PEG did not rest solely on Liz's dislike of her mother's control. She also felt strongly attracted to the promise of intellectual excitement among peers. She thought, "How cool would that be to go to college?" She was very eager to "live with a bunch of other girls who were really smart, really different, unique people. I remember being really excited the day I got there. Wow, you know, I'm finally here; this is going to be so great." Liz welcomed the opportunity to nurture her intellectual curiosity among other young girls who loved to learn.

Developing deep friendships and knowing that there are others who grapple with the same kinds of problems can be hugely beneficial for gifted children who feel isolated. Previously, the Bennetts had permitted Liz to go to summer camp with other academically talented children. As many gifted children can attest, spending a summer with equally bright and inquisitive children can compensate for a lot that is lacking at home and at school. By allowing Liz to attend the summer camp, Mr. and Mrs. Bennett helped their daughter feel validated in her intelligence and at ease with other children her age. When Liz later learned about PEG, she already had experienced the delight of academic challenge and being among true intellectual peers. Her awareness made her a prime candidate for considering early entrance at Mary Baldwin College. Despite their strained relationship with their daughter, Liz's parents "remained in place" while she stretched her wings of independence in college. Later, as an adult, she found it easier to return home on her own terms.

Rachel Sinclair grew up with her much older brother in a single-parent home. Although she felt that her mother was "incredibly supportive and went to great lengths to make sure that I had the opportunity in almost any activity that piqued my interest," she also felt that her mother was "somewhat overbearing when it came to academics." Because Rachel was apathetic about her intellectual abilities as a child, her mother would "constantly remind me of my intelligence and abilities, which was somewhat counterproductive because I simply took them for granted and did not ascribe any particular importance to them."

Rachel's mother became quite perturbed with her daughter when Rachel was in first grade. "She was probably either frustrated with my lack of effort at school or with the workings of an educational system that would not identify me as gifted, or both." At some point, Ms. Sinclair said to Rachel, "You're very bright. You know that, don't you?" "I remember inferring that *bright* was synonymous with *smart* and saying 'yes' in an attempt to pacify my mother." Rachel reflected that she "did not appreciate it at the time, but that was the first affirmation of my abilities."

Perhaps because Ms. Sinclair was an African American single mother, she felt the need to be especially vigilant about Rachel's academic progress, given her awareness of her daughter's extreme intelligence. Historically, gifted programs in the United States have under-identified culturally diverse students, and this was the case in the early 1990s when Rachel was in first grade and white students received a disproportionately higher number of gifted services than did students of color.[7] Ms. Sinclair may have worried that unless the school staff saw excellent achievement, they would not recognize Rachel's giftedness.

Unfortunately, Ms. Sinclair's tone was not as effective as she may have hoped. In the heat of her upset, she did not give Rachel the opportunity to engage in a reciprocal discussion about high academic achievement. Even at the age of six, Rachel had her own perspective but muffled it to placate her mother. Yet despite the mother-daughter friction over this issue, Rachel was later thankful that her mother helped her recognize her intelligence early.

Calling her pre-PEG years "a difficult experience," Rachel explained the roots of the conflict with her mother. "My mother is the oldest of six children and has always been used to being responsible for and in charge of everyone else." Rachel thought that part of what she experienced was typical of adolescents. However, she said, "Considering how integral my independence is to my identity now, it is no small surprise that living together has never been a good situation for us. Now, having accepted that, it is easier for us to relate."

Rachel needed someone else in the family to encourage her direction. "My aunt became a very important person to me at this time and remains so today. She has proven to be a profound source of unconditional love and wisdom." A PEG administrator remembered how Rachel's mother and her aunt both participated in the admissions interview, noting how uncommon it was to have an aunt present. During the interview, Ms. Sinclair mentioned her sister's closeness with Rachel and how much her sister could contribute to the interview process. Despite Rachel's discomfort with her mother's assertiveness, the administrator thought that Ms. Sinclair was generous and wise by promoting the special aunt-niece relationship.

Ms. Sinclair supported all of Rachel's interests and was very concerned with her performance in school, but she could not provide the emotional comfort and acceptance that Rachel craved at the time. Without the backdrop of the love that comes from truly understanding a child in all of her aspects, neither Ms. Sinclair nor the Bennetts communicated with their daughters in ways that made them feel fully validated. Although Ms. Sinclair did encourage the connection between loving aunt and adoring niece so that Rachel received the extra emotional support that her mother might not have been able to provide, Rachel wanted more unequivocal encouragement from her mother. Similarly, Liz felt that her parents did not convey a sense of unconditional love when she was a young adolescent.

Rachel retained her commitment to making a difference as an adult, but it took her about six years to find her interest in organizational psychology and to make the decision to apply for graduate work. In adulthood, Liz became a lawyer for poor clients, despite her parents wanting her to take a more prestigious job. Although Liz felt that she had disappointed her parents, she remained true to her values.

These two women's histories suggest that the pursuit of purpose may be more difficult when parents do not allow free expression of opposition, even though they may support their child's interests. Feeling fully accepted by parents seems to help the development of a sense of purpose, yet the two PEG participants who did not feel that validation still remained empathetic to others and still contributed to the welfare of others.

Ties to Purpose

Responsive parents engage in "holding on" by appreciating and confirming their child's unique self, "letting go" by contradicting their children when necessary to provide boundaries and guidance but ultimately allowing them to follow their interests, and "remaining in place" by accepting their children and providing continuity even while sometimes being rejected. To create the best environment for their children's development, the "real challenge is knowing when to play which role, why, and to what degree."[8] Successful parents can thus be described as those who "seem able to acknowledge, balance, and integrate all three roles by using approaches which promote the growth of children."

Researchers warn against parents who want to attain their unfulfilled dreams through their children. Narcissistic parents often "justify their intrusive actions as advocating for their children."[9] In contrast, healthy parents "are aware of their own needs in the adult development process and use reflection and self-restraint to refrain from becoming overly involved in their children's lives." Families who fail to respect boundaries interfere with the steps that children must take to flourish.

Ironically for PEG parents, the "holding on" process of helping their children find an appropriate challenge resulted in them facing the need to "let go" of their daughters much sooner than anticipated. Despite their feelings of excitement and relief at having found an acceleration opportunity where their daughters could be fulfilled and challenged, they also felt sadness at the prospect of having them leave home earlier than expected. In doing so, however, these parents helped nurture the girls' independence and self-reliance—valuable qualities for college success and for the growth of purpose. They then waited patiently for their daughters to reach out to them on their own schedule to share their newfound skills, confidence, and maturing sense of self.

CHAPTER 4

The Influence of Family Values

The 14 women in the PEG study were fortunate to have parents who modeled independent and vigorous lives as the girls grew up. These young women had a clear understanding of their family's highest values and absorbed the moral frameworks that upheld them. Sometimes the lessons the daughters learned translated into choices that their parents did not fully welcome, but ultimately, the love that buoyed their relationships trumped initial parental reservations. Most of the PEG study women whose families had backed them firmly as youngsters felt competent and proactive in setting and achieving their personal goals.

Parents and Family Friends as Role Models

The parents and close family friends of the PEG study women revealed several themes in their life behaviors: unconventionality, healthy skepticism, independence, trust, hard work, self-sacrifice, expressiveness, and closeness. This is not surprising; research has shown that these behaviors are often found in families of eminent individuals of both genders.[1] For the PEGs, seeing these qualities in their parents undoubtedly helped the women to solidify their own values, to pursue happiness, and to maintain their sense of purpose.

Unconventionality and Skepticism

Lucy Jacobs pointed to her mother as the one who inspired her approach to life. Lucy's parents divorced when she was young, and both parents remarried. "My mother's pursuit of an unconventional, no-holds-barred lifestyle has been at the root of my own assumption that my happiness should come before conformity to societal expectations," she said. As a PEG undergraduate, Lucy went through a wrenching soul-searching process that helped her acknowledge her homosexuality. Even though her mother would have preferred that Lucy marry a man and have a more conventional family, she supported and accepted her daughter's sexuality. "I feel incredibly lucky and grateful about the example of her life," Lucy stated, "more than I think she knows."

Lucy also grew up with her mother's liberal values, which "definitely had an impact. I was never taught that Black people are different from white people, for example, and I grew up absorbing the idea that some people in our country who have lots of money and power are not very nice." Her mother frequently voiced skepticism about politicians and their motives. "In short, I grew up with a very vocal critical thinker, and I suppose I can say it turned me into one, too." Lucy's belief in social justice was rooted in her mother's outspokenness; however, being a quieter person, Lucy expressed her protests in her writings and found personal ways to help others.

Independence and Trust

Most of the PEG study parents trusted their children's judgment and encouraged their autonomy, but one student's relationship with her mother particularly exemplified this trust. Both of May Crane's parents trusted her and let her interests take the lead, but it was May's mother, a psychiatrist, who was the bigger intellectual influence. "If I were into Greek mythology, Mom would borrow all of the books out of the library, take me to the museums to see the paintings, and take me to see *Clash of the Titans* in the movie theater," May recalled happily.

Dr. Crane was her daughter's biggest advocate because she "always stuck up for me. If I told her that I was frustrated because my classes were too simple, she'd make the school give me harder spelling words or a more advanced math book." May was very unhappy in school and thought that her mother probably recognized the detrimental psychological effects of the unchallenging curriculum. "This is insane, but my mom would let me stay home from school whenever I wanted (once for 21 days straight when I was seven)." May said that she was probably depressed at the time but also that her mother "believed that I learned more on my own than in school. When I was 13, Mom let me cut school to go to museums in the city since I was showing an interest in seeing exhibits. She'd call in sick, and we'd have a great day together." Soon, May was allowed to go alone because her mother trusted her "to just go to the museums and back." Ignoring convention when it got in the way of her daughter's healthy development, Dr. Crane believed deeply in nurturing May's interests, and May learned early to follow her passions and become autonomous.

May appreciated her mother's viewpoint that since the world was difficult, home life should be easy, and she felt the strong, positive support of both of her parents. "Neither of my parents ever put me down; they always told me how smart and special I was. I was never compared to anyone else."

May's mother continued her enthusiastic support after her daughter enrolled in PEG. May was only 17 years old when her mother permitted her to live on her own in one of the biggest cities in the United States. "Between my junior and senior year, Mom let me live in the city to attend university summer classes, which became the cornerstone of my contemporary art knowledge. I'm still friends with an art critic from that time!" Dr. Crane had "let go" of her daughter so she could become a self-reliant adult. Her encouragement strengthened May's desire to become an art professional when she was just seven years old. By age 13, May knew that she wanted to be an art dealer. Years later, when some well-meaning college professors tried to persuade her to go into academics rather than business, May stayed true to her wishes. She became an art dealer at the young age of 18. With strength of conviction beyond her years, May followed her dreams.

By absorbing the independent spirit and the allegiance to learning that her mother had modeled, and by developing good interpersonal skills, May was able to thrive, despite having to work for some demanding, unreasonable bosses. When she could no longer tolerate the abuse, she decided to go into business for herself. Freedom of choice was one of the top reasons she felt purposeful as an adult, she said. Dr. Crane's consistent faith in her daughter helped May trust her own decisions.

Hard Work and Self-Sacrifice

Nikita Escher believed that despite her father's difficult professional life, he always worked hard and provided everything his family needed. But after many years of service and just five years shy of retirement, her father lost his job. Unlike some of his colleagues who could afford to wait for the money that might result from a lawsuit lodged against the company, her father had to find work quickly. "I remember months of him working at [a home improvement store]. He would do anything for us, and I will never forget that," Nikita remembers. When he got a better job, Mr. Escher had to commute to another state, which greatly reduced his family time. "It must've been incredibly difficult and exhausting for him, but he never complained and was always excited to see us when he came home." With his focus on his family's well-being and specifically on his children's education and growth, Mr. Escher became Nikita's prime model of graciousness under fire.

From her father, Nikita developed a life philosophy of maintaining a positive attitude and living fully. "Part of this philosophy is forgiving and forgetting," she explained. "You can't enjoy your life as much if you are holding onto bitterness. This includes blaming yourself when things don't go as well as you expected." Carrying this mindset into her adult career, Nikita became known as an extremely capable and diligent employee, as well as an efficient team leader.

As an engineer, she felt that she was improving society. Being an effective and successful worker helped serve her sense of purpose.

Expressiveness and Closeness

Not all role models of the PEG study women were relatives. Claire Hagan's mother's best friend, Sharon, was important to Claire as a girl. A successful businesswoman, Sharon was like an aunt who provided great warmth. "I thought she was *so* cool. I was totally enamored with her! She was always very sweet to me, and I remember most that she was so open with her affection," Claire said. "We practically made it a game to find ways to express how much we cared about each other." Hugging was one of her favorites. Claire loved both the physical and verbal expressiveness of Sharon's warmth. Having grown up in a less expressive family, Claire felt that Sharon brought a lot of happiness to her childhood. "I thought so highly of her, and it made me feel so special that she liked me, too."

When Claire, now a biology professor, described her students, she spoke with the concern of a caring adult, just like the concern and attention she had experienced from Sharon. During her interview, she repeatedly spoke of the importance of establishing a nurturing professor-student rapport. Perhaps in part a reflection of her childhood relationship with Sharon, Claire worked hard to create close bonds with her students.

Values

In addition to exhibiting admirable characteristics that influenced their daughters' behaviors and attitudes, the PEG study parents modeled key values. By acting according to their principles, parents taught the importance of lifelong learning, risk taking, resilience and resourcefulness, and non-materialism. As a result, their daughters inherited these core values.

Lifelong Learning and Education

The PEG women described themselves as enthusiastic, lifelong learners, having come from homes where intellectual curiosity was highly valued. In their families, the excitement of learning was integrated into daily life.

Georgia Sullivan felt a pervasive intellectual energy at home. She described the typical dinner scene from her childhood as an example of her family's encouragement. "Dinner hour was a combination of laughter and serious discussion. Many dinners were interrupted by searches for reference books to resolve tricky questions or issues. My family always acknowledged me as intelligent and encouraged my reading, curiosity, and lessons."

For the Sullivans, coming together to eat was the perfect opportunity to meld playfulness with inquisitiveness. Georgia associated learning with fun. As an adult, she had "great knowledge and even greater capabilities to learn. I have great skills for working with people, and I know how to accomplish things." These skills aided her well in her role as an environmental and disaster reduction consultant, which she felt contributed to the betterment of the U.S.

For Kristen Edwards, also a consultant, the values of intellect and education were so deeply ingrained in her childhood home that it was "an environment that almost took the seeking of academic challenge for granted." Kristen attributed that atmosphere to her parents, who were "well educated in all senses of the word—not just academically." She felt that because her parents understood the world more broadly, they could truly appreciate knowledge and insight. Kristen disliked feeling ignorant and realized that attaining her dreams was an ongoing process. As a result, she was strongly motivated to continue learning and growing.

A voracious reader, Jessica Holmes also enjoyed learning life skills and praised her parents for promoting them. But in addition to traditional learning, Mr. and Mrs. Holmes taught their daughter that "you don't have to learn everything from books or in school. When you're an adult, academic abilities aren't everything, so my parents always encouraged me to develop practical, everyday skills like cooking." As an example, Jessica recalled "always hammering and drilling stuff around the house," after she requested—and received—a power drill one Christmas. Her parents' outlook and training prepared Jessica to take care of herself. Her competence and experience meant that she could travel independently to study in foreign settings because she was self-reliant.

The Sullivan, Edwards, and Holmes families all exemplified the kinds of environments and attitudes that shaped these highly intelligent young women, who were delighted to learn both academic and life skills. By making learning a shared, joyful experience, creating the tacit expectation of academic challenge, and teaching practical skills, these parents built scaffolds for their daughters' later pursuits and lives of purpose.

Risk Taking

Armed with a substantial knowledge base, as well as the confidence to find answers to questions on their own, the PEG women learned the value of taking healthy risks, and their parents encouraged this behavior. By managing obstacles and unfamiliarity, the young women could continue to challenge themselves and make good life choices. The parents valued risk taking so that their daughters would become responsible for their own happiness.

Of course, all of the teenagers demonstrated their risk taking by enrolling in PEG at Mary Baldwin College. Most of them felt trepidation about leaving home and starting college so young. A number of them wondered if they were smart enough to manage the course load. Even Madison, who at 16 was one of the older PEG freshmen, worried about her ability to handle all of the college pressures. "Once I was accepted, I was terrified. 'Do I go?' This was a huge risk. Layers upon layers of anxiety were building up." Madison was concerned that her decision was irrevocable and that she would never be able to compensate adequately if it turned out to be a bad decision.

Most of the PEG study participants knew how large a leap they were taking. Luckily, their parents reassured them. Madison's mother said, "If you hate it, you don't have to finish it. You can make it count as high school credit and still graduate on time." She asked Madison to commit to one year and to give it her full effort.

"Mom asked, 'Can you do one year?' And I could. I remember the relief and the satisfaction of having made that decision—a big one." Madison, like the other PEG alumnae, risked the consequences of her unconventional decision to attend college early by skipping the lock-step progression of high school. Making that scary but highly promising move resulted in dynamic personal growth that bolstered her core values and competence. Having survived that difficult choice and having felt the enormous relief that came from making up her mind, Madison was better prepared to make other tough decisions once she entered college.

Claire Hagan was one teen who braved even greater risks. When she was still 14 years old and had just completed her freshman year at Mary Baldwin, her parents encouraged her to take an internship at a biological field station in a foreign country. Working with adults on real-world scientific problems fueled Claire's excitement about her biology major. The experience also gave her the confidence to tackle other problems in her field. Claire's parents believed that she could take this large leap of experience and do well, and she did. Her step into unfamiliar territory (both literally and figuratively) gave her the opportunity to mature intellectually, socially, and emotionally in a relatively short period of time.

Resilience and Resourcefulness

Risks can lead to failures, and the PEG women learned that resilience and resourcefulness are a necessary part of the journey to become purposeful adults. Most of the girls were lucky to have parents who modeled these traits, but lessons can be learned in a variety of ways.

Lucy Jacobs was primarily in charge of the care of her siblings and of the chores in "an emotionally turbulent and financially distressed household." As the oldest of six children, she developed resilience and resourcefulness by default because her mother had to spend a great deal of time away from home due to her job. Lucy's stepfather suffered from post-traumatic stress disorder and was emotionally abusive to the children and their mother. Not only did

Lucy feel "very much alone," but she also was highly stressed about money as a child and young teenager. "I was acutely aware that we were struggling, and things felt precarious most of the time," she said. Despite her ordeal, the experience helped Lucy to become smarter about her goals of "financial and emotional stability and a relatively simple life." She learned how to find resources to cope with her household challenges and to bounce back emotionally from isolation and abuse.

Focus on Non-Materialism

Most of the families of the PEG women maintained a non-materialistic focus on doing what makes one happy. These parents emphasized following one's passions to make life meaningful and satisfying.

Darcy Maddox explained that her family "always championed being happy over all else." Despite a loss in pay, her father retired early so that he could fish. Her mother divorced her father to pursue her own dreams, and her sister became a teacher because that was what she truly wanted to do. "My family harbors no love for money or for the fame of success," she stated. They were comfortable enough to live well among loved ones without having more mate-rialistic ambitions. "That definition of success in life has allowed me to grow fearlessly and without pressure." Darcy said that her family considered her equally successful on her first day at PEG, on the day that she left college early one term because she was only 14 and missed her family, and on the days that she called them "while touring Europe on an enlisted soldier's meager salary because I was happy. It is a simple outlook that allows for big dreams."

The pressure-free focus on self-fulfillment made Darcy feel that she was in command of her destiny. At the time of the study, she was a 24-year-old who had already long served the military, had been frequently promoted, had received her Master's of Science degree, and was investigating both law school and history Ph.D. programs as her next step. Her family's emphasis on seeking hap-piness by pursuing that which is personally meaningful gave her the freedom and confidence to use her great potential at the pace and in the venues she chose.

The PEG study families de-emphasized fame, fortune, and status but lauded other qualities in their daughters. "My family prizes good character above all else," Georgia said. How she conducted her life was more important to her family than exactly what she did with it. May, like many other PEG study women, felt that her family conveyed to her the importance of treating people decently and kindly. Kristen felt that she had always been cherished and considered that "an incredible base to build upon." Kristen had a brother with Down Syndrome, but her parents never lost sight of her need for validation as a gifted child amidst the strenuous demands of parenting a child with very fundamental needs. Julia's parents believed equally in respecting individual differences and valuing the family as a unit. Julia knew that "there was the family, and then there was everybody else. Whether I hated my brother today or not, if somebody else came up and started hitting him, I was going to hit back." Nikita also embraced this concept. When she was about five years old, she and her two-year-old sister, Penny, got into a fight. Their mother took Nikita aside and told her that she should not hit Penny because she was much smaller. She explained that Nikita could hurt Penny more than Penny could ever hurt her. "That really stuck with me because after that, I was her protector," Nikita remarked. She had learned the important lesson of taking care of people "who are smaller or weaker. I still try to mentor people and help them to gain strength and confidence so that they are able to do the same for others." Nikita took her mother's moral lesson to heart and as an adult tried to strengthen others so that they could multiply its positive effects.

In each case, the PEG study women were taught as youngsters that qualities beyond the materialistic were of paramount importance. Their parents encouraged them to become compassionate individuals, which allowed them to experience how personally rewarding it feels to do something for the benefit of others. These parents' modeling and communication of their strong, positive values led their daughters to embrace them as their own.

Moral Development

Research has shown that gifted children may be more prone to grapple with moral issues at younger ages than their peers.[2] Gifted education expert Barbara Clark notes that, as a result, "the early appearance of social conscience that often characterizes gifted children signals an earlier need for development of a value structure and for the opportunity to translate values into social action."[3] Families that reinforce gifted children's moral selves may help provide the foundation for their children's desire to change the world for the better. It is not surprising, then, that morality was a common theme among the PEG study families. The women's parents and grandparents conveyed their ethics through their principled behavior.

According to psychologist Michael Schulman, morality does not mean avoiding punishment or seeking a tangible reward. Rather, it is about doing the right thing. Empathy, principles, and moral affiliations are three sources of moral motivation. People act morally because they identify with the feelings of sufferers, are committed to high ideals of behavior, and/or emulate "good" people.[4]

Schulman says that morality may be both "'taught' and 'caught.'"[5] Parents can both teach and model moral values that reinforce their children's instinctive morality. To enhance moral development, they may create a home environment where their children feel encouraged and valued. Schulman explains that children best internalize parental rules when they are treated "with warmth and sensitivity" and have parents who "explain their rules clearly, give firm correctives, but do not rely on physical punishment."[6] A cooperative, not an obedient, child is what moral training should produce, he contends. Children who feel accepted and know that their parents want the best for them tend to take reprimands seriously.

Julia Hix, a secondary school science teacher, grew up in a family that exemplified many of Schulman's suggestions. Her parents believed in providing a clear framework of right and wrong, but they also gave Julia and her brother choices to make within that framework. This balance of structure and choice gave the children a sense of safety and freedom. Bad behavior had appropriate consequences, but Julia's parents were consistent in explaining why they were disciplining her, and this is significant. "Simply giving a child 'prohibitions without explanations' works against the development of altruism," notes Schulman.[7] Parents who establish trusting relationships that are grounded in love, respect, and support give their children a better chance of becoming adults who care about and want to help others.

Julia's parents made their moral beliefs explicit: "Take something you stand for, and if you believe it, then what everybody else believes doesn't affect it." Julia learned that if she felt something was morally wrong, then she should take action to correct the situation, even if it meant going against the majority. When she got to PEG in the late 1980s, Julia wanted to play soccer, but MBC didn't have a team. When she asked to play with the local all-male team, an administrator assured Julia that she would try to make arrangements, despite the obstacles. Every time Julia checked on the status of her soccer request, the administrator told her that she was working on the issue. Put off by the recurrent delays, Julia took matters into her own hands and made her case directly to the team—and succeeded. She became a starter and earned the respect of the players. She had righted a wrong and forged the way for women to play soccer locally.

Assuming Responsibility

Assuming responsibility is part of moral development and was a common theme among the study women's families. Not making excuses or blaming others for one's mistakes is an important quality to acquire to become a mature adult. The PEG women wrote about their profound sense of responsibility and the desire to act according to their high, ethical ideals.

Ruby Kelp, a poet, recalled a childhood incident that made a lasting impression on her and affected how she behaved at college and in adulthood. She was in second grade and had forgotten to bring in her completed homework. The Kelps lived very close to the school, so she called her mother and asked her to bring it. Mrs. Kelp refused Ruby's request. "Later, she explained that it would have been unfair for her to bail me out when so many other kids had parents who worked during the day or lived too far away to bring their work for them." Ruby said that she learned a powerful lesson at a young age that "my work was my responsibility and that I should not rely on other people to take care of it for me. I really hated having to sit inside that day during recess as punishment for not bringing the work."

By explaining why she refused to accommodate her daughter, Mrs. Kelp helped Ruby absorb the concepts of fairness and responsibility. By the time Ruby reached PEG at age 14, she had already learned to be accountable for her actions. "In college, one of my professors told me that he appreciated that I never made excuses if I didn't have work done," she said. The professor reinforced what Ruby's mother had already taught her.

Paying the Consequences

Many teenagers do not understand that to assume responsibility, they have to pay the consequences of their behaviors, but Julia Hix did; her parents emphasized that principle. Both Hix children participated in family decision making and could disagree with their parents, but they had to be aware of the impact of their decisions. When Julia was deciding about early college entrance at age 14, Mr. and Mrs. Hix said that they wanted her to be happy but also to realize that there would be different consequences depending on her choice. Understanding the implications of her decision made it "a lot more real—that what I was doing was affecting everybody else in the family," Julia said. It also helped her see that if she went to PEG, she would have to make a full year's commitment. Knowing these two things "made me take the decision more seriously." Julia was able to imagine the effects of her decision because her parents helped her understand what it would entail, and this lesson prepared her to shoulder the responsibility of her life-changing choice.

Serving the Community

Many of the PEG study participants said they were grateful to their families for giving them self-confidence as children. That gratitude acted as a powerful motivation for the young women to help others feel good and become self-reliant.

Julia Hix's parents modeled their belief that an individual's energy, thoughts, and actions can make a real difference in the world. "Family values were communicated mostly by example. Nobody said, 'These are our values; learn them,'" recounted Julia. Her grandfather was just one of many family members who volunteered in his community. "My grandfather works in a soup kitchen, and I can see the difference it makes. Children come in there and at least once a day they have a hot meal. He also delivers meals to the elderly." Watching the effects of her grandfather's efforts inspired her. All through her college and adult years, Julia was an avid volunteer who devoted large amounts of time to helping others.

Nina Carpenter spoke at length about her parents' ethos of serving others and about their influence on her thinking and volunteering, and she shared her parents' desire to make the world a better place. One of her community contributions after graduating from PEG was the establishment of a regional association for peace and social justice.

Prolonged engagement with purpose requires the ability to reflect accurately about one's life and to evaluate whether one is living according to a deeply held belief system. Parents who both voiced and lived their values provided powerful role models for their children. The moral lessons about assuming responsibility for one's actions, accepting the consequences for those actions, and helping others became entrenched in the PEG women's hearts because they saw their parents living according to those principles. Not only did most of the parents support their daughters' intellectual interests and accomplishments, but they also encouraged their children to look beyond themselves to the greater world to see how they might be of service.

Most of the PEG study parents made their daughters feel that they had something substantial to offer the world. The idea of "making a difference" stemmed from those home environments. For many of the women, the message from their parents was: "Don't just say what you think is right or important; stand up for it and make changes. Count for something in life." With this foundation, PEG and Mary Baldwin College then propelled these young women forward and encouraged their commitment to purpose and to making a difference.

CHAPTER 5

School Issues and the Struggle of Being Different

Despite the prevalence of preschool attendance, going to school begins formally for most children when they enter kindergarten. The PEG study participants, like other gifted children, were happy, well-adjusted, and enthusiastic about the prospect of going to school. Their natural curiosity and questioning would finally be rewarded with full days of learning and exploring knowledge. Unfortunately, like far too many gifted children, most of the PEGs were quickly disappointed with their school experiences.

Feeling Different

Once grouped with same-age classmates, the bright picture of school that the PEG girls had imagined began to darken. Passionate about information, eager to share their excitement about learning, and often interested in subjects that did not interest their peers, most of the girls began to feel different from other students and experienced some unease as they moved through primary school. Julia's mother described how her daughter was different from her classmates: "She never had time for frivolous stuff; she played with blocks to build things and liked puzzles—things she had to figure out." Unlike most of the other children at school, "she was nearly always serious as a child; she didn't laugh a whole lot. Julia was happy, but she was always a little beyond her years."

Julia may have been more serious as a child than most of the other PEG study participants, but she represented the underlying earnestness of the PEGs' desire for true intellectual discovery. As often happens with gifted children, many of these young girls felt bored and frustrated with classes that did not challenge them or probe topics deeply enough.

Besides enduring an inappropriate match of curriculum with her ability, Julia was also aware that she was somewhat different from the other children, and she distinguished between being different and caring about being different. "Not caring what everyone thinks is one thing, but feeling okay about being different is something else. Feeling okay about being different comes along a lot later!" Julia didn't have a choice about being different, and it was "definitely not okay to be different" in school. Even though she had a few primary school teachers who tried to support her, she continued to feel different as she got older. Unlike many girls, she was unconcerned about external appearances, and by middle school, her disregard of fashion set her even further apart from most of the student body. Noticing that she was building an emotional wall and beginning to act destructively, Julia's parents worried about her.

When Julia entered PEG, she was relieved to find others with the same excitement about learning. She no longer felt like an outcast. Despite the new, positive environment at PEG, it took Julia many years to feel completely at ease with who she was. The damage she had suffered to her sense of self had been profound.

Bullying

Most of the PEG study participants suffered from some sort of bullying in their home schools—physical attacks, verbal abuse, and/or isolating tactics. Early on, Claire became aware of being unlike the other girls and didn't have much fun socially. She didn't fit in very well; she had only one close, smart friend. She was teased constantly as she rode the bus home. "Getting home, I would walk up the driveway crying on many occasions. I don't even remember why they picked on me; they just did." But adults didn't worry about bullying too much when Claire was growing up, and she remembered "spending a lot of time outraged at the unfairness of things."

Claire's sense of justice developed early, as is the case for many gifted youngsters.[1] As a seven-year-old, she confronted a 12-year-old boy who was aggressively teasing his 11-year-old sister on the school bus. When Claire tried to intervene, the boy "got really mad and slapped me across the face, very hard. I just turned around and sat down and was quiet; his hand left a red mark on my face." Standing up to a much older boy stemmed from her deep emotional response to unfairness of any kind.

As she got older, Claire remembered "always either being in fear of being humiliated or being humiliated." Her mother reassured her that she needn't care about fashion, Top 40 radio shows, or TV shows and that she was "not weird for caring about school or loving to read or wanting to have philosophical conversations." As an adult, Claire understood the lesson her mother had tried to teach her: "to trust myself, to be myself, and to not care too much about what other people think, but I'm not always able to stop caring, even now." Mrs. Hagan helped Claire stay true to her intellectual and moral self, even when she suffered emotionally from rejection.

Madison said that the hardest years of her life were from ages five to 12. Knowing she was different, she spent most of her time "figuring out exactly why I was different and what I could do about it." Her parents' and friends' support in elementary school boosted her self-esteem, but her greatest life lessons "were from the kids who made fun of me. There weren't many of them, but they were consistent and cruel." Madison later concluded that coping with her tormentors had given her the strength to handle many difficulties. "It really can be true that that which doesn't kill you makes you stronger," she said. As a child, Madison eventually realized that "I was just fine the way I was—that I was smart, unique, pretty, and resourceful. I didn't need anyone else's approval; I only needed mine." The bullies' harassment "could not break me, but I had to continually grow stronger to prevent that. That foundation of strength is still there today."

By turning her persecution into perception, Madison gained insight. She understood that becoming resilient was a cumulative process that continued through college and into adulthood. Perhaps partially as a result of these childhood experiences, Madison became a medical doctor who provided caring treatment to people who often were victimized.

Coping in Middle and High School

In a study of bullying, Peterson and Ray found that gifted children are bullied predominantly because of their intelligence.[2] Sylvia Rimm notes that bullying based on a child's excellent school performance transforms "the child's strength into a weakness and a potential source of shame."[3] As school bullying increases, Rimm, Peterson, and others feel that "gifted children may be more susceptible to the emotional damage that bullying can inflict."[4]

The Peterson and Ray study indicates that bullying for gifted children is most intense in sixth grade, when students simultaneously endure being teased about their intelligence and their appearance. Middle school is a critical time because it is when children begin to form their identity. Close friends usually aid in that development, but adolescents can be distressingly intolerant of any deviance from the norm. According to Miraca Gross, "This can be problematic for gifted adolescents who differ, in most areas of their development, from the majority of students in their chronological age cohort."[5] Gross cites research which found that gifted students who perceive themselves as different lose self-esteem.

Middle school raised the social and emotional stakes for most of the study alumnae, as it does for many gifted students. The PEG study women reported intensified teasing, humiliation, and torment in middle school by students who disdained their academic interests and different priorities. Since this is the time when students often turn away from their families to seek affirmation from their peers, the importance of social acceptance intensifies.[6] The excessive pressure to become part of the mainstream may hurt the moral character of gifted children who do not get adequate social and emotional support. Resentment about poor treatment in school can make gifted children bitter. If their hostile surroundings break their spirits, then the chances that gifted children will retain their empathy toward others decreases. Most of the PEG women eventually rebounded from the abuse, but others grew defensive and distant.

Bullied gifted children in the Peterson and Ray study reported getting little or no support from teachers and administrators, even when the staff knew that such intimidation was occurring on school grounds. The children often were told that they should be able to figure out their own problems because they were so intelligent. Such a response shows a painfully inadequate understanding of gifted children's development. While they may be quite advanced intellectually, gifted children do not necessarily have more highly developed social and emotional coping mechanisms. They are asynchronous in their development, meaning that their intellectual development may be advanced compared to their age peers, but their social development may lag behind that of those same peers. Abandoning gifted children to survive on their own is unconscionable and can lead to serious or even devastating consequences. Madison, Claire, and Julia were all fortunate to have support from loving, caring adults. Without it, the cruelty they endured might have led them to depression, suicide, or other negative behaviors.

Trying to Fit In

For many gifted children, the only escape from bullying is to try to fit in with the rest of their age mates. However, fitting in comes with its own set of stressors. As the gifted young women in the PEG study went through school, many of them who chose academics over popularity suffered socially. But the ones who capitulated to social pressures suffered differently as they tried to fit in. One of Darcy's PEG application essays poignantly offers the perspective of a 13-year-old middle school student who feels forced to disguise her true self: "I feel stifled here. I try to talk with my peers, but that fails when I realize they don't feel like talking in depth." When she offered a different opinion on a topic, the other students usually laughed at her and were dismissive. "I have learned to be accepted by my peers by putting on a front and disguising my real thoughts." Because Darcy wanted to discuss issues seriously, she struggled to find real friends.

Gifted education researcher Sally Reis calls this type of dilemma "affiliation vs. achievement"—the push-pull that young teenage girls feel between wanting to be popular and also wanting to be academically accomplished.[7] Today, fewer girls may "dumb themselves down" to become more popular,[8] but that may depend on school attitudes and a selection of advanced course offerings. Although there has been a big increase in the percentage of girls who enter science, technology, engineering, or math fields, many girls still shy away from pursuing those subjects as both undergraduate and graduate students.[9]

Two of the PEG women mentioned the dangers of conceding too much of one's true self to gain acceptance. Kristen said that from kindergarten through sixth grade, she was fearless and tried lots of new things, but at 13, she became "more worried about what people thought." As an adult, she found it difficult "to be disappointed in my own courage and to realize that I was willing to compromise in order to be liked. I think it is a stage of my life that I am still learning to correct."

By the time she finished middle school, Lucy was headed for serious trouble. Staying in high school past her freshman year "could have done significant, irreparable damage to my personal health and well-being," she said. "I was a Goody Two Shoes Teacher's Pet who wanted to be well liked by my peers, and I sought peer group acceptance by turning toward 'bad' behaviors." By ninth grade, she was beginning to experiment with drugs, alcohol, and sex. Lucy said, "I believe that this behavior would have escalated had I stayed where I was."

The Struggle to Be One's True Self

Each woman in the study had tried to become her "true self" before she attended PEG, but the lack of close friends and academic peers stymied that process. To achieve popularity with the "in" crowd, Darcy, Kristen, and Lucy donned social disguises that conflicted with their personal values. Julia encased herself in an emotional fortress to avoid the pain of rejection. Relinquishing the true self led to self-alienation and even to destructive behaviors for some of the women. Without a basis for authentic connection, friendships remained relatively artificial for most of the girls until they arrived at Mary Baldwin.

Anxiety about being an outcast can be debilitating. A gifted child may wonder if she can survive all the teasing, bullying, and loneliness. May said that she used to think "that I would be a friendless, loveless person because I was such an outcast as a child— I never fit in. I never had close friends who shared my interests. I felt like everyone outside of my family was constantly annoyed or confused by me."

Pushing oneself to fit in can result in self-denial for a gifted child. Estrangement from the true self in childhood and adolescence may lead to difficulty developing self-knowledge and self-acceptance, two critical qualities in the development and pursuit of goals. If a person becomes too emotionally wounded, it may sap her ability to cope with great difficulties. The likelihood of depression increases. Motivation to act decreases. To be other-directed and purposeful, most individuals must first gain a healthy inner strength to withstand later duress.

In contrast, standing apart from the mainstream may be a positive trait; it may contribute to original thinking about society's thorniest problems, and it may afford insight into gifted young women.[10] Being alienated from many peer groups as they grew up may cause gifted individuals to feel others' pain more deeply than the average person. If they get the academic and emotional support they need in time, gifted young women may be able to draw on their acute observations and empathy to find and implement innovative solutions for humanity.

Social Development vs. Socialization

Part of the problem of how to address gifted students' social needs is a lack of understanding of the terms used when discussing this issue.

> *Lack of socialization is one of the first criticisms raised by many home school opponents, but psychologist Linda Silverman notes the important distinction between socialization and social development. Socialization is the ability to adapt to the needs of a group, the ability and desire to conform. Social development, on the other hand, is the process of getting to know and be comfortable with oneself and one's beliefs so as to better contribute to the needs of the group. The difference is between going along with the crowd and not making waves or standing out (socialization) and cooperating when necessary for the common good but also being willing to stick one's neck out to make a positive difference (social development).*[11]

As young girls, most of the PEG study women struggled against socialization in its conformist sense and strived for social development in its independent aspect. Only by becoming socially developed (as opposed to being socialized) does one gain the clarity of one's position and the determination, motivation, and courage to stand up for what one believes and values. To sustain a sense of purpose often requires contradicting conventional wisdom.

Anti-Intellectual School Settings

For highly gifted students, school can sometimes deter complex learning. Most of the PEG study participants reported public school environments that were anti-curiosity and that undercut a true love of learning. Julia said she was treated like a nerd when she asked thoughtful questions about the academic material. Claire agreed.

"People would roll their eyes or make me feel like a trouble-maker for asking the questions that I really wanted to ask." Many of the study alumnae characterized themselves as being intensely curious, wanting to find things out for themselves, being truth-seekers, natural inquirers, and passionately interested in things. They were unhappy and frustrated throughout much of their formal schooling. Continuing in the public school system might have seriously dampened their inquisitiveness because it was socially hazardous to show the depth and earnestness of their real desires and interests.

May in particular felt significant discomfort from her teachers. "It was the teachers who often disliked me for being more work for them or else felt that they had to prove that I wasn't as smart as reported." Responding to her hostile environment, May didn't volunteer answers in class or share her grades with other students. "When you do well, you make other people feel bad." Trying not to be confrontational, she began to submerge her true personality. She hid her insight and academic success, "though I did find that I quietly enjoyed winning every award, or always being the finale for the piano recital, or having a slightly scary reputation."

May was lucky that she had a history teacher who "really did adore me." The teacher recognized her high intelligence and made allowances for her. She automatically got A's on all of her work because he knew that she was so smart that she didn't have to prove herself. "It's twisted and wrong and unfair, but that little gesture made me feel good. Finally someone told me that he could see that I was special." May said that no one in school ever praised her because they didn't want her to "get a big head, but at that point, I had heard so many negative things about myself that it was a very touching, perverse act of kindness."

Resilience researchers point to the power of the individual teacher, as May's story so aptly illustrates. Gifted children need recognition of their advanced abilities and insights. Even though May hid her true abilities from other students, she felt validated by that one teacher. He provided a lifeline that made school somewhat tolerable. Teachers can provide critical support and opportunities for students to become strong and resilient. "Research confirms unequivocally the power of one person to make a difference."[12]

Most teachers in the United States get little to no training in gifted education before they begin teaching.[13] As a result, even well-meaning teachers sometimes hurt gifted children unintentionally. A teacher who does not understand gifted children's characteristics may damage, rather than vitalize, students' self-esteem. During middle school, one PEG study alumna (who didn't want us to identify her in this instance, even with a pseudonym) took an accelerated math class at the local high school. Bussed from that building back to the middle school every morning, she was teased frequently. "Eventually the middle school resource teacher caught me in tears as I headed to my regular middle school classes. She determined the source of my upset and lectured the offenders." The next morning, the teasers "were very careful to be nice and polite, but that was actually worse. I decided then that I was completely separate." The teacher, who felt empathy, inadvertently increased this student's feelings of isolation from her classmates because she reinforced the girl's identity as "different."

It is imperative for teachers to learn to appreciate the unique talents and particular social and emotional needs of highly gifted children. Through their support, teachers may set an example of true inclusion in their classrooms. Respect for intellectual differences and characteristics should apply to gifted students as much as it does to children with learning difficulties and/or culturally diverse backgrounds. Caring teachers who create open learning environments and accept gifted children for who they really are can have long-lasting and significant effects.

Teachers Who Made a Difference

Paul Torrance, a renowned creativity researcher, conducted a longitudinal study about predicting creativity in elementary school children. Among the important influences that helped the children become creatively gifted adults were the teachers "who made a difference." The adults Torrance surveyed described characteristics that they attributed to these teachers, such as "being made to feel comfortable with their creativity and feeling of uniqueness; being given activities that provided practice in creative skills; sharing the joys of creative attainments…and being acknowledged for making creative contributions." The productive, creative individuals were grateful to any teacher who helped them realize and then maintain their creativity. Torrance reported on one teacher in particular who encouraged "the children to grow, to be the most of what they could be, to be comfortable, especially highly creative children who were regarded as 'different.'"[14]

Some of the PEG study women recalled wonderful teachers who recognized and appreciated their differences. Lucy had many teachers whom she loved, but it was her third-grade teacher, Mrs. Dimini, who was "the clearest influence on my intellectual and creative development." Truly grateful for the acknowledgment that Mrs. Dimini gave her talents, Lucy said, "She loved the stories I wrote and would pin them onto her bulletin board each week as examples of great work. She wrote enthusiastic, specific comments on my stories and poems about how and why they were good." Mrs. Dimini's specific feedback not only helped Lucy understand what she was doing right, but also validated her ability. Literature and writing subsequently became lifelong passions for Lucy.

Julia also had influential teachers. Her mother recalled, "Her kindergarten teacher and then Mrs. Forster, her first gifted program teacher, both encouraged Julia to be herself and let her know that it was okay to be bright; it was okay to like to read." Both teachers were very intelligent themselves, and they nurtured Julia's abilities and encouraged her. As an adult, Julia still remembers the complex lessons and the profound effect of Mrs. Forster's outlook and support. "She was probably the first teacher that really encouraged everyone to go their own direction, to learn whatever they wanted to learn," she said. Mrs. Forster conveyed the message that "learning was just a wonderful thing. She thought so, and so everybody there in the gifted program thought so, too."

Gifted students are fortunate when they have teachers who are highly attuned to the needs of individual children and who create open and productive environments where students can thrive. In an in-depth study on the roots of success and failure in talented teenagers, psychologist Mihaly Csikszentmihalyi showed that students were most highly influenced by teachers who were enthusiastic, who created learning experiences that promoted "a close fit between challenges and skills," and who had the "unusual ability to perceive the emerging needs of often insecure young people."[15]

Teens in the Csikszentmihalyi study stressed the importance of supportive elementary school teachers. "Favorite childhood teachers were especially remembered for their reassuring kindness and genuine desire to be helpful."[16] Classroom life could be improved at all levels by the "cultivation of passionate interest as a primary educational goal"[17] because that type of class promotes a love of learning that is intrinsically satisfying. All students, including the most gifted ones, can flourish under these conditions.

By the time talented teenagers enter high school, most of them "experience apathetic or lackluster instruction with an especially acute sense of disappointment."[18] Because so many of them have developed avid interests in particular areas, gifted students are more likely to be "intolerant of teachers who go through the motions."[19] Similarly, the PEG women's emotional well-being was tied to the satisfaction of their intellectual needs. Despite encouragement from a few inspiring teachers, the PEG study women noted major deficiencies in their elementary, middle, and high school educations. However, they blossomed under teachers who appreciated their abilities and who freed them to pursue their interests.

Risks to Goals, Hope, and Empathy

The inner construction of purpose includes three major components: goals, hope, and empathy. Finding purpose entails setting and attaining goals. Pursuing goals depends on the hope of creating and achieving them. Acting upon humanitarian goals requires empathy for the plight of others.[20] When any of these components is impaired, purpose becomes harder to acquire and maintain.[21]

Most of the study participants enjoyed certain teachers or aspects of school, but they also suffered intellectually, socially, and/ or emotionally. Negative elementary, middle, and high school experiences put at risk the goals, hope, and empathy of these girls and held the potential to hurt the study women's academic work, their psychological well-being, and their sense of purpose. Inadequate academic challenge fed their sense of loss and affected their behavior. Unsupportive school environments often discouraged them from personally meaningful achievement and jeopardized their ability to empathize.

Effects on Academics

Hope is essential for students to fulfill their academic promise. Not only does hopeful thinking increase students' sense of self-efficacy and motivation, but it also helps them "to stay 'on task' and not be blocked by interfering self-deprecatory thoughts and negative emotions."[22] Uneasy in their uncomfortable pre-college learning environments, many of the PEG study women began to lose hope. How could they pursue their potential when they often had to hide the most passionate parts of their nature? Most felt that they were stagnating or regressing academically because of low-level curriculum and the threat of repercussions from teachers or classmates. As their intellectual needs were thwarted, their self-confidence began to diminish. As critical thinkers, the study women wanted to seek answers to questions that most mattered to them. When those instincts were quelled, the route to purposefulness was jeopardized.

Highly gifted students can be at risk as much as students living in poverty or students with learning disabilities. Researchers describe the potential hazards for at-risk students: "Imagine the negative ripples—lost opportunities, unfulfilled talents, and sense of failure—that may flow over a lifetime for some students who drop out of high school or college."[23] Whether gifted students literally drop out of high school or just "check out" mentally, the risk is that they will lose their love of learning, lose sight of their goals, lose their sense of empathy, and lose the desire to improve the world. It is a sad fact that many eager, extremely smart students do not experience a welcoming intellectual environment during their school years. The emotional and social impact they experience adds a further, heartbreaking dimension to their loss. The loss of their creativity and high ability to our society and the world is incalculable.

Effects on Well-Being

Feeling unaccepted and having to suppress their enjoyment of learning threatened some of the PEG study women's excitement about life. "Hope is crucial for psychological health. Hopeful thought entails the ability to establish clear goals, imagine workable pathways, and motivate oneself to work toward goals."[24] When motivation and enthusiasm are missing, preserving a sense of purpose becomes difficult.

Children who cannot envision fulfilling their goals may stop planning productively for the future. Researchers conclude that there is a "growing consensus that the perceived lack of progress toward major goals is the cause of reductions in well-being, rather than vice-versa."[25] The anti-intellectual forces that encumbered these gifted girls often made them feel as if they could not succeed in school according to their own standards, values, and interests. Deprived of genuine ways of being, their self-esteem often withered. Had they not been able to enroll in college early, the blows to their sense of satisfaction could have further reduced their energy to pursue lives of purpose.

Adolescence is the time when children may be most idealistic and energetic in forming and aiming for their dreams. Visions of a better world may inspire children to create purposeful lives. To hold onto their aspirations, children need to feel that they will endure despite their troubles.

Transforming Suffering

Life without meaning is life without purpose. Although some people emerge from difficulties stronger than they were before, excessive negative experiences can cause gifted children to lose their sense of meaning. Ostracized and alone, most of the gifted study women withdrew to emotionally safe places, whether at home or within themselves, at some point in their childhood. While all of them survived emotionally and even excelled academically, the PEG study women were often angry and sad as young girls because they longed for truly kindhearted friends and stimulating academic work. By the time they were considering enrolling in PEG, many of them were at their breaking points.

Most of the gifted youngsters who prevailed against social and emotional injuries in school had parents, other relatives, or adult friends who consistently celebrated their individuality and provided enough positive reinforcement to convince them that they were unique in the best ways. To balance the focus on their talents, the adults also underscored compassion for others and responsibility for one's actions. Finding just one or two friends who understood and appreciated them also made a critical difference to the girls' well-being. For those fortunate children, suffering was transformed into empathy.

Part III

Life During PEG

CHAPTER 6

Intellectual Development and Social-Emotional Needs

Enrolling in PEG was one of the major turning points in the study women's lives. It was a place where they could discover, examine, and be their true selves without risking ridicule. Attending the early entrance college program helped some to reinforce their sense of purpose and others to develop it. During her PEG directorship, Dr. Rhodes adopted the philosophy that giftedness was not an end in itself but rather a means to living purposefully, and she encouraged students enrolled in PEG to develop their talents for self-fulfillment and for the benefit of others.

Madison summed up how many of the girls felt: "Suddenly, I wasn't just passing time until my real life began. My life developed purpose and direction. Every day held new adventures and new experiences." For Darcy, PEG was a godsend. Her public school's gifted program had just disbanded for lack of money, and she felt desperate about finding a suitable place to learn. When she and her family discovered the program, "All our hopes were answered." Enrolling in PEG was transformative; many of the girls were leaving behind debilitating experiences and behaviors and turning toward exciting, new, and healthy choices.

Leaving Dissatisfaction Behind

As part of the PEG admissions process, the study women had to write four essays to demonstrate their intelligence and maturity. Asked why early college entrance would be appropriate for them, most said that they wanted greater academic challenge. However, the social and emotional costs of their previous intellectual isolation were apparent in the descriptions of their home schools.

Liz was 14 years old when she entered Mary Baldwin College. One of the reasons she wanted to attend PEG was to make more friends. "Living with others of the same intellectual caliber would aid me greatly because I could enjoy their company, learn more about others, and absorb influences and opinions," she wrote in her application essay. Darcy, at 13, explained that although her school classes were "quite enough challenge" for most of her peers, she was painfully bored. To keep her mind engaged, she developed a strategy. "I sit very quietly and observe people. I analyze people's actions and their words. Now it is natural to study people inconspicuously." Observing people surreptitiously, however, did not make school more satisfying.

Georgia wrote her application essay when she was just 12 years old. In it, she emphasized the importance of emotional and social comfort while learning. "The amount of liking and respect that one receives from their teachers and classmates plays an important role in their education. There are still some people who think that enjoying school is stupid, dumb, and impossible." Georgia astutely urged teachers to express their regard for all of their students, including the most advanced or unconventional ones.

At 16, Rachel was an older and more experienced applicant. As a Black teen, she had felt the sting of prejudice in her schooling and wanted to be in a place where she would receive support "in becoming the person I strive to be." She wrote, "African American females still face difficulties despite some people's efforts to create equal opportunity. African Americans are discriminated against, mostly because of conscious, or unconscious, stereotypical beliefs." When she was young, Rachel "had several opportunities denied me because my teachers believed I was not suitable for a program for brighter children. In their view, my ethnicity would work against me to the point that it would not be beneficial for me to be placed into those programs." It wasn't until Rachel applied to PEG that she finally realized that her home school had simply not recognized her advanced intelligence. She later said, "I came to perceive myself as very average. Anything outstanding that I did was a fluke at best. Though I would not assume to be the intellectual superior of my peers, I have since grown to be assured of my intelligence."

Rachel also wrote about growth through education. "In every person's life, there is a time for coming into, for becoming, and for leaving all things. In my view, this is integral to the process of continual growth." Rachel saw education as a "sort of 'how to' book on the subject of self-discovery." Invaluable lessons could be culled from education, which could then lead to enriched experiences in life and were vital parts of growing, she concluded. Whereas "the road the majority takes through high school and college seems paved and sterile, PEG is like the invitation to take a scenic trail." With high hopes for her future at Mary Baldwin, Rachel wrote that it would be "an experience that is the very epitome of growth."

Like Rachel, Darcy appreciated the growth that education could afford her. She noted that "education can lift a whole society. It challenges the individual and teaches them so many lessons on perseverance and self-discovery that contribute to the wisdom achieved later in life." Clearly, being able to enter an environment that supported intellectualism and nurtured a passion for lifelong learning was pivotal for these teens to develop into purposeful young women.

Building on the Foundation

Although all of the young women shared a curiosity and enthusiasm for learning, several of them highlighted key aspects of PEG that specifically appealed to them and that they saw as major advantages to entering the program.

Rekindling the Intellectual Spark

Madison typified the girls' excitement when they arrived on campus. She felt grateful to "learn that I loved to learn—I'd really forgotten that." Public school had almost driven away her natural enthusiasm for learning. Similarly, Lucy said she was "rescued from a public school system that was slowly killing my love of learning and leading me to deny my 'smarts' for social reasons." Claire said that the college experience of being able to ask any question she wanted without derision was "refreshing." Providing a rejuvenating boost to languishing minds, PEG rekindled that joyful spark of intellectual engagement. Going to PEG, Nina explained, "completely helped, in that I did not 'waste' three years of my life in a blah high school setting, but sent me on my way to learn and grow in an exciting environment."

Promoting Authenticity and Community

Julia enjoyed the other PEG students' attitudes toward learning—an invigorating change from her former classmates in middle school. "For most of us, it was the first time we'd been in a group that was interested in academics. It was okay to ask a question, even if nobody understood it, much less could come up with an answer." Happily, she discovered that college was quite different from middle school. "You're in an environment that actively encourages curiosity and learning, rather than suppresses it." Among intellectual girls, Julia could be her true self. Ruby recalled that "there was a spirit of cooperation that I hope still exists today." The women did not feel self-conscious at PEG, so their mutual support increased.

Benefits of Single-Sex Education

Looking back, Julia felt that a single-sex college greatly benefited the women in math and science. It could be cultural, Julia said, but "in a mixed group, when it comes time to manipulate, to actually do hands-on stuff, the people who step forward tend to be men. When it's all women, you don't have that option." Other PEG study participants agreed that the women at Mary Baldwin

College seemed to get more encouragement for non-traditional female fields than they may have at a co-ed college.

Self-Concept and Fitting In

While some people assume that putting gifted children together in a program makes them conceited, the effect is actually often the opposite: the students' academic self-concept may initially decrease. When a highly gifted student is placed in a class with average-ability peers, she is likely to see herself as the smartest, easily outperforming her classmates. But when she is placed in a class with other very bright students, she may be somewhat shaken to learn that there are others as capable as she is, and some even more so. Her self-esteem may drop as she struggles to reassess her identity. However, once she realizes that she is in a group of very high achievers (and therefore must be very smart to have been included in that group), her self-concept improves—this time with a degree of humility that may not have been present before. Working with other high achievers, setting very high standards, and striving to maximize their potential thus ultimately promotes a high academic self-concept, which has a positive role in students' subsequent achievement.[1]

The study women's experience was similar. Being with other girls who had a variety of high-level abilities helped put their talents in perspective. As May said, "In regular school, you can easily dominate, but in college, the level is amped up, so you learn that you're not a science whiz." On the other hand, she could better appreciate her strengths. "If you can compete at something at college level, you must be pretty good at it for a teenager."

A few of the study women eased their transition to the much heavier academic college course load by taking some lower-level classes as freshmen. But most dove right into the rigorous schedule of college lectures, readings, and experiments. Coming from schools that did not teach the students how to conduct research or manage large-scale projects efficiently, the young PEGs had a steep learning curve.

Although PEG and MBC had academic and advising systems in place to support the radically accelerated students, ultimately the young women were expected to develop the skills and accept the responsibility for the heightened challenge. Claire became overwhelmed with work right away, but she got enough support from older PEGs to cope with assignments effectively. As May implied, the students' strength of mind was evidenced by their ability to manage a full college course load as early teens. Once the students combined their academic smarts with their determination to succeed, they pushed themselves to more advanced and complex levels of intellectual challenge.

Kristen said that the PEGs used to joke about being "eternally dissatisfied" because they knew that they could always do better in their course work. Despite this, the girls enjoyed being in the company of bright peers and grew from the experience. "PEG is humbling," Kristen remarked, "because you realize how many of those young women are smarter than you are, but it also makes you aware that you do have a lot of potential."

Before PEG, Rachel was "content just to get by in school and had little motivation to do well." At first, she was happy to be in PEG because it was new and exciting. She was thrilled to be on her own among girls with whom she could relate. "It eventually helped me to realize what it meant, in the academic sense, to be gifted. Having never been previously identified as gifted at my former schools, this was a significant leap in my self-awareness." Once Rachel had a sense of her competence and felt comfortable among her true peers, she became deeply invested in her learning and flourished.

Exposure to other highly talented and driven young women promoted enormous growth in some of the other girls as well. Jessica said that she had an "extraordinary period of development" at PEG. She felt that PEG automatically raised the bar on her academic, social, and athletic skills. Among other high-performing girls, Jessica worked her hardest, made the most of her opportunities and abilities, and learned from her peers.

Meeting the intellectual challenge of keeping up with the other PEGs and doing the college coursework "really pushed me to go further than I would have gone in public school," Claire wrote. "And then being able to succeed was really rewarding and gave me a lot of self-confidence." The PEG peer group helped her set "really high goals and then achieve them." The motivational key was not just being in accelerated classes; "it was being around all the other girls who were doing the same thing. Seeing them, seeing the ideas that they came up with, I enjoyed pushing myself to further fit in."

Claire came to MBC with an inferiority complex. "I thought that I didn't really belong there, so I felt like I had to show that I belonged." Ironically, feeling less capable than her PEG classmates made Claire work harder to reach their level, and when she chose to fit in to the nurturing and challenging intellectual environment, she grew. Fitting in no longer meant having to change fundamentally to fit others' expectations of her behavior and interests. Instead, it meant working toward high standards. Fitting in, which many of the girls had avoided prior to PEG, was now viewed as a positive behavior.

As the gifted young women progressed through college, they discovered different dimensions of their own and others' knowledge, interests, and abilities. Recognizing that the PEGs had different strengths and talents "helped me grow a lot," said Claire. Similarly, PEG showed May that people can be smart in different ways. As an adult, "that translated into being helpful to others." May was proud that she got along with so many different types of people and felt that PEG had helped her hone her social skills as a young teen.

Increased self-awareness helped the young PEG study women become better students. With a clearer mental picture of their talents, a drive to earn their place among other gifted women, and the openness to learn from peers, they were primed for pursuing their potential with energy, direction, and discipline.

An Intellectual Peer Group

In retrospect, the PEG study women recognized the intimate connection between social-emotional well-being and intellectual development. When their minds were appropriately stimulated, their social confidence and emotional health improved, and vice versa.

Claire mentioned the critical importance of having friends whose attitudes about learning and academic challenge were in sync. "Going through the PEG program would have been much more difficult without having a peer group to share it with. The most important impact was that it helped me realize that I wasn't alone." The teenagers formed deep, meaningful, and long-lasting bonds while they were grappling with increasing levels of responsibility, autonomy, and intellectual exploration. Knowing that they were not alone gave them the strength and courage to thrive in their radically accelerated program of study.

Commitment to Learning and Respect for Professors

The underlying ethos of the young women's academic journey was their commitment to learning. Nina observed that her PEG peers and their professors were all seriously devoted to "learning as a way of life."

May recalled "very warm professors who made me feel good about my talents and myself. Despite my griping at the time, I was allowed a lot of intellectual autonomy—I could throw myself head-long into whatever interested me." She reflected, "Allowing someone to do in-depth study in a topic they're interested in is a gift—discovering what you're good at, at a young age, is a gift." May felt fortunate to have "professors who really liked me and were very supportive. I got so much confidence from them." May's professors put her at ease in college and encouraged her fervent interests, which deepened her already strong commitment to learning.

Nina "never regretted even the slightest thing about my decision to attend PEG. It opened my life up." She cherished the atmosphere that welcomed her exuberance for learning. Her professors appreciated "my joy and enthusiasm for their subjects. Their respect for me, even when I was so young and wore silly costume-y clothes to class, allowed me to explore subjects unabashedly." Instead of being scorned for her imagination and expressiveness, Nina was praised for her passionate pursuit of knowledge. As a young teen, she felt valued for her love of learning. Had she stayed in public school, Nina may never have allowed herself to be so open; she may never have received that kind of unmitigated, positive reinforcement of her creativity. But with the MBC faculty's encouragement, Nina and May, like the other PEG study women, continued to grow intellectually as self-motivated learners and independent thinkers.

Timely Academic and Artistic Opportunities

No matter what their earlier schooling experiences, almost all of the PEG women described themselves as voracious readers, even those who majored in the sciences. Arriving at PEG in their early adolescent years, the girls were exposed to a large variety of books in the library, in the bookstore, in classes, from their professors, and among new friends. Their intellectual worlds blossomed immensely, which fed their great need to learn deeply.

The sudden abundance of academic and artistic opportunities awed the young women, and they took full advantage of them. Nina, for example, loved to "create and show art, teach, play and perform music, try theater, see New York on inspiring art trips, and be a counselor at MBC summer camps for Japanese students and at Science Camp." The diversity of these types of experiences allowed the PEG students to explore knowledge and themselves while also learning organizational and interpersonal skills. The PEG students felt that they would not have had a chance to grow in so many dimensions simultaneously if they'd stayed at their former schools.

Madison believed that the availability of so many academic opportunities at PEG helped encourage her to try new disciplines. "I learned that I was good at math and science, not just in English." Discovering her advanced math-science abilities at age 16 directly influenced Madison's decision to become a doctor—a decision she may never have made if she had continued to believe that she was accomplished only in the humanities. Being exposed to so many opportunities allowed Madison to choose a career that she may never have otherwise chosen, and she was able to focus her learning toward her goal of entering the field of medicine.

The ability to begin paving their career paths early worked in favor of many of the PEGs. Claire developed advanced analytic and academic skills in her mid-teens because she started college so young. Her future as a professor benefited from her head start. Similarly, May said that by the end of her sophomore year, she had figured out her major and "really fell into a good rhythm with my classes and could visualize goals for the future." She had known that she wanted to enter the art field for several years, and by age 16, she had a firm idea of the steps necessary to become an art dealer. Graduating college at such a young age gave her valuable early experience in her field. Her sense of purpose was taking shape and gaining strength.

Attitude toward Learning

Soon after they enrolled in college, the girls realized that learning would no longer be so easy. Deeming her algebra professor ineffective and the class below her skill level, Nikita "blew off going to class several times and rarely paid appropriate attention." The budding engineer was very upset when she got a B at the end of the semester. "That may not sound so horrible, but it was the worst grade that I ever got in a math class in my entire college career," she said. Nikita quickly realized that she needed to adjust her attitude and work habits. She became conscious of the "power my attitude can have on my ability to perform, so I find myself checking my attitude and adjusting it if things don't seem to be working out the way I hoped." Understanding that principle at age 14 helped her become an honors graduate in mathematics. As an adult, she was given great responsibilities as a young software engineer.

Nikita also realized that her attitude about education improved when she matched her learning style to her studies because it maximized her strengths. "I am a very physical learner. If I take the time to write out facts as I read or hear them, then I am much more likely to remember them." Graphic organizers also helped her absorb knowledge. Studying in ways that favored her personal learning styles made college easier. PEG helped Nikita become aware that the learning environment was also critical to her academic success. For graduate work, she chose "small universities where I could know my professors and learn a lot through their mentorship that I couldn't learn simply by reading or sitting in class."

Despite an overwhelming desire to do well in her courses, Nikita ultimately learned that the most important person to satisfy academically was herself. She wanted to meet her high standards on her terms. She hated freshman English because she felt that the professor had a very narrow way of seeing things. "I would rather get bad grades than create something I think is less than my best work to suit someone else," she said. For Nikita, intellectual integrity meant that her work had to be personally meaningful.

Leadership Skills

All of the study women developed enhanced academic and interpersonal skills during their time at PEG, but Mary Baldwin College also emphasized women's leadership, which is key to developing purpose. During the admissions process, the PEG admissions staff had looked for leadership potential in candidates' personal qualities and accomplishments. They wanted girls with intellectual ability, effective communication skills, sensitive interpersonal and intrapersonal skills, problem-solving abilities, passion, and persistence as a framework for successful leadership. The students who were selected to enroll in PEG exemplified each of these qualities to some degree. Most of them quickly joined campus groups and rose to the top, often elected as leaders by traditionally aged and early entrance students alike.

Although many of the girls arrived with great leadership potential, the college played a significant role in promoting their talents. Dr. Rhodes modeled leadership by routinely sharing her vision with young PEG students. Leaders, she told them, do not have to be charismatic; people with different personalities also can be effective leaders. By looking carefully at our individual strengths, we can find our own ways to lead.

Given useful direction and assistance, almost all of the women involved in the PEG study became campus leaders. By starting in the smaller, safer PEG community, the young teens practiced leadership skills without the sting of serious consequences when they made mistakes. After they felt successful in a smaller sphere, they gained confidence and ventured into the larger world of the MBC campus.[2]

Joining the traditionally aged students in clubs and sports, the PEGs were exposed to some of the 200+ leadership positions that were held by women at MBC. There were female student leaders, faculty women as role models, and women in the highest administrative posts. As the study participants moved to the larger MBC sphere, they encountered greater challenges. No longer were they solely interacting with other PEG students; they had to meet the demands of the older and more experienced students. Instead of just having PEG advisors in smaller PEG groups, the young women now interacted with regular faculty advisors in the larger MBC organizations, and these advisors did not have special training in gifted education. The faculty expected the PEGs to function at a college level, so these advisors were potentially more intimidating than the much smaller PEG supervisory staff. To ascend to leadership positions, the study women had to reach or exceed everyone's expectations, and they did.

When she first arrived at PEG, Claire didn't think that she could be a leader because she didn't "have the right personality for it." She said that although she and her peers often made fun of the required leadership class as young teens, she did learn a lot. "Having to think about and discuss the qualities of an effective leader, going through all of those self-exploration and assessment exercises, and learning interpersonal communication skills helped me understand how I could be a leader." Claire said that as an adult, "I still don't see myself as a great leader, but I know that I can do it if I want to and/or need to." Despite her modesty, Claire was an active adult leader as a professor and in her local community. PEG had helped prepare her to lead.

Of course, not every study woman participated in leadership roles while attending MBC. May valued working for the school newspaper, yearbook, and literary magazine because there was "a real end product with a deadline to complete it by" but didn't find student government or other forms of leadership meaningful. "I never wanted to lead people," she said. She wanted to "be helpful and supportive, but I don't kid myself that I know what's best for people. I've always felt this way, and it has nothing to do with PEG." May wanted to create a better world, but she preferred bringing about change on a smaller, more personal scale. As an adult, her kind and generous spirit made her a leader by example.

PEG and MBC combined to create an atmosphere that encouraged its students to give back to the campus and to society. By sharpening the young women's awareness of their leadership potential, the college helped them to see how they might contribute meaningfully to other communities in the future.

Spiraling Model of Purpose

In 1960, the renowned psychologist Jerome Bruner introduced the idea of a "spiral curriculum" in his book *The Process of Education*. He wrote that "any subject can be taught effectively in some intellectually honest form to any child at any stage of development."[3] This belief yielded the principle that "a curriculum as it develops should revisit these basic ideas repeatedly, building upon them until the student has grasped the full formal apparatus that goes with them."[4] Bruner's ideas helped form the constructivist approach to education, which posits that students build their sense of meaning based on prior knowledge and through interactions with others. A child compares her hypotheses with real experiences and arrives at new understandings.

The PEG study women's experiences suggest a spiraling model of purpose, which evolved along with their intellectual, social, emotional, and moral development. As very young teenagers, they enrolled in college with vague and often unarticulated senses of purpose, but by graduation, they had constructed a much stronger

internal scaffold for meaning. At PEG, the young women encountered challenges in every facet of their lives: in their studies, in their
friendships, in their emotions, and in their values and outlooks.
By growing in each of these spheres, they began to envision their
futures more clearly. Eventually, these women could picture their
goals and felt more secure about how they could enact their dreams.

Whereas many study participants began college with unformed
or generalized ideas of their futures, some finished college with
specific goals. Those who lacked specificity still felt capable of
forging their paths and controlling their futures while coping with
obstacles. They believed that their increased self-confidence from
their PEG experience allowed them to wait until they were ready to
choose the path that best suited them. Echoing the voices of many
of the PEG study alumnae, Nikita wrote, "Choosing to go to PEG
is the biggest educational factor influencing my life. Mary Baldwin
College really shaped my personality by giving me confidence and
helping me to find out what I really wanted from my education and
career." PEG helped Nikita decide which graduate school to attend,
"which in turn influenced my career and life." Although not all of
the study participants had as clear a vision of what they wanted to
do upon graduation, most felt well-directed as they finished their
senior year.

Darcy traced her evolution through PEG where she began as "a
clueless kid who did not know the full challenge that I had agreed
to try to accomplish. I did not know what I wanted to do with my
life or what career field I wanted to venture into." All she knew was
that she wanted "to do something important, noble, or worthy—but
with a child's enthusiasm of saving the world." After graduating,
Darcy chose to enter the military, which for her "partially fulfills
those expectations of doing something noble." After seven years,
however, feeling ready to spiral upward even farther, Darcy was
"searching for the next big challenge."

PEG affected Ruby's life in many positive ways. At Mary
Baldwin, she met her closest friends and fell in love with literature.
"It was where I was introduced to big, beautiful libraries and where

I got the opportunity to study abroad, which changed my life. It was where I became a leader and where I grew into being a strong woman." Ruby was grateful for the inspiration to love scholarship and to experience the world much more fully and openly than she could have ever imagined when she enrolled in college at age 14. "My love for academia grew in PEG under the generous guidance of MBC faculty," she said. Ruby made a powerful perception: "More than achievement, a sense of investigation and personal growth is what makes gifted young women turn into successful women." Ruby's education had fueled and reinforced her lifelong desire to pursue knowledge and purpose.

CHAPTER 7

Caring Community, Social Self-Growth, and Moral Development

What was life like for the PEG students? They lived in a caring community that bolstered their well-being. Many mentors guided them, older PEG students prepared them, and a coterie of true peers understood them. The various components of PEG college life reinforced the central message that the young women were valued and appreciated. Feeling validated, respected, and worthy was essential to the women's emotional health. Their strength grew as they entered a college community where most of the faculty and staff took their ideas seriously, treated them as responsible individuals, and believed that they could handle academic, social, and emotional challenges. Being in an early entrance college program enhanced the healthy development of these young women.

Researcher Kathleen Noble speculated that placing very smart girls in a supportive and encouraging college environment during their formative years might help protect them from the harshness of the adult world. She cited the finding that the most salient factor for gifted adolescents' talent development is the social milieu in which they "learn to recognize their talents and take them seriously or, conversely, learn to abandon talents and aspirations."[1] Without a caring community, young gifted students might too readily waste their extraordinary promise. Noble also cited adolescence research that established that "during no other developmental period does the peer environment exert as powerful or pervasive an influence on self-concept." The PEG study alumnae were primed for the enormous benefits of an enthusiastic cohort because they were in the right place at the right time.

Caring Community

By living together in the PEG residence hall, the young women had a place where they could develop and practice effective communication skills on a daily basis. Students in the program shared a learning environment where they were expected to treat each other with respect so that they could constructively contribute to a caring community of true peers. In this way, the program affirmed the individuality of each young woman, yet maintained a sense of community. "Just the thrill of being independent and setting my own goals, working to attain them, and living this self-contained, independent life was amazing to me," said Liz. PEG's caring community made her feel safe because of its nonjudgmental intellectual atmosphere. She commented, "Although I didn't always realize it while a student, I was lucky to be there, and it was a safe place for me."

Guidance and Support

The young freshmen realized quickly that they had to be responsible for managing their college work and responsibilities, going to classes and meetings on time, participating in required sessions, communicating effectively with their peers and adults, and contributing to dorm maintenance chores like cleaning the kitchen. For some, it was the first time they had to juggle so many tasks on their own. For others, it was a continuation of lessons learned at home. For all of them, it was an enormous degree of responsibility to assume as very young teenagers. Every successful phase of self-management, however, made the PEGs stronger and prepared them to rise to the next level of accountability for their lives.

The PEG administration structured the program to meet the asynchronous needs of these extremely intelligent, very young students. While encouraging them to function intellectually as adults, the PEG administration also recognized that the girls were young adolescents who still required supervision. At the ages of 13-16, most of the girls' exposure to different lifestyles, opinions, and knowledge was quite limited when they first got to college. The PEG students also needed special social and emotional programming and support that was quite different from programs for traditionally aged college students.

Although parents usually decrease their control of their high school children's behavior in gradual stages, the PEG students stepped into an open campus at very young ages with no direct parental controls and very little experience with that sort of freedom. To help ease the transition, the PEG administration somewhat restricted their social lives in their first two program years, for instance, by imposing curfews. Otherwise, the students might have encountered adult situations for which they were unprepared.

A few study women resisted the imposition of rules while they were undergraduates. They believed that they should be treated as adults personally since they were being treated as adults academically. In classes, the PEGs had the same accountability as the older students. Socially and emotionally, however, they were not ready to take on full adult responsibility. The young women often did not realize that despite their normal (or sometimes very mature) psychological development, they could not be safely released without restrictions into the regular college community. Keeping them together in the residence hall for one to two years helped the staff prepare the young women for the bigger demands of adult life and effectively monitor their progress. Despite their resistance, most of the girls understood the concerns that the PEG staff had for their adolescent well-being. In addition, these young women still felt that they had more freedom and independence of thought and action, in general, than their public high school contemporaries.

Resident Advisors, Administrators, Peers, and "Near Peers"

PEG residence advisors guided students through college individually and led groups to improve their interpersonal skills. PEGs who were a year ahead in the program ("near peers") often told the incoming freshmen what to expect in college so that they could cope better. They also supported the incoming students. As a young Filipino woman with self-described quirky ways, May didn't feel comfortable in the town of Staunton. "I was unhappy being weird in a small Southern town," she said. PEG upperclassmen invited her to their non-PEG residence halls, which "were a nice, safe haven for me. It was good to get some guidance and wisdom from them, since they had been through lots of the same things."

None of the PEG women had lived with so many highly intelligent and intense people in such close quarters before, and they had never depended so greatly on friends for emotional support. Away from home, the PEGs became interdependent. Darcy said, "We PEGs helped raise each other." Claire agreed. "We'd talk about all sorts of stuff and cry. There was always somebody who was having a crisis. One night you would be helping someone, and another night someone would be helping you."

Of course, not everyone got along all the time. However, the PEG administration taught conflict resolution to deal with roommate problems—skills that Claire said she has used ever since. The study participants also applauded their exposure to different lifestyles because it taught them to appreciate and get along with a wide array of people.

Claire particularly appreciated the efforts of Christine Garrison, the first PEG director, to help her believe in herself. "She was just a great cheerleader. She always made you feel that you could do whatever you wanted." Claire remembered sitting in her office, overwhelmed and upset. "Christine said, 'Claire, you're awfulizing again.' She introduced that word into my vocabulary and it has always stuck with me." Problems that seemed huge and insurmountable really weren't, Claire realized. The morale-building and emotional support that the PEG staff provided to the young study women contributed hugely to their success in the program.

Mentors

Mary Baldwin/PEG staff, faculty, and peers mentored the girls from the beginning to the end of their college experiences. Nikita's music professor, to whom she attributed "Renaissance sensibilities," helped her recognize "a whole world of experiences" that she had never had, much less considered. He inspired her to be "more aware of new experiences and ideas and more open to trying new things."

Darcy was grateful to her role model, Dr. Ellen Grant, for teaching her about life at the tender age of 13. Observing her professor convinced Darcy that she "could be an independent, educated woman with great friends and a good life." Dr. Grant taught Darcy how to write well and encouraged her dream of attending a well-known foreign university. In Darcy's senior year, she took an independent study with her mentor that was "my single most enjoyable educational class of my college years." By showing Darcy how to enjoy all aspects of life as a woman, her mentor imbued her with a vision of numerous, complex possibilities.

Mentors at MBC helped their students determine their path for the future by providing them with inspiration and specific knowledge about opportunities. Gifted education researcher Abraham Tannenbaum wrote about the need for gifted children to know how to be in the right place at the right time to take advantage of available options.[2] As an example, Jessica raved about the "fantastic" class she took with Dr. Sylvia Downing, an economics professor who later became her advisor. Downing's teaching excellence was a prime motivator for Jessica's switch to an economics major. To prepare her for an academic career, Downing suggested that she attend a summer school class at an elite university, an opportunity she would have otherwise missed. "Sylvia made sure I took all the math classes I needed to get into the grad school of my choice."

Dr. Downing taught Jessica to apply her energy efficiently in the most productive directions. "More than any person besides my parents, Dr. Downing has influenced the direction of my career and my life." Jessica's mentor encouraged her to reach as high as she could academically, informed her of the steps she needed to take to further her education and career, and supported her until she accomplished her goals.[3]

Ruby appreciated that her advisor, Dr. Ives, was deeply interested in both her academic and emotional health. Not only did he instill his compelling "point of view about politics and issues of justice and international human rights," but he also helped her cope with self-consciousness about being a PEG. Despite her young age, he treated Ruby as though she were the same as his other students. He helped her choose classes and warned her about a professor who was unfriendly to PEGs. Dr. Ives not only influenced Ruby's thinking about justice, but he also ensured that she would find the most welcoming classrooms to develop self-confidence.

Claire was impressed with her professors' willingness to meet often with students to expand their thinking.[4] Her psychology and biology professors, Dr. Conti, Dr. Brigand, and Dr. Rudin, all had generous open-door policies. Claire relished the chance to "shoot the breeze with them for half an hour or 45 minutes." They were incredibly busy, but "they never said, 'Oh I have to go do this now,' or 'Come back later.' My PEG friends and I would stay talking to them for hours sometimes." Given how many women were, and continue to be, reluctant to pursue science careers, the professors' extra attention significantly solidified Claire's desire in her mid-teens to become a biology professor.

In the program's initial years, mentoring opportunities were more structured, and PEG enrollees learned about possible careers from a required Model Women series. Professional women talked informally about their personal and career decisions and answered PEG students' questions. In subsequent years, PEG students were invited, but not required, to participate. Lucy embraced the program's focus on self-reflection. Having been tempted to experiment with drugs, alcohol, and sex before she enrolled in college, Lucy said that "the program's emphasis on personal awareness and development came at just the right time for me." Through the series, PEG students could think deeply about the kinds of lives they wanted and how those goals needed to influence the choices they were making. In the safe PEG environment, some of the young women like Lucy turned toward more constructive college activities. At the age when their peers were just starting college, most of the PEG study women felt prepared to pursue their futures.

Transfer of Trust and Receptivity to Adults

For the most part, the study women grew up in homes where there was mutual trust. Not only did the parents trust the children, but the children also trusted their parents. Once they arrived at Mary Baldwin and got adjusted, these young women were more likely to trust adults, which made them more receptive to ideas at odds with their own. They also were more likely to listen to adults' powerful stories of lessons learned through various choices and decisions. They were receptive to, and grew from, their mentors' ideas, guidance, and support. The few non-study PEGs who complained that they did not have an adequate support system may not have sought and absorbed adult advice. In her 16 years with the program, Dr. Rhodes noticed that some PEGs learned only through direct experience and lost the opportunities to use other people as their human resource guides. However, by listening carefully, many study participants learned through vicarious experience, enabling them to avoid going through every adolescent pitfall personally.

Building Strength and Courage to Face the Outside World

The study participants had their share of life losses, disappointments, and challenges before and during their time at PEG. Three sets of the study women's parents divorced. One student had a sibling with special needs. Other families experienced considerable financial stress. Most study alumnae depicted PEG as supportive of them through significant personal and intellectual trials. At this crucial stage in their development, the young women needed a safety net so that they could shore up their strength to face the real world. PEG helped them become braver.

Jessica felt that being in PEG was a kind of haven but also an initial crucible because of outside attacks. Students like Jessica, who were African American or from other culturally diverse backgrounds, described how strange it was to be in a small, Southern, predominantly white, rural town, where a few residents were malicious toward them. Their distinctive personalities and substantial intellects compounded their differences. "A lot of people said very nasty, hurtful things like, 'You must be a freak' and 'Your parents must abuse you,'" she said. Fortunately, her home base at Mary Baldwin provided solace. The program "taught me to persevere, taught me how to fail and start again, taught me how to be disciplined, taught me how to seek out the new and innovative, and taught me how to find joy in life." By learning how to cope with problems in a community environment of support, Jessica further developed the reserves of courage and strength necessary to thrive as an adult.

Darcy said that PEG prepared her for military life because it made her feel adaptable and capable of meeting challenges. "PEG provided strong roots which made me feel as if I could take on challenges and not fail completely." In the military, Darcy discovered that she could "take on obstacle courses; run fast, hard, and long; jump out of planes; take up new and challenging hobbies; travel abroad; and mediate internal strife over duty and ethical beliefs." Having met and mastered challenges as an early college entrant, Darcy was prepared to face all kinds of physical and mental tests.

The tenacity and determination she developed at PEG helped Darcy to meet challenges that at times seemed insurmountable. She relayed one particular story with pride. While in the military, she was required to complete a 12-mile march with a "combat-loaded rucksack" as quickly as possible. Her 22 companions were all male, and she had been an average soldier in basic training. This particular challenge stung Darcy because she knew that her fellow soldiers didn't expect her to perform well. They even listed the odds against her—that she was wearing the wrong boots, hadn't "rucked" in six years, hadn't been able to exercise lately, and "more than anything, was a girl." Darcy said, "I consciously made the decision that I would not embarrass myself and I would be successful." And so she was. Darcy finished in fourth place, less than 10 minutes behind the seasoned male soldier wearing appropriate boots who finished first. Her success at PEG, she said, was due to that same quality of determination. For Darcy, PEG created a foundation of strength and courage, readying her for an entirely new world of problems to solve, tasks to accomplish, and places to visit.

PEG was not perfect, but it was a predominantly safe and supportive community where the young study women could express themselves freely and pursue their interests passionately. Emotionally, they were well on the way to discovering and developing their true selves. As they built their courage and self-confidence, the PEG study women got ready to take on the world as very young college graduates.

Growth of the Social Self

Central to the study participants' healthy development were the positive relationships that they formed among both their sister PEGs and the traditionally aged MBC students. Although some MBC students showed insensitivity to the PEGs, Georgia and others talked about the importance of their older classmates. "I created connections within my PEG peer group, but I also created friendships in the broader MBC community. Having both groups around me throughout college made a difference." Exposure to a wider social circle helped Georgia "practice making friends and keeping them." Most of the study alumnae, however, forged their strongest and longest lasting friendships with other PEGs because of shared intellectual curiosity, social-emotional growth, and the PEG experience.

Despite many people's concerns about the social and emotional well-being of accelerated teenagers who will miss their proms, senior week at the beach, and graduation itself, research indicates that these students do not often miss those high school events.[5] They find equivalent social experiences at college. The study participants had mixers with boys their own age and attended other social functions while at PEG. Many of them were active in sports during their undergraduate years. MBC organization members and club officers welcomed the girls and the contributions they made. Most of the study women felt that radically accelerating through school was well worth missing some of the traditional high school events that others assume would be so important to their psychological and social health.

In a seeming ironic twist, among the greater population of PEG students, those who fit in socially and were accepted at their home schools tended to take longer to see PEG as a positive experience than those who had not been accepted previously. Making a smooth transition to PEG meant possibly losing old friendships that the students were not willing to abandon. In holding on to their old friends, they had a harder time making new ones in college. On the other hand, girls who struggled in their home schools were often the ones who blossomed immediately at PEG because having a friend or several friends was a new and rewarding experience.

Finding True Peers

Ruby described the emotional transformation that began when she enrolled at Mary Baldwin College. Frustrated and isolated in public school, when she came to PEG, she felt the most normal that she ever had among peers. "Suddenly, 'who I was' was okay. While other people saw us as oddities, among ourselves we were so relieved to finally be who we were: curious, smart, witty, odd, challenging, revolutionary, goofy, and gifted."

The PEG girls displayed asynchronous behavior, which is common among gifted children and adolescents. When a teenager's intellect outpaces the development of other skills, such as her judgment or her social awareness, it often alienates her from other teens who might not appreciate that sometimes rapid variability. Claire said that it was fun to have friends who could act like silly young teenagers one moment and enter a serious intellectual discussion the next. Having peers who could so readily move from one mode of communication to another made it easier to get along well and to develop close friendships.

Not only could the young women be their true selves at Mary Baldwin, but also they finally were valued for it—a very intense reversal from their earlier school experiences. In some ways, PEG was the institutionalized version of a supportive home environment. Darcy, who was close to her family, spoke about PEG as being her "home away from home and my stability." Liz had struggled with her parents before she entered college, so PEG became a welcome surrogate home. The women were all extremely happy to be with "very smart, unique girls" and to meet rigorous academic and social challenges with peer support.

Many of the PEGs had difficulty relating closely to other public school students at their home schools, but they had no trouble finding friends at PEG. According to May, there was "an extreme, concentrated set of social dynamics" among the PEG students so that they were all "bonded together forever like army buddies." She reveled in finding people "who really had things in common with me, who understood me." Able to trust the other PEG women, May "learned about loyalty to friends and that you have to stick up for each other to get by." May's strong image of army buddies to describe the PEGs' lifetime connection explains the study alumnae's "We're in this together" attitude and kinship. Each woman highlighted the enormous impact of her PEG friendships.

The students' passionate feelings sometimes created divisiveness, but Claire remembered that she could strongly disagree with her sister PEGs yet not be abandoned socially. Having friends who remained emotionally connected and who accepted her viewpoints meant a lot to her. They bolstered her self-confidence and reflected the healthy process of social development that occurred at PEG. Standing apart did not mean being excluded.

Friendships made during Rachel's time at PEG "had an incredible resiliency. What I remember most is how sharing the values and aspirations of my peers was truly inspirational." Being among girls who could envision great things for their lives helped Rachel believe that she could do whatever she set out to do. The growth of her "self" relates to the "possible self," which represents the individual's idea of "what she might become, what she would like to become, and what she is afraid of becoming."[6] This concept provides the link between thinking about one's ambitions and the motivation to do something about them. At PEG, Rachel spent most of her time building her self-efficacy after having had very poor motivation and lackluster performance in public school.

Social Flexibility and Diversity

Rather than limit themselves to smaller cliques, the study alumnae made friends with PEGs from lots of groups. Their social flexibility was linked to their personal appeal. Openness made them good absorbers of others' experiences. Their optimism, couched in both quiet and more outgoing individuals, was contagious. They thrived on the variety of personalities and backgrounds of the women in the PEG residence hall and in their classes. They embraced diversity to learn about the world and themselves by comparing their similarities and differences with others.

Highly energetic and accomplished, Jessica described her friends as "extraordinary people." They differed in race, occupation, and interests, and she extolled their courage to be themselves and to experiment. "They're willing to try, they do what they do well, and they also do what they want to do. They're not confined by societal expectations." Because PEG enrolled students who were ready to buck societal expectations about schooling, Jessica found like-minded friends. Entering college early, she said, "definitely forced me to become an independent thinker. And it also taught me how to cope emotionally with social disapproval [in the community outside of MBC]." Jessica's choice led to self-assurance about her beliefs and herself.

Kristen remarked that coming in contact with girls from such diverse backgrounds in such close quarters had a big impact on how she saw the world, as well as her level of respect for different people's ways of being. Those lessons stayed with her in adulthood. About to be married, Kristen yearned to live abroad, and her fiancée was supportive of her goal. Kristen wanted to learn more about how others lived in circumstances quite different from her own. Similarly, the other study women wanted to investigate and expand their worlds as adults because of their exposure to new ideas and lifestyles while students at PEG.

Some PEG study alumnae were content to work toward improvements in their local communities. Others wanted to make a broader impact. Interacting with PEGs from different cultural backgrounds tested the young women's flexibility of perspective. The more that they empathized with people who had considerably different belief systems, the more they wanted to venture out into the larger world to investigate and understand foreign cultures. Their ever-expanding worldview fed their hunger for travel and helped them envision global change.

Five Elements of Strong PEG Friendships

The PEG girls created powerful, lifelong friendships at Mary Baldwin College. The strength and length of those friendships resulted from the deeply affecting experiences that the study women shared as young teens. Five factors formed the infrastructure of the relationships, giving them a depth and intensity that might not otherwise have been present:

1. *Being away from home.* For most of the students, living away from home in early to mid-adolescence is emotionally difficult. Most young teenagers aren't fully ready to live apart from their families at that age. As a result, the PEGs bonded closely with one another and relied on each other as they learned independent living skills. Going through episodes

of homesickness together helped them support one another with empathy and kindness.

2. *Living together during a formative adolescent development period.* The close proximity to other adolescents who were coping with the same emotional, social, and academic issues allowed the PEG girls to experience developmental milestones with a group of others who truly understood their struggles, as well as their achievements. This shared understanding helped to nurture their friendships.

3. *A shared past experience of being hurt or wounded.* So many of the young study women had been alienated from their home school classmates that they now shared real empathy. They knew the emotional and social toll that the other women had experienced because they had experienced it themselves. Sensitivity and vulnerability were common qualities among the PEGs, which underlay their compassion and firm friendships.

4. *Having to explain themselves and PEG.* Some of the study alumnae experienced some negative reactions as accelerated college students, especially in the early years of the program, when the outside community and some traditionally aged Mary Baldwin students and faculty criticized the program and the girls. The girls banded together as a unit against these outside criticisms, offering one another support and allowing each other to vent their anger and frustration. They also discussed among themselves ways of handling their conflicts, with the help of some coaching from the PEG staff. Supporting each other in these ways helped solidify their friendships.

5. *Their uniqueness affirmed and prized.* Many friends, staff, and MBC faculty valued the PEGs, which made their lives more enjoyable. The sense of safety and celebration allowed the girls to express their true selves more readily. The PEG environment encouraged authentic expression and real

trust, and profound attachments formed because the young women did not have to hide their struggles of self-discovery and their newly growing identities.

At Mary Baldwin College, the study alumnae became a true cohort because they all shared the unique PEG experience at about the same age, time, and place. The young women then carried the PEG community's affirmation with them after they graduated. Whenever adult life tested them, they knew that they could rely on a coterie of gifted women who shared the experiences that had shaped them.

Postponing Serious Romantic Relationships

Some of the PEG study alumnae dated, but others felt that being at a women's college had distinct advantages that did not involve men. Georgia said that being in a single-sex environment allowed her to practice her learning skills without simultaneously trying to practice her romantic skills. Having entered college at age 13, Georgia still had plenty of time to date when she graduated at 17.

Liz saw her lack of interaction with men while she was at PEG as a mixed blessing. "I didn't really seek out a lot because I didn't really want to date somebody from the local colleges," she said. When she got to law school, Liz was "behind the curve socially" but also appreciated that during her time at MBC, she could "focus more on developing my character and my interests. It was detrimental in a social sense, but I've dated a lot since then, and it's just something that comes with practice."

Ruby felt that she needed to grow romantically when she graduated from college. Her inexperience made her apprehensive, but postponing romantic relationships may have better suited her writing goals. In an important study of talent development, gifted teens understood the conflict between productive work and peer relations and were more sexually conservative than were their classmates. American adolescents' sexuality concerns may be excessive, the authors warned. "We might rather say that it is the talented teens who are liberated from the need constantly to attend to the artificially fueled sexual concerns that take up their peers' energy and time."[7] Delaying romance until after college allowed Ruby to focus on her education, which helped her to realize her ambitions of being a poet and a college instructor. Ruby attained those roles as a happily married woman before she turned 35.

Because they graduated so young, most of the study women felt that they had time to catch up romantically if they had not been dating while at MBC. Postponing intimacy gave the young teenagers time to satisfy their intellectual curiosity and determine their own values and beliefs before they got lost in someone else's goals and desires. With a firmer sense of self, the PEG study participants were better prepared to have mature relationships based on stronger self-awareness and self-knowledge.

Self-Exploration, Self-Awareness, and Self-Reflection

To maintain a lifelong sense of purpose, one needs to grow, which requires self-examination, self-awareness, and self-reflection. According to psychologist Robert Solomon, being reflective and aware leads people to recognize "how much of life is out of one's hands, how many of life's advantages one owes to other people, and how indebted one is or should be to parents, friends, and teachers."[8] Claire commented that at PEG, she was introduced to "formal self-exploration and the setting of personal goals for growth and development."

Madison remarked upon how she became more self-aware while at PEG. Early in her experience at MBC, she learned that her determination, assertiveness, and verbosity both helped and hindered her social life. As a young student, she hadn't fully realized the negative impression she was making. With some self-examination, she recognized that the strong personality and intellect that made her very successful academically could be detriment socially. She said, "I had to learn the distinction between confidence and arrogance, assertiveness and aggressiveness. I had to learn how to be a receptive listener as well as an articulate talker." Beginning this process in college helped Madison become an effective medical student because she related better to people.

While at PEG, Lucy went through a process of self-exploration, examining her firmly held beliefs by being open to education and different people's perspectives. In her junior year, Lucy was strongly against abortion. After taking philosophy, psychology, and literature courses, "I changed my mind and decided I was really pro-choice. I am still amazed that I could experience such a fundamental shift, and it has made me question the certainty of all my convictions." Thinking deeply about people's contrasting viewpoints contributed to Lucy's self-examination because she developed a much greater sensitivity to, and more complex understanding of, people's needs and rights.

As an adult, Ruby knew that thinking carefully about her values, motives, and behaviors contributed to the woman she had become. Self-examination led to self-awareness. She said, "Self-reflection has been an important way for me to determine how I want to proceed in personal and professional relationships. I think it is valuable to observe how what I (and others) do has consequences for those around me." Ruby observed that people "often pursued their personal goals to the exclusion of everyone else, and it seemed to be at a great cost down the road." Ruby's sensitivity to the effects of her actions on others sometimes limited her efforts on her own behalf, she said. Yet this quality made her feel true to herself, even if it meant the seeming sacrifice of "getting ahead" in traditionally successful ways. Self-reflection helped Ruby and the other study women to achieve clarity about their sense of purpose.

Moral Development

Self-reflection can lead to moral development, as Ruby so aptly illustrated. Moral development is often more fully realized and more deeply felt in intellectually gifted children earlier than in their age peers.[9] For many of them, the need to act consistently with their values is urgent and pressing. Many PEG study participants acted according to the values that were important to them, no matter how others responded. At least two types of moral growth—societal and personal—occurred among the PEG study women while they were undergraduates. Some championed the rights of disadvantaged groups in society. Others underwent personal moral tests of their values and behavior.

Championing Moral Causes

As leaders in the Mary Baldwin community, the PEG study women headed a number of honor societies and organizations that promoted social justice. Ruby co-chaired the campus chapter of Amnesty International (AI) in its early years and believed strongly in its purpose. According to its website, "AI's vision is of a world in which every person enjoys all of the human rights enshrined in the *Universal Declaration of Human Rights* and other international human rights standards."[10] AI acts to prevent and end "grave abuses of the rights to physical and mental integrity, freedom of conscience and expression, and freedom from discrimination." In her mid-teens, Ruby was already focused on human rights issues.

Her advisor, Dr. Ives, had strongly influenced Ruby's concern about justice, but it was her older brother who reinforced her interest and impetus. She said that her brother was a good role model for trying new experiences and getting involved in vital moral issues. "He even led the anti-war demonstration at State University for the Gulf War. We went to peace rallies together in Washington along with the whole family," she said. Ruby's principled behavior reflected the combination of her personal moral sense, the knowledge and inspiration she received in her advisor's class, and the support of her family.

As a bisexual college student in the mid-1990s, Nina was well aware of the prejudices that restricted the lives of gay and bisexual people. Her women's group brought more awareness to the Mary Baldwin and greater Staunton communities about the anguish that lesbians face. Through her involvement in a Staunton church choir, Nina did a lot of outreach. Dr. Rhodes recalled that many heterosexual PEG students became members of the women's group because they were moved by the plight of their sister students. Gifted expert Barbara Kerr refers to this phenomenon: "Gifted young women are often very idealistic or even iconoclastic."[11] Not only did the PEGs' sense of fairness contribute to their participation, but they also may have appreciated the opportunity to exhibit their intellectual independence and test their values. Most eminent women, Kerr explains, needed to get involved in non-mainstream groups that allow for a greater flexibility of thought.

Nina was remarkably courageous, especially at her age and on a predominantly conservative Southern campus, to create such a group. By providing a free forum for reflection about sexuality, she helped women cope with the many oppressive experiences of their daily lives. Nina and Ruby helped to make their respective groups self-sustaining. Both are still vigorous campus organizations.

Personal Moral Tests

Claire recalled a personal moral test. The Ku Klux Klan had received a permit to march in the city's downtown area. Despite warnings from the college president not to attend because it would give the Klan too much attention, Claire felt strongly that a protest should be made. A large group of young women from PEG stood on the sidewalks holding candles and signs in protest. Later, they attended a service with the other protestors. "It was an amazingly moving experience," Claire recalled. "I was so proud to see a good turnout of students and faculty." The courage that Claire developed as a young teenager translated into her commitment to acting on moral stances as an adult. With strength of conviction, Claire developed and maintained her sense of purpose despite many hardships that she later endured.

Authentic Growth

As high school students, the study women probably would not have been exposed to self-awareness workshops, nor would they have had the opportunity to meet with the steady stream of talented and accomplished professional women and mentors from various fields who met with them at MBC. The special opportunities available to the PEG students prompted this group of girls to think deeply about what they wanted from life and how to focus their talents.

Part of the women's inward journey entailed determining what their belief systems were, what they most valued, and how they wanted to conduct themselves. Tests of faith and conviction resulted in stronger understanding of their needs and capabilities. Through experience and self-reflection while at PEG, the study alumnae developed and enhanced many personal characteristics that underlay their success as graduates. They gained strength of conviction, courage to welcome challenges, humility regarding others' gifts, openness to change, and the sense that they could accomplish their goals—qualities that they felt PEG supported and nurtured.

In a community where they could truly explore their ideas and unique characteristics, the study women engaged in authentic growth. When they made mistakes in their social interactions, they got honest feedback from their peers and the PEG staff. With trustworthy friends and adults to bounce ideas off, the study participants had a greater chance for genuine self-discovery. In the process of finding their true identities and pursuing their real interests, their development was healthier than it might have been in situations that provoked false selves to emerge.

Having been validated and valued, having negotiated the social and emotional complexity of their cohorts, and having succeeded at their studies, these young adolescents developed a healthy sense of self-confidence. Through the encouragement and guidance of mentors, staff, and friends, the PEG study women began to develop a firmer sense of their worthiness, value, and credibility. The caring community helped them to feel worthwhile by taking their social, emotional, and intellectual concerns seriously. In meeting and exceeding sophisticated and complex academic and personal challenges and expectations, the study alumnae could see the credibility that they were establishing on campus. By becoming so well-integrated into college life, their sense of belonging and effectiveness at Mary Baldwin increased. With stronger belief in their self-efficacy, the women's minds and spirits became more attuned to their individual senses of purpose.

Turning Points

Each of the study alumnae said that arriving at PEG signified a major turning point in her life. As Claire, who entered PEG at age 14, stated, "PEG-aged students are at a much more formative stage in their development than traditionally aged students." Claire wondered if she would "have been as receptive and responsive to PEG" if she had "experienced a similar environment four years later." If she had entered a program like PEG at age 18 instead, then the influences of staff, administrators, college professors, and her classmates might not have had such a profound effect on her life. By later adolescence, she might have built up certain defenses intellectually, socially, and emotionally that would not have allowed her to be as open to new ideas and experiences as she had been as a young adolescent.

Various aspects of the PEG early entrance program affected these complex individuals. Pointing to only one change does not truly reflect the multi-dimensionality of each woman's experiences, but it may provide a glimpse at the various ways in which the PEG alumnae began to enhance their self-image and explore their immense potential.

- ✔ Lucy turned away from self-destructive behavior to a constructive sense of self.

- ✔ Rachel switched from being academically unchallenged to being highly productive.

- ✔ Georgia turned from frustration in school to happiness and fulfillment in college.

- ✔ Madison turned from trying to "get a life" to actually living that life.

✔ Liz turned from feeling vulnerable at home to being in control at college.

✔ Nina and Darcy turned from intellectual boredom to intellectual excitement.

✔ Kristen and Nikita turned from their limited life experience to a richer and more varied exposure to people and possibilities.

✔ Ruby turned from feeling weird and isolated to feeling normal and appreciated.

✔ Claire turned from ignorance of her potential to a new awareness of her capabilities.

✔ May turned from a lack of female friends to the closeness of her PEG peers.

✔ Jessica turned from educational convention to adventurous pursuit of knowledge.

✔ Julia turned from her self-imposed emotional fortress to the open friendliness and acceptance of the PEG community.

PEG helped these students reach turning points that led to healthy changes and growth in their emotional selves. Only after they reached these points could they direct their lives toward true meaning and purpose.

Part IV

Life After PEG

CHAPTER 8

Benefits of Early College Entrance

Young College Graduates

People often wonder how students who radically accelerate and enter college early manage in the world as such young graduates. Do they find employment? Do they have enough maturity to get along well in the workplace? Do they take time off to travel or explore other areas besides academics? If they attend graduate school, do they fit in? The PEG study women had a variety of responses to those questions, most of which were quite positive.

Following graduation, the PEG alumnae experienced the same kind of trepidation that regular college graduates might feel, yet their optimism and sense of self-efficacy were strong, having finished college two to four years earlier than their age peers with honors, leadership experience, and good, supportive friends and mentors. They had learned important lessons in developing their considerable gifts, which would serve them well in their adult lives. Some of these young women chose the path of graduate study in order to realize their dreams. Others recognized that they needed more life and work experience before they enrolled in higher-level educational programs and either sought employment or took time

off to travel. All embraced the exciting challenge of personal decision making as they set complex yet realistic goals.

Coworkers, bosses, graduate advisors, and classmates responded
variously to the early graduates' age. Some bosses accorded equal
status to the new employees, regardless of how young they were.
Many graduate school classmates took the PEG study women's
youth in stride. But for some of the PEG women, the experience of
"always being the youngest" persisted. Most of them kept a sense
of humor about their circumstances, however, or made changes
in their environments when their situations became intolerable.

Most of the PEG study women were happy that they had saved
a few years by skipping some or all of high school; they felt it was an
advantage. Georgia said, "PEG was extremely influential in making
me the person I am today mostly because the early completion of
my undergraduate degree fed my urge to accomplish more and
compete with a wider range of people." She and others felt that they
had gotten a head start on achieving their goals and broadening
their world.

Kristen offered a different perspective on graduating from
college early. "Learning and experiencing life takes time," she
said. After college, Kristen realized that she did not need to push
herself even though she had entered college early. "Acceleration is
only good if you plan on using that 'extra' time as a bonus, not as
a launching pad for another round of running ahead. Eventually
you have to learn patience with yourself." Kristen described needing
time and space to "catch up with herself" and considered it one of
her weaknesses to always "look forward to new goals rather than
enjoying the successes I have." Although she did not want her life
to stagnate, Kristen was not willing to sacrifice balance and joy by
pushing herself according to anyone else's schedule.

As the PEG study alumnae matured emotionally and clarified
their priorities, they began to adapt to new social realities. Their
attitudes toward work, family relationships, friendships, and life in
general evolved. They made peace with being much younger than
others in their fields. By traveling throughout the world, the PEG

study participants continued to look outwardly. They also considered building families and worked to maintain balance as their lives became more complex. Ultimately, their social and emotional growth made them more committed to giving back to society.

Being Academically Well-Prepared

Nina described her confidence when she finished college. "I felt proud and confident of my abilities and not embarrassed about who I was. PEG made me feel very normal," a viewpoint shared by many study women. Having built their confidence and sense of self in their undergraduate years, most of the alumnae left college feeling better adjusted and much more assured of their intellectual and coping abilities than when they had first arrived as freshmen.

As a doctoral candidate in a selective graduate English department, Lucy said, "I feel better prepared academically than I think I would have felt had I attended a traditional program at a traditional age, but this is hindsight, and who can say?" Lucy tempered her statement to reflect her singular experience, but as a scholar, she was well-equipped to assess the Mary Baldwin teaching methods: "I do know, based on my study of metacognition and self-efficacy models in education, that PEG seemed firmly grounded in constructivist pedagogies devoted to active learning and development of self-regulated learners." The students at Mary Baldwin were encouraged to seek the answers to their own questions, to make meaning of the information they found, and to monitor and control their learning process. Deeply introspective, Lucy also relished "the emphasis on reflection in PEG, which seems to have been especially helpful for me!"

For skeptics who might question the value of a Mary Baldwin College education, Darcy proudly compared it to better-known universities. Her seven-year military career and her studies for a Master's of Science in Strategic Intelligence prompted Darcy to applaud the PEG academic experience. "I have written analytical papers and have been reassured by my ability to write, my deductive reasoning, and other cognitive skills that were nurtured at Mary

Baldwin College. I have felt that my education is easily comparable, if not superior, to those higher in rank and position than I." Darcy felt as well-prepared to handle mental challenges as anyone else in the military. Her army achievement record was so consistently excellent that Darcy was promoted every time she applied for advancement.

Graduate School

Like many of the PEG study women, Claire graduated from Mary Baldwin College at the young age of 17. Although she did not feel ready to face adult work, she did feel ready for graduate school. Early graduation provided her the opportunity for professional growth and helped her to be flexible in her career path. "After taking a year off after college and then spending six years in grad school, I was still relatively young (25) when I started my first teaching job." After five years teaching at one college, Claire moved to a different one and said that she felt like a brand new professor. She was the "right age for it," yet she had already accumulated five years of college teaching experience. "I think my early start made it less difficult to start over at a new college once I realized that the first college was not meeting my needs. If I were older, I don't think I would have been as willing to move on." She also felt comfortable waiting four more years for tenure. Her greater professional flexibility was a bonus.

Liz entered law school when she was 18 years old. The university was much larger than Mary Baldwin, so she became "a small fish in a big pond." She didn't discuss her acceleration much, so age was a concern only when she went out to socialize with her friends at a bar. When asked why she wasn't drinking, she would answer matter-of-factly, "'Well, I'm not really old enough, and here's why.' You'd always get the response, 'Oh, that's interesting. How'd you do that?'" Liz would then explain that she had entered college early, and conversation would resume without fanfare.

Not every young woman was fortunate to have such acceptance of her young age. After entering her doctoral program, Julia had problems with her thesis advisor. "Age was part of it. His son was the same age as I was and was struggling in high school. And I was a graduate student." The advisor expressed so much resentment in his treatment of Julia that she ultimately left the biology program. "I was yelled at and humiliated in public and told that I would never graduate," she recalled. Leaving graduate school was beneficial for Julia, though, because it had been the wrong path for her; it had not fit her true interests. She had worked for nine years in a major medical research lab and had taught college-level biology, but when she changed direction and instead taught science at a private middle and high school, she discovered that she was an outstanding educator. Having always wanted to teach, she had found her niche and was happy.

Jessica also experienced difficulty during her graduate studies at a prestigious university. As one of only two African American women in the heavily foreign-student populated and competitive economics department in graduate school, she felt ostracized due to her nationality, race, and gender, despite being at an American university. The comfort and acceptance she had experienced at PEG had allowed her to learn much more effectively than she did as a graduate student. Even though she did well in grad school, she felt relatively unsuccessful academically. But Jessica did not lack talent; she lacked a caring intellectual community. Despite her struggles, Jessica persevered and earned her Master's degree, graduating with honors.

Other Options: The Military

After graduating from MBC, Darcy was accepted into graduate school, but she decided against it because "I could not reconcile the image of myself studying for another degree while lacking real-world experience, especially since I felt so young." So she joined the Army instead. Initially, age seemed to be an obstacle in her career path; she wanted to be a commissioned officer but was too young. Barred from an officer position, she enlisted as a soldier. Grateful later for not having been granted her original wish, Darcy explained:

"I have been challenged and placed in positions and units that would not have been available to me as an officer." In addition, she earned her Master's degree "courtesy of the United States government due to my assignment to the Defense Intelligence Agency—a position that likely would not have been available to me as a young officer." For Darcy, youth ultimately benefited her—being a soldier had turned out to be a better way to learn and grow, and she quickly rose through the ranks and continued her formal education.

The World of Work

The PEG women's self-confidence, patience, and perseverance in their work were the foundation for their ability to assume increased responsibility, establish their credibility, and progress from wunderkind to equal worker. Having honed their leadership skills during their undergraduate years, they made valuable contributions to their new work and study settings. As they moved forward into the world, they took on the full brunt of adult responsibility. They knew that if they persisted patiently, they would ultimately make meaningful contributions.

No matter what professions they entered, the young PEG women became accountable for daunting tasks, and their extreme youth made their accomplishments all the more remarkable. Each new experience increased their effectiveness, underscoring their capability and desire to act on behalf of others. The more responsibility they assumed, the more successes they achieved, and the more they shared their talents, the more they grew in their self-assuredness. Given their profound wish to improve life for others, the PEG study participants became well equipped psychologically to press on to create purposeful lives.

Establishing Credibility

At a world-renowned company, Nikita was given major responsibilities as a young, 20-year-old engineer. It was her first job, and she was the youngest person in the company by 10 years. Most of her colleagues were in their forties or older. Because of her young age, Nikita initially had a hard time gaining enough respect from her work team to be effective. However, "by the end of my time there, I was not only part of the team, but I was jokingly called 'Nikita the Hun' for my work enforcing the proper reporting of progress of the project." Nikita had established her credibility successfully. Guided by high standards and self-discipline, she transformed her older colleagues' skepticism into true admiration for her organizational and leadership talents.

When May entered the working world of art dealership after graduating at age 18, she was delighted that her much older colleagues took her seriously. Her boss's confidence and openness helped her readily learn the business. "He allowed me to do very important tasks from the start. For example, I did all of the writing, I handled all of the critics, and most importantly, I was able to interact with collectors and sell them art." Even though she was overworked and underpaid, May always received praise and support. "My opinion was valuable to my boss, and knowing that gave me confidence." She stayed at her first job for almost seven years because her boss was willing to give her responsibility and mentor her. Reflecting on her youthful experience, she said, "It warms my heart when I remember how these major Impressionist dealers would talk to an 18-year-old like she was a 'real' person."

May was grateful for all that the men at her job taught her: "what makes a good painting, what makes a good investment, how to identify fakes." Having become so close to the these male mentors, May "considered them my uncles" and called them for advice after she started her own business. Arriving from PEG with a solid art knowledge base, effective communication skills, and a passion about her field, May established her credibility by fulfilling her roles with excellence. She handled hundreds of thousands of dollars worth of art, a heady responsibility for someone who was still technically a teenager. She kept asking for and receiving increasingly demanding responsibilities and succeeded. Later, as an independent art dealer, she continued to challenge herself.

Even though Liz described herself as shy and reserved, she established herself early on in the legal field as dependable and trustworthy. These qualities, along with her intellectual competence, enabled her to become the youngest secretary that her county bar association had ever had. She said, "It's almost unheard of for someone who is 24 years old to do something like that." But Liz knew that her colleagues were at ease with her in that position of responsibility because "they see me as a person who will do what needs to be done." She took pride in her work ethic. Having developed self-reliance at home, she had further developed her problem-solving skills, her positive sense of self, and her life of independence at PEG, which contributed to her growing self-confidence. Liz had the competence and credibility to act purposefully.

Taking on increased responsibility was emblematic of the PEG study alumnae's need to be challenged by their work. Nikita said that she really liked her engineering job because "it offers new and interesting challenges every day." She gained self-assurance from her professional successes and supportive coworkers: "This confidence makes me willing to try difficult things." All of the women's worthwhile accomplishments meant grappling with tough problems and responding with creative solutions, which made them feel capable of reaching their goals.

Fighting Gender Constraints

Liz had to fight gender-based preconceptions and her colleagues' predictions that she would not succeed as a defense lawyer. She didn't fit the "typical profile of a lawyer" or of a "good old boy" where she worked. "You know," she explained, "you hang out with your friends, golf, and play poker, and that's not me." Facing the obstacle of being left out of the male network, Liz said that she had to "make my own way and chart my own career path. There aren't really any other women in town who do what I do." The women who are in criminal law in her region of the country "tend to be prosecutors. They tend not to represent defendants, and I think that would be true in other areas of the United States as well."

By challenging herself as a quiet woman in an unusual legal role, Liz developed her skills and self-confidence. She relished surpassing her employers' low expectations for her. At the first firm where she worked, "They told me, 'We would never put you in a courtroom. You just don't have courtroom demeanor,' but a year and a half later, there I was trying a case." Arguing her first jury trial was "incredibly exciting," she said. She felt enormous pride from performing such a personally difficult assignment.

Liz's joy came from pushing herself beyond others' expectations and her own natural tendencies. "I'm not by any means a gifted public speaker. My job forces me to constantly refine and hone my public speaking skills because I have to go to court every day and speak on behalf of other people." Jury trials frightened her the most because they were the most "important things you can do as a lawyer." She tried not to think about the weighty responsibility in court because "it would be too overwhelming to sit and think, 'I'm arguing to these 12 people about the fate of this one person.'"

Taking her responsibility seriously and motivated by the desire to aid impoverished people whom society often neglects and disdains, Liz forced herself to grow in her skills and self-assurance. She knew that consistent challenge would increase her ability to protect her clients' rights. In addition, by demonstrating her sincere concern for their well-being, Liz hoped that she might empower them to take more responsibility for their own lives.

Love of Work

Despite—and in some cases, because of—challenges and obstacles in the paths toward their career goals, most of the PEG study alumnae found their work intensely satisfying. Rachel summarized how these young women felt about their professional work: "I love to love what I do. I will never be content to just have a good job if it is not work that allows me to continually grow." She wanted to spend her time meaningfully, so she routinely evaluated her work situation to ensure that she was growing. For Rachel and many of the others, their personal and professional lives were inseparable. She said, "I do not think I could have a truly satisfying career if I did not find it personally satisfying, and I could not have a satisfying personal life without a satisfying career."

Jessica also described how much she loved to work and defined it as much more than just an individual job at a particular point in time. At the time of the study, Jessica was teaching economics at a small-town college. "I love working. I love not only writing and research, but I love organizing," she said. She wanted to lead people by working on community projects and also by creating a small, alternative newspaper "because that's an entrepreneurial outlet for my energies. I want to have work that I love, whether I'm doing needlepoint or playing music or writing a story—it's all important to me." Volunteerism was as much Jessica's work as was her profession. Even her personal hobbies were part of the work that she considered important to her life.

Working toward the Future

Not every young woman in the study was fortunate to find work that she loved right away. Although Rachel was not ready to start her career immediately after graduating from MBC and felt that she chose her job as "a matter of convenience," she found that the work allowed her to grow and enabled her to find her direction. She stayed with her retail company for several years because she "was able to move into new positions that were personally challenging and that allowed a great deal of independence." She also liked the company and the kind of people it attracted. Even in a position that was not part of a planned career, Rachel wanted autonomy and challenge. By staying with the same company for several years, she was able to observe the dynamics among people and productivity, which helped her to choose the field of organizational psychology as her next career goal. It had taken time and perseverance, but she finally had discovered her true calling.

Travel and Time to Explore

Travel was a common goal for almost all of the PEG study alumnae, whether it was before, after, or even as a part of their graduate school or work experiences. They wanted to explore the United States and foreign countries. Not content to play the tourist, the women described traveling purposefully and actively planning for their trips.

Madison's medical training in foreign lands gave her a good dose of reality. The most valuable lessons that she learned "rarely came from lectures. They were from friends, classmates, roommates, my travels during breaks, and my experiences with patients who touched my heart and reminded me why I was in medical school abroad when I forgot." Somewhere along the way, Madison's worldview took a 180-degree turn. "My view of things has changed from how the world fits into my life to how I fit into the world at large." As she left her adolescent perspective behind, she felt more like a part of the global community.

"I rarely travel just to travel. It isn't that worthwhile to me," Madison continued. Instead, she hoped to work as a doctor in many countries. "While I'm in each place, I want to meet the people and become a friend." She already had gained some insight. "Living abroad taught me a lot about how the rest of the world views both America and Americans. Strangely, this has made me both more critical and more appreciative of my homeland." Madison wanted to travel with serious goals but said she would take advantage of whatever fun opportunities arose. "I wouldn't go all the way to Africa for a safari, for example. But you'd better believe that while I'm there for a medical rotation, my friends and I will be going on the best safari we can find!"

Because of her Irish ancestry, Ruby relished the opportunity to learn more about her family heritage during a trip to Ireland in high school. The visit overwhelmed her. "I had a very distinct feeling of being at ease and at home in Ireland. I vowed that I would return to live there one day." True to her word, Ruby spent a college semester in Ireland. "I came to love the local region and began to understand and appreciate Irish culture through my studies and travels within the country." After that extended stay, she returned to Ireland every few years "to widen my understanding of the culture and the social changes it continues to undergo."

Nina's focused, in-depth traveling started when her parents took their family abroad to live for several years. "It was a very emphatic kind of travel," she remembered. Ensuring that their children understood the significance of their stay, Nina's parents "were always explaining some of the economic and cultural differences for us." The family traveled frugally, "so that made our trips even more exciting because we saw a lot more of the cultural differences than we would have if we had stayed in fancy hotels." Like Madison, she valued the closer look she could get at a country's daily life.

Nikita had made it a mission to visit every state in the United States and every country on the globe. She wanted to make enough money to retire at age 40 and then travel the world. Having time to explore the truer picture of the locale was paramount. "I would want to take my time and explore all of the local culture and flavor instead of rushing around and only having enough time to see the tourist spots," she said. "So far, I have visited 26 states, Jamaica, England, Austria, Hungary, and Holland." And she was eager to keep going.

Traveling abroad helped the PEG study women understand people's differences. As college students, their peers' diverse backgrounds had instilled the desire to travel. As adults, they saw an even greater variety of ways of living and approaching human problems. The alumnae's exposure opened their minds and hearts to new ideas and greater acceptance of cultural practices in other countries. Learning in the context of people's real lives meant that the women gained a greater depth of insight about what they saw and heard. It led them to be more critical thinkers about their own culture and often contributed to a stronger sense of purpose. With a more finely honed understanding of other cultures, the women could determine how they might contribute meaningfully to foreign nations or to their own country's needs.

Starting Families

In addition to having extra time available to travel, one of the benefits of graduating from college as older adolescents is that the study alumnae had plenty of time to think about marriage and children. Accomplishing so much at such a young age allowed the PEG women time to fit much into their lives before having to worry about the proverbial ticking of their biological clocks. They also had extra time to develop their careers before making those life-changing commitments. By the time of the study, a number of the women were in their late twenties and early thirties and felt ready to start a family. Some were poised to do so; others were just planning. Some still were not ready, and a couple of them didn't want children at all. Whatever their feelings, the women's early academic and career experiences allowed them to set more liberal timelines for themselves concerning when (and if) they wanted to start a family.

Characteristics of Successful Women

The PEG study women graduated from Mary Baldwin College poised for success. They all exhibited, to various degrees, the characteristics that enhanced their ability to rise to the top in both their professional and their personal lives. Having proven their diligence and determination to conquer challenges as undergraduates, they emerged from college with the self-confidence of women who knew they had the ability and the fortitude to meet their goals in life.

High Personal Standards

Setting high personal standards was a common feature among the study participants. At PEG, demanding academic coursework, motivated peers, and supportive college faculty and administrators had raised the young women's self-expectations as they graduated from college. Nina said that "the high work standards, methods, and results from my PEG experience translated to a sense of determination, confidence, and ability in my job."

Nikita was proud of winning the award for Outstanding Graduate Student (Master's of Software Engineering) when she finished her degree. "I worked very hard in my Master's program to keep myself to a high standard of excellence. I managed to keep a 4.0 GPA for the duration of my Master's so that I graduated with honors," she said. "I also formed the software engineering student association and served as its president, was a member of Upsilon Pi Epsilon [the international honor society for the computing and information disciplines], and worked in the software research lab." While still a graduate student, Nikita and her team published a research paper of critical importance to lifesaving devices. Just as she had done at PEG, Nikita maintained her academic excellence while also leading and serving her community. She contributed purposefully to others and enhanced the development of her talents simultaneously.

High Expectations of Others

The women's high expectations also extended to others in the post-college world. Nina said, "I expect a lot from people. Living and learning with such intelligent and enthusiastic girls at PEG fostered my expectations and experiences now, both with women and men."

However, having high expectations can be a detriment when applied too strictly. Alumnae like Liz and Jessica reported that after a few years out of college, they stopped being quite so hard on themselves and softened their expectations of others. Liz learned how to forgive herself and others more readily for any intellectual, social, or emotional flaws that she observed. Her more mature, accepting attitude eventually led to better friendships and work relationships.

Pushing Past the Comfort Zone

Most of the PEG study alumnae realized that they had to actively pursue growth after graduating from Mary Baldwin College. For many, that development required pushing themselves past their comfort zones. Kristen, an associate at a consulting firm, said, "I am controlling, I know I like structure, stability, and routine, but at the same time, I know this weakness well enough that I purposely place myself in situations of change and flux." Countering her natural inclinations, Kristen learned more about what it takes to succeed. "Losing out on a graduate school scholarship competition was probably a major turning point for me. Up to that point, I hadn't failed in much of anything I'd tried," she said. "My being 'smart' was not enough in the face of people who were dedicated and willing to sacrifice. It is a lesson I am still learning. When things come easily to you for so long, inertia can set in." Just as a gifted student who is left unchallenged in school does not develop the proper study habits for the time when they will be necessary, Kristen needed a wake-up call to stimulate other important personal qualities besides her intellect.

Conscious of the potential trap of complaisance, Kristen forced herself to make regular and significant changes in her life. "I learned how to live in the 'real world,' to have a job and be independent. I also learned how to rise above serious challenges and to sabotage my insular tendencies by planning adventures." During her first year of grad school, Kristen moved to a country where she "knew no one, did not speak the language, and had no idea where I would be living. I learned that when push comes to shove, I am very efficient and capable." From her self-imposed adventures and challenges, Kristen grew in her self-knowledge, self-reliance, and self-efficacy.

Feeling insecure about getting an MFA among others who were very talented writers, Ruby challenged herself by entering a creative writing degree program. She said that it was the first time she felt that she might fail. But she overcame her worries, produced high-caliber writing, and won prizes for her poems. She learned that safe choices may undermine goals and visions, whereas being vigilant and consistent about self-challenge contributed to her purposeful progress.

Eleanor Roosevelt said, "You must do the thing you think you cannot do." These courageous young women perpetually put themselves in challenging circumstances, rose above their limitations, and overcame their weaknesses.

Dealing with Setbacks and Uncertainty

Some of the PEG study women encountered serious impediments to their progress. One woman could not matriculate at a highly selective, private university as a graduate student for lack of funds. Another was thwarted in her advancement by a selfish and powerful supervisor. Jessica encountered a difficult scenario when she was working for a prestigious business magazine. One day, while she was waiting for a flight in an airport, "I got a phone call from one of my co-workers saying they had just fired my boss and were considering eliminating my position.... You have no way of knowing what's next."

Because Jessica's working contexts shifted so quickly and radically, she learned to cope with uncertainty and change. She soon left the magazine and began teaching economics at a small college where she had to develop new relationships with colleagues and students. Shortly thereafter, she headed to business school in a foreign country where they spoke a different language and where she would have to establish friendships yet again. As Jessica's story reflects, regardless of difficulties and delays in reaching their life goals, the PEG women showed great resilience, persistence, and commitment to creating a life with meaning and purpose.

Self-Knowledge and Choice

To be happy and fulfilled, gifted women must have good self-knowledge and make important choices.[1] Liz fought her parents' objections by becoming a criminal defense lawyer. They wanted her to have higher status and more prestige in her law career, but Liz followed her personal values and made a conscious decision to work with disadvantaged people. Ultimately, she said, her parents became more comfortable with her choices.

Demonstrating the same kind of independent spirit, Kristen trusted her opinions, not those of others. "I am a questioner and seeker of truth. I am not willing to take much at face value. I need to learn things for myself and am not willing to take other people's opinions or viewpoints for my own." Ironically, Kristen said that her skepticism made her more open to new experiences and people. Reliance on her own observations and reasoning made her feel comfortable in most situations. With a strong personal philosophy, she hoped to remain "true in her work" and to her need for self-fulfillment. Kristen knew how she wanted to live her life.

A Sense of Accomplishment

Ruby expressed great satisfaction with her accomplishments. Completing her Master's of Fine Arts in Poetry "was a great achievement. I had taken three years off between my BA and grad school to work and travel and continued to work while I went to graduate school." Ruby was proud of her ability to juggle so much in so little time.

Similarly, at age 22, Nikita realized how much she had achieved in the five years since she had graduated from Mary Baldwin. "In that time, I have helped my company prepare global resources for Y2K, earned my Master's degree in Software Engineering, and spent almost two years working on a big program." Because she aspired to be a team leader, Nikita also spent a lot of her time "helping out with special events planning and creating engineering instruction."

Eleven years after graduating from Mary Baldwin, Georgia, a senior analyst in the field of environmental disaster, was self-assured and optimistic about her intellectual abilities and practical skills. Grounded in her faith, she also relished her loving relationships with friends and family. The positive influences made Georgia feel that she would continue to find new avenues of meaningful challenge and direction as she got older.

These women, like many of the other study participants, were able to accomplish significant goals and achievements at a relatively young age because they had eliminated up to four years of unnecessary schooling. PEG had allowed them to graduate young with a solid base of knowledge and leadership skills, as well as the confidence to forge ahead on their paths to purpose.

CHAPTER 9

Community and Making a Difference

No matter what choices the young women made after graduating from college, they seemed most alive when they were fully using their talents and actively involved in making a difference. Most had experienced a remarkable level of involvement at PEG, which helped them test their limits, and they perpetuated that pattern of intense engagement into adulthood. Each of the women spoke from the heart.

Describing her best qualities, Nikita said, "I appreciate most my honesty and true caring and respect for people. If I could spend all my time taking care of other people and making them happy, I would." An avid volunteer, she participated in activities that "help co-workers to really get to know one another and foster a sense of community at work. One of my purposes is to help other people learn and be inspired like I have been." As such, Nikita advised a group of fifth-grade girls who participated in a science and technology fair. "It is important to encourage girls to try science and math because they can often be intimidated and lose opportunities they might really enjoy simply because of stereotypes."

Imagining her future during an early interview with Dr. Rhodes, Julia said that no matter which career she ended up pursuing, she always envisioned herself "making a difference in somebody's life, whether it was teaching science to middle or high school students or making discoveries in a medical lab." Julia, who had begun a Ph.D. program in medical genetics, ended up teaching secondary school biology. Not content to be an anonymous cog in a bigger wheel of institutional effort, she said, "I want a job that makes me feel as if I, and not just the organization I am part of, make a huge difference."

Lucy could not imagine living a life without purpose. "I am someone who is supremely conscious of how short life is; I am terrified of dying with regrets that I did not at once suck life dry and leave something better than I found it."

Ruby said that making a difference was the core of her life. She and her husband shared the belief that "our lives are a gift, and our gifts are meant to be used to help others." However, she pointed out the importance of maintaining a balance between personal happiness and serving others: "If I'm personally fulfilled, then I am free to turn my good energy outward." Being at peace meant that Ruby could use her energy productively by serving people in her community rather than wasting energy on a troubled self.

Georgia wanted to get the most out of life both privately and publicly, and she discussed personal happiness in the context of helping others. "I am interested in work and volunteer projects that make a difference, while also challenging me to play full out. I know that making a difference in my community or in the world is critical."

Madison said, "My purpose, most importantly, is to give more back to the world than I have taken from it." Her empathy was apparent in her service ethic. "I have always known that I desired to lead others through servitude. While I, like all people, can be rather selfish, 'the suffering masses' are not anonymous, distant ideas whose fate is not tied to my own." Madison could imagine herself in their position "being hungry, oppressed, scared, and even angry. I suppose you could say, 'There but for the grace of God go I.'" Madison connected intensely with misfortunate people in downtrodden circumstances. As a medical student, she was "very much devoted to providing medical care to people in under-served communities and developing countries."

Believing genuinely in her ability to improve people's lives, Madison said, "Perhaps it may seem naïve, but I still believe that I can change the world—if not the world at large, then at least the world of each person whose life I enter. I want to see the world and know that I truly lived in it and was never content merely to pass through." Recognizing that the essence of helping others is first understanding them, Madison was poised to learn about foreign cultures and beliefs. By paying close attention to patients' needs and contexts, her contributions could then be sensitive to the reality of their lives.

Sharing Madison's interest in global issues, Jessica spoke of a time when she would be able to effect change on a broader basis. "I do really care about things like world peace and hunger and globalization and inequality of income and things like that," she said. She hoped "that one day I will have the skills and talents and contacts to do something, even a little something, about those sorts of issues." In the meantime, Jessica continued to act locally as she dreamed globally. "When I deal with people, to me it's about friendship and trust and reliability and the sense of responsibility to others." When her work precluded her deeper involvement in large-scale issues, she looked for gaps in community services with the aim to fill them inventively.

All of the alumnae were grateful for their college educations and wanted to give back by making a personal impact on their communities.

Selfless Service

Lucy recalled that some of her sense of justice developed as a result of self-interest. When she got involved with ACT UP, the AIDS activist group, she often held up signs at protest marches. "This involvement was mostly about me trying to find myself, carve out an identity, and find a niche. But I sure learned a lot about empathy, passionate commitment to a cause, and (unfortunately) the reaches of injustice."

Protesting on behalf of other people was one facet of Lucy's motivation, but she just as readily ached for those who did not have her skills and talents. Deeply fascinated and moved by language, she planned to volunteer at the Communicative Disorders Clinic in her town. "My worst fear is aphasia [an inability to speak, read, or write], and I can't imagine how lonely and terrifying it would be to be unable to communicate what you're thinking and feeling." Overcoming her personal fear, Lucy felt drawn to help others with language disorders.

Like Lucy, many of the PEG study women wanted to help the less fortunate. Julia taught swimming at a YMCA where children from disadvantaged homes needed much more than swim instruction. She incorporated healthy life lessons into the swim lessons, along with a warm understanding of the children's personalities and their families, to encourage optimism.

Working professionally with people who did not have support systems motivated Liz to help them beyond the confines of her public defender's job. She spent a lot of time thinking about justice and what it truly meant. "I like helping people who otherwise are not going to be helped." Her community purpose was to alert her professional law colleagues to the humanity and rights of her clients. "I see a lot of people who have substance abuse problems, mental health problems, and educational difficulties as well. And I think those are things that a lot of people don't think about. They're quick to condemn the kinds of people I work with." Liz described how people discussed her clients as "terrible." They wanted to "strip them of all their parental rights or throw them in jail, lock them up, and throw away the key," she said. "It's my job to say, 'Hey, no. Look, I work with these people.'" She tried to make others understand her clients more sympathetically. "And then the flip side of that is when I point out their condition, I have to make it better. I have to do what I can do to volunteer and help those people."

As a literacy coach in her community, Liz helped less fortunate people improve their lives, not just represent them in court. Aware of how easily her clients could fall prey to abuses of the legal system, Liz taught them to become better self-advocates. "Our legal system is not particularly helpful to people who suffer from debilitating mental illness or substance abuse or a number of other problems." Liz was particularly disturbed that 25% of adults in her county were functionally illiterate. When someone hands a form to a non-reader in court, Liz said, "What do they do? They just sign it. They've probably signed a waiver saying they don't want a court-appointed attorney, or signed a plea transcript saying they're guilty. They have no idea what they just signed." Upset that "people get taken advantage of because of things that they can't really help," Liz tutored individuals in reading. Her sense of purpose was so strong that she didn't just legally defend her clients' rights, she also actively worked on the more pervasive problems that they faced.

Literacy was as big a cause for Ruby as it was for Liz, and Ruby also served as a literacy coach. "I no longer see my intelligence as the thing about me that is most valuable. I think my perception and compassion are really more who I am," she said. Those personal qualities made her more effective when aiding others. She used to view someone's level of intelligence as the "ultimate, defining characteristic of a person," but she then realized "that intelligence is only as good as the person who carries it." How she used her gifts, rather than what her gifts were, was most important in life.

May displayed perhaps the most direct connection between her childhood suffering as a highly gifted girl and her goal for other gifted people. May wanted to stand up for very smart people who could not stand up for themselves. "Because I grew up such a nerd, I instinctually always root for the underdog." May was bothered that too often it was the "beautiful and rich people who succeed in the world, so I do favors for people I think are brilliant: I'll work for them for free, I'll give them my time and energy."

Balancing Work, Personal Life, and Service

To keep themselves on track, the study participants worked hard to juggle their myriad commitments. Their work, personal lives, and community service were equally important to them. To maintain their equilibrium, the women had to consider the competing forces in their lives and make the appropriate adjustments.

Balancing their lives was a major goal for the majority of the PEG study alumnae. Some women felt that their lives were imbalanced, yet all were either actively seeking balance or could envision when they would be able to achieve greater balance in the near future. The women recognized that imbalance was an indication that either they were being pulled in too many directions at once or in one direction to the exclusion of others. To be effective as producers, volunteers, and friends, they needed to sustain their social, emotional, moral, and physical health for many years to come. Because these women had so many diverse goals, they realized that achieving balance in the varied aspects of their lives was important for their continued well-being.

For Georgia, life was a "balance among work, volunteering, and personal commitments." She said that she was "pretty successful" at combining her career with a satisfying personal life. However, "every so often, I allow work to intrude into my personal life. Every time (so far), I've had a friend or family member notice and call the imbalance to my attention." Georgia had a "righting" technique to keep her life balanced.

Like Georgia, each study alumna felt at one time or another as if some aspect of her life needed adjustment so that she could stay on track. With long-term vision, strong values, and important goals, the women were able to cope with major imbalance because they counted on the time when they would be able to exert greater control. By sticking to quality of life as a focus, they were able to choose which activities to pursue and which to ignore. Study participants who felt that their lives were slightly off-balance made efforts to regain that balance as quickly as possible.

Ruby's life philosophy entailed balancing service to others with personal happiness. She'd seen lots of people "who are so burdened by the troubles of the world—environmental degradation, political injustice, etc.," that they would not allow themselves to feel personal happiness. She said, "That personal despair only adds to larger problems instead of solving them." She felt that focusing on happiness gave her emotional energy to help others. Ruby represented most of the PEG study women who spoke about enjoying their lives at the same time as they sought to make a difference.

PEG and Purpose

The young women's commitment to balancing their work, personal lives, and volunteerism was impressive, and their experiences at PEG were important factors in helping them to accomplish this goal. Darcy was grateful for the care that PEG provided her as a young teenager: "PEG established expectations of what a community should provide—a shared goal, common vision, and a support network." Residence in a nurturing environment helped them realize the power of being an active member of a vital and close-knit society. While the PEG students were determining their goals and envisioning their futures, they experienced PEG as a model purposeful institution. Their valuable early college entrance experience made them want to be part of similar communities in the future.

PEG's legacy lay in the way it helped the study women develop their sense of purpose. They took with them into adulthood the need to be their true self and the understanding that they were "not defined by their intelligence," as Rachel said. Instead, "one's passion is the source of true genius." The women had learned to seek appropriate support academically, socially, and emotionally from their peers, their professors, and the PEG and MBC staff. In their adult years, they then used those self-advocacy lessons to seek out new sources of support. They discovered that they could not trust everyone equally and appreciated those true friends who wanted them to succeed. Madison said, "I know I have learned to be more selective about who earns my trust and friendship—not every environment is like MBC."

The PEG experience echoed the best messages of support and caring from the students' families and acted as a counterbalance to the negative influences of their younger school days. As the soothing tones of acceptance resonated within, the study women felt grateful for the cultivation of their talents and their dreams. Despite the vicissitudes of their lives, the PEGs' early foundation of trust and nurturance reinforced the women's deep desire and ability to make a real difference in society.

Gifted individuals are often deeply driven to develop their talents to the greatest extent possible. Infused with this sensibility, the young women experienced tremendous talent growth during their college years. As undergraduates, the study alumnae resolved, either consciously or unconsciously, to help others grow in their self-assurance, skills, and talents. By first doing the work of growing strong and of satisfying their personal needs to fulfill themselves, the women were then able to look outward to see what other people needed. Even though many of them began college with compassion, it was still essential that during college these young women received enough bolstering of their psychological well-being to prioritize service to others in their adulthood.

Having been spared the frustration of staying in high school and instead rocketing to much greater intellectual heights at the right time, the students felt academically challenged in ways that made them highly energized and motivated. They felt nurtured in a community that really understood their needs and desires. Part of the PEG program legacy was the power that it gave the study alumnae to repay society for all of the enrichment that they had experienced. Through their selfless giving, they demonstrated that their lifelong intentions were to create lives of service.

Part V

Case Studies
of Five PEG Women

CHAPTER 10

Madison Kennedy: Parenting Excellence and Coping with ADHD

Dedicated to global medicine and trained in a specialized program abroad, Madison Kennedy was a first-year pediatric resident in a very poor area of the United States in the winter of 2005. Just a year earlier, she had spent two months in Africa, becoming familiar with diseases unique to that country and seeing first-hand the deprivation in which some of the residents lived. In a country rife with AIDS, Madison had a hard time watching children suffer with no access to treatment. Malnutrition distressed her, too. "Did you know that African babies' hair will turn blonde when they are malnourished?" she wrote in an email to her family and friends. "It's one thing to read about it in an email and another to see it every day in your patients and have to watch children die who would have lived in the U.S. or Europe."

Madison's exposure to the horrors of untreated illness deeply affected her sense of empathy and led to new perspectives. "I never realized that malaria is thought of here much like the flu back home, even though it's way more dangerous. It's just that common." Madison's eyes were opened to the dire health conditions in Africa, and her heart was filled with compassion.

A Brief Biography

Adopted at birth by a loving couple, Madison grew up as an only child in a home of modest means but unlimited encouragement and support. Her parents, Carla and Henry Kennedy, had wanted a baby for five years and felt extremely grateful when she arrived. Their daughter's exceptional intelligence was apparent early, despite her frenetic energy and difficulties with math. Both parents worked hard to help her succeed in school, but in spite of their best efforts and her high achievement, Madison was bored. Ultimately, she told her parents that she could not stand another year in high school. So at age 15, she applied to the PEG program, enrolled just as she turned 16, and enjoyed a productive college education.

Motivated by her love of medical genetics and undeterred by her struggles in science and math as an undergraduate, Madison applied to an international medical school that was affiliated with a prestigious American university so that she could study global medicine. During one of her classes, a doctor described the symptoms and associated behaviors of Attention Deficit Hyperactivity Disorder (ADHD),[1] and Madison realized that she suffered from that disorder and had spent her childhood struggling against it. By taking medication to offset the ADHD symptoms and by continuing to grapple with her resultant learning differences, Madison graduated from medical school. She then entered a pediatric residency in a region of the U.S. with a high proportion of disadvantaged families, which she thought would help prepare her to work in developing countries.

Loving Adoptive Parents

Excellent parents "make their home a stimulating and safe harbor where gifted children know there are always people who love them, who understand their dilemmas, and who care."[2] Twice-exceptional children—those who are gifted but also have ADHD or a learning or behavioral disability—need a great deal of reassurance and support because they grapple with the paradox of being intellectually advanced while struggling in other areas. With parental encouragement and positive actions, children often can overcome obstacles and develop inner strength that will serve them well when they are on their own.

Carla Kennedy liked to cross-stitch, and after adopting Madison as a baby, she stitched a poem that has remained in the Kennedy home for more than 30 years. A valued memento, the framed embroidery piece expresses Carla's loving sentiments as an adoptive mother:

> *Not flesh of my flesh*
> *Nor bone of my bone*
> *But still miraculously my own*
> *Never forget for a single minute*
> *You didn't grow under my heart but in it.*

Being adopted was not a big issue for Madison. "It was not a very interesting fact of my life growing up. I was like, 'Yeah, I'm adopted; whatever.' I didn't care," she said. From the studies she read, Madison didn't think she was typical of adopted children. For instance, she did not fantasize about her birth mother. She always knew she was adopted and was satisfied with the family she had. She believed that living securely in a happy household with parents who loved each other may have lessened her desire to discover her biological parents. "Perhaps because I was accepted unconditionally as part of the family, both immediate and extended, with no restrictions or conditions, I always felt that I knew where I came from."

Instead of feeling stigmatized for being an adopted child, Madison felt that she was more fortunate than other children because she was adopted. Her parents turned adoption into "something special" because they kept conveying to her that she was "this perfect, precious thing." Her parents' story of choosing Madison was part of the positive emotional foundation that "made the rest of life a lot easier."

Growing up in a home with parents who thought of her as a cherished gift, Madison developed healthily. She successfully managed the transition from public school to early college at PEG, medical school abroad, and her pediatric residency. Despite rough spots along the way, her parents' academic and emotional support, their expectations and values, and their strong relationship with Madison contributed greatly to her well-being.

Academic Support

Although Madison had ADHD, neither her parents nor she knew it when she was a child. As she struggled with math in primary school, her mother spent innumerable hours by her side so that Madison could complete her homework assignments. Over the years, Madison gradually became more independent and self-confident in her math abilities. Grateful for her mother's tenacity and both of her parents' acceptance, Madison learned that she did not have to excel in everything and that she could master the skills and concepts that frustrated her if she worked assiduously.

Carla and Henry were strong advocates for their daughter's academic needs. "The local school system was not providing adequate stimulation for me, so my parents sought outside resources such as summer enrichment programs," Madison said. With little money for non-essentials, Carla and Henry sacrificed years of vacation so that Madison could attend four summer gifted programs. Making that sacrifice was worthwhile, they said, because the experiences helped Madison grow intellectually, socially, and emotionally.

Although her parents were mostly "hands-off" during her time at Mary Baldwin College, Madison recalled how she teamed with her mother that first semester when she was 16 years old. " I had no idea what classes to take or how to balance all of the requirements and my interests," she said. "Together, we came up with a schedule that accommodated both." Madison's parents helped her "find the strength to keep studying, working, and attending classes—to honor all of my responsibilities, even though I would still be exhausted and frustrated."

Once she graduated from Mary Baldwin College, Madison decided to attend medical school in a foreign country. Despite having been accepted into a medical school in the United States, the foreign school's opportunities for studying tropical diseases and the prestigious coupling with a top-ranked American medical school were overwhelmingly inviting to Madison. "I can't say that my parents were thrilled about me moving to another country, especially one with such a volatile history," she recalled. Yet both parents recognized how much their daughter needed to pursue her dream. Madison was only 20 years old when she left to study medicine in a country with a vastly different culture and language. Although her classes were held in English, most of the people in the community did not speak it well or at all. Despite homesickness and initial discomfort, Madison eventually adapted and settled in.

Emotional Support

Madison attributed her adaptability to a "rock solid emotional foundation" from her parents. Happily married long before Madison was adopted, they "made a good team, and I never had doubts that their love was unconditional." Performance in school did not affect how her parents treated her; they did not withhold love if she did poorly. "A lot of families say there's unconditional love, but I don't think that all families have it," she said. Madison never realized how rare her family was until she attended college and saw students who were the products of unhappy, dysfunctional marriages and broken homes.

Carla and Henry's daily demonstration of love meant that Madison never thought about being anything other than what she was. "I converted oxygen to carbon dioxide—I did good," she said jokingly. Her existence gave her parents great joy, and their reassurance boosted her confidence so that she realized, while still in school, that she did not need other people's approval to feel good. "The two people I looked to most in my life never denigrated me for being the core of who I was." Carla and Henry worked with Madison on self-esteem, self-confidence, and self-acceptance during early childhood. "Everything I'll ever accomplish will always come back to them," she said.

Although she usually avoided self-pity, Madison remembered calling her parents when feeling depressed one night after working an 80-hour week as a pediatric resident with her ADHD condition exacerbating her problems. They responded as constructively as they had when she'd been at PEG, promising to give her the tools she needed to get through her distress. "It's the kind of support that builds you up but doesn't pull you back. Some people don't know the difference, and I'm lucky that my parents did." By encouraging her to take personal responsibility, Carla and Henry helped Madison develop the inner strength that she needed to face increasingly difficult life situations.

Parental Expectations

Madison had a clear idea of her parents' expectations as she grew up. "They definitely expected me to do the best I was capable of. Laziness was not tolerated." Carla and Henry insisted that their daughter move positively and productively in life. "Whatever my path was, I sure as heck had better be on that path, but they didn't dictate what that path was. I didn't have to be a certain thing."

Carla and Henry also taught Madison what to expect of herself. The first time Madison did not receive an A was in tenth grade. "I flipped because I'd always expected myself to get A's because that's just what I knew I was capable of doing." However, Madison did not beat herself up when she did poorly on tasks that were truly hard for her, as long as she had done the best she could. While teaching their daughter to persevere with arduous tasks, Carla said, "We always encouraged her to reach for the stars" and proudly mentioned that Madison was the first student in her county to attend a prestigious gifted summer enrichment program out of state. Counterbalancing Madison's struggles was the steady parental message that with effort, she could do anything.

When Madison's poor behavior warranted it, Carla and Henry guided her to think about what she was doing. "Sometimes as a little kid I would say silly or stupid things, and kids made fun of me for that. Mom would say, 'Just stop and think about what you say first so you say what you mean.'" Carla also helped Madison to become realistic when her deep sense of empathy and enthusiasm prompted her to dramatic action. "I was the bleeding heart little girl who wanted to financially adopt little children in Africa through those organizations where money never actually gets to Africa," she recalled. Carla respectfully discussed the matter with Madison rather than dismiss her daughter's wish. "She explained to me why it was silly and that I could do it, just not in that way. I was never discouraged from being sympathetic or from being a good friend."

Summarizing her parents' expectations, Madison said that they wanted her to be honest with herself, work hard, and do her best in whichever field she selected. "My mom and dad only wanted me to be happy, responsible, well-rounded, and open minded." These expectations reflected the Kennedy parents' values, which they modeled daily.

Parental Values

Carla and Henry's parenting philosophy was part of their life philosophy: "Work hard, play hard, and live life to the fullest." Underlying that perspective was the belief that "You should be committed to whatever you choose to do." The Kennedys used that same approach to parenting. "We took responsibility for our lives and hers. While we didn't sacrifice everything, *we* raised our daughter—not grandparents, nannies, or tutors." The couple felt that Madison's commitment to all aspects of her life was greatly influenced by their commitment to her.

Both parents valued family, unconditional love, knowledge, honesty, integrity, compassion, caring, and commitment. When Madison was six years old, Carla left home for three months to care for her aging mother; the strain on both parents was substantial. "The last six weeks, I never came home," Carla remarked. "What did that show her? A commitment to family, giving, returning a part of what was given to me by my mother, the knowledge that Nanny was being cared for, and when all else is gone, family will be there." Madison's parents lived their values, even when those priorities meant making big sacrifices.

Carla and Henry also emphasized that Madison should respect everyone and not judge them. Respect was earned by taking responsibility, so honesty was key. Madison learned what would happen if she ever lied. "If you mess up, you fess up," Carla used to say, "because if you don't and I find out, you are in so much deeper trouble. You take responsibility for your own mistakes."

Madison's mother had a college degree, and even though father had not graduated from high school, both parents considered education to be the "key to unlocking every opportunity." Carla modeled that value by going back to school to get a second degree while Madison was in college. Carla said, "Was I challenged to do my best?! And I did, because I'd asked the same of her."

Carla and Henry also taught Madison about giftedness—that in and of itself, giftedness is not worthwhile unless it is honestly and ethically earned. Carla said, "Where is the pride in accomplishment without those moral values?" Carla and Henry both "communicated these things through our daily living. Parents can't say one thing and do another," said Carla. The Kennedy family sought to live consistently by their personal values.

Through her own moral sense and by modeling the values exemplified by her parents, Madison grew as a principled and compassionate person. Her values of decency and empathy shaped her responses to environments. Her first sub-internship in a U.S. hospital was such a bad experience that she almost left pediatrics. She abhorred the attending physicians' lack of caring for the medical students and interns they were supposed to be training. When first-year residents made beginners' mistakes, the supervising doctors were callous. They alternated between micromanaging and leaving junior staff to flounder.

Disheartened, Madison worried that her values could become distorted in such settings. "I was thinking, if this is what pediatrics is, I don't want to be that kind of person." Although she began to make plans to enter a different medical field, she ultimately found a good match for her sensibilities in a program with a vastly different philosophy. Madison's new pediatric residency embraced her values of warmth, generosity, and encouragement. The doctors' approach included concern for the whole person. When first-year residents made mistakes, the attending physicians did not belittle them but rather taught them the correct procedures. The attending physicians wanted the residents to thrive in their work. "They were so down to earth and so nice, and I knew instantly that this was what I had been looking for originally and that I'd finally found it."

Not only did Madison feel more comfortable psychologically, but she also found it easier to absorb and apply information. "I think I learn more in an environment where I feel free to ask questions. If I think I'm making a mistake, then I don't have to be afraid to go ask the supervising staff. I think it's safer for the patients." Just as she had learned well in the caring culture of PEG, Madison flourished in the nurturing hospital residency.

Parent-Child Relationships

The Kennedys expressed their gratitude for life in general and Madison in particular. Both parents had lost many relatives early in their lives. Those tragedies gave them an appreciation of life based on the realization of its brevity and of the primary importance of family ties over material possessions. Being good parents was paramount to them. Carla underscored that no matter how much of a challenge it was to raise Madison, "it is my privilege to be her mother. I know no greater gift." Her parents' gratitude for their daughter's existence was fundamental to Madison's well-being and reinforced her awareness of the gift of life.

Characterizing her relationship with each of her parents, Madison said, "My mom and I are more like equals, and I'm my daddy's little girl." Madison's father worked for the same company for 33 years to bring stability and security to the Kennedy home. Carla sold real estate, but her priority was always Madison. When she advocated strongly for her daughter, she ignored other people's negativity. "I'd hear the snickers, but I didn't care, and when my goal was realized, I was committed. So was Henry." Carla had a close relationship with her daughter; they could discuss anything. "Madison was always answered honestly with the content only being tempered by age appropriateness and readiness," she said.

Carla also commented that Madison "kept me on my toes" when she was a child, which helped her grow as a parent. But after Madison graduated from college, Carla acknowledged that "My greatest growth has come the last eight years as her world has expanded. If I want to continue to be an influence, an ear, a voice, I have to grow with her." Always educating herself to the fullest extent possible about Madison's experiences, Carla grew in tandem with her gifted daughter.

Carla's advice for other parents of gifted children was that they should trust their own instincts and "seek counsel from those in a position to guide." But even more important, she said, "obtain the knowledge you need to be your child's number one advocate. Stay current with legislation and all resources out there. If you don't do it for your child, odds are no one else will." Madison's mother also underscored responding sensitively to the actual child and not to what a parent might want her to be. "Let the child set the pace; don't push, but support and encourage." At the heart of the matter was the need to give the child the gift of the parent's self. "Give them your time, give them yourself, not just money and things. And listen to what they say."

Coping with ADHD

Growing Up

Although Madison had a suspicion before medical school that she might have ADHD, it was not until she was in a child psychiatry class that she was certain. She met all of the criteria her professor listed. In retrospect, she could identify her childhood behaviors that were consistent with ADHD: "not being able to sit still in class, running around like I was driven by a motor, not being able to finish one task before starting another, interrupting people."

Carla recalled how tough school life was for Madison at that time. "Madison's self-esteem was low, she was bullied, and she had more current knowledge than several of her teachers. She was a challenge in the classroom, and they didn't want the challenge."

Luckily, Carla helped Madison with behavior modification strategies. Madison admitted, "I did have a lot of assertiveness and sometimes even aggression, but my mother knew how to channel it." Carla and Henry also set ground rules for behavior. "I always knew what was expected of me. The goals of the house were very clear, like you have to do your homework before you play, which is both behavior modification and goal setting. There were consistent rules, rewards, and punishments." As a result of their combined efforts, Madison excelled in school.

Madison was always the smartest student in her class. However, attending her first summer gifted enrichment program with other equally bright students caused her to doubt her intelligence. "All of the other students were doing much better in their classes and learning faster than I was, so I thought, 'I guess I'm not that gifted.'" Other students could sit in class all day and study for several hours at night, but Madison did not have similar stamina or the ability to concentrate.

So when PEG accepted her for early college entry, Madison was both thrilled and terrified. She was exhilarated because she had taken a huge risk and gotten into the program, but she was also plagued by self-doubt: "What if I go and I hate it and I've lost this year of high school?" she asked her mother. Madison worried that she would then be afraid to return to high school. "I was building this tiny little molehill into this huge mountain," she said. Carla reassured her daughter by telling her that if she didn't like it, she wouldn't have to finish all four years. Madison remembered her mother saying, "'All you have to do is commit to one year, but you have to give that one year everything you have.' She asked, 'Can you do one year?'" And Madison answered, "Yes," feeling relieved and satisfied for making the big decision to go.

ADHD "Happy Land"

"College is really ADHD happy land. You're rarely in the same class for more than an hour or two, and you're studying different subjects at once," Madison stated. With her love of learning and high energy level, she felt at home at PEG. Being at an all women's college helped her socially, too. "Everyone is always talking at once anyway, so no one really minds if you're not all that great at paying attention to everything they have to say." Still, Madison's self-doubt emerged when she started having more problems with her condition.

Having ADHD made it hard for her to stay organized, but Madison found some advantage to her non-linear thinking patterns. "I could think quickly and about many different things at once. I could come up with unusual solutions because the mind of an ADHD person rarely travels in a straight line." Madison turned her impulsivity toward generating community service projects and her hyperactivity toward participating in more classes, activities, and sports.

Compensatory Strategies

Madison's academic weaknesses might have impeded her progress, but she compensated inventively.[3] Calculus was intimidating, and she needed to find a way to pass the course. She made a *quid pro quo* with a traditionally aged student named Ellen. As a teaching and laboratory assistant in chemistry lab, Madison lessened Ellen's load of "grunt work" and checked her basic math. In exchange, Ellen tutored Madison in calculus. "So we complemented each other, and I went from being a D student on my first test in calculus to a 4.0. And I understood it; she didn't do it for me; I passed the test on my own." Ironically, Madison later became a calculus tutor and got paid to help other students.

Cell biology was another difficult class. Overall, Madison's GPA was between 3.7 and 3.8, but in that class, she was earning a much lower grade. "If I couldn't pass that class, I knew I couldn't make it in medical school." Choosing to take all of her other finals in two days, Madison spent the rest of her time during finals studying for her cell biology exam. When she took it, she missed only one question. The professor gave her an A for the semester. From his viewpoint, she had earned it. "He gave me the grade for what my knowledge was coming out of the course and my ability to use it," a grading policy she greatly appreciated.

Medical School

Attending medical school in a foreign country was very trying, and Madison's first year was especially tough. "Just the sheer culture shock, the overwhelming unfamiliarity and difficulty, the magnitude of what you've undertaken hits you like a ton of bricks," she recalled. That initial year was the longest and the hardest, with hours and hours of classes per day and the expectation that the students would readily absorb the knowledge.

Behavior Issues

Fortunately, Madison's medical school friends helped her with her ADHD without insulting her, and she appreciated their patience and forbearance, a contrast from her general experience. "People have accused us [individuals with ADHD] our whole lives of being poor listeners and interrupting and being hyper," she said. But Madison was able to listen to her friends' advice about her behavior without becoming defensive. "They were able to point out to me exactly what I was doing and how they, as my friends and fellow medical students, would like me to fix it." Grateful for their sensitivity, Madison said that a lot of other doctors were less lenient with people who had ADHD "because the symptoms are so counter-intuitive to the mind of the average person going into medicine." Had her friends not been so considerate, Madison probably would have had to deal with increasing criticism, "which would have become very difficult."

Learning Issues

Once Madison entered medical school, her old compensatory strategies no longer worked. "I suddenly needed to be able to study long, very detailed information for hours on end, and I couldn't." People without ADHD do not realize that "if you just think you have to sit down and study for hours on end, it is actually physically painful," she explained. She described the symptoms: "Your muscles will tense, your stomach will clench, your head will start to hurt, you'll start to yawn, you'll get tired, and you'll get hot." It's as if the body is trying to make the person think that she's sick to avoid the terrible "experience of trying to force yourself to do this thing that your mind is not geared to do."

Medication was the cornerstone of Madison's ADHD management, but her personal strength helped as well. "Through sheer force of will and having chutzpah to power a nuclear missile," Madison said, "I plowed my way through and somehow managed to scrape by. But it was hard and often painful, frustrating, and even frightening."

Since Madison was a medical student who was trained in biofeedback and behavior modification, she decided to monitor and train herself. She thought about the advice she would give a patient and then followed it herself. On good days, she studied for 45 minutes and took a 15-minute break. On bad days, she studied for 30 minutes and took a 20-minute break, reasoning that 30 minutes of study was better than none. Studying for shorter times on the bad days also helped her psychologically: "If I knew there was an end, I could make myself get started."

New Compensatory Strategies

To compensate for the huge amount of reading she had to do in medical school, Madison developed her own set of strategies. First, she obtained books that contained the key points she needed to study. "They were pared down to the bare bones basics," she said. Next, she figured out that she had to attend class lectures, unlike her roommate, who could skip them and still manage to learn the material successfully on her own. Madison also realized that she could not study for long periods of time each night because it was too tiring. If she did not finish her studying on a particular night, she didn't fret about it. She knew that her strategy was making it possible for her to "go to class, take notes, and study again the next day." She needed to conserve her strength for the long haul.

Another tactic was to become "ultra organized" to compensate for "being innately disorganized." Madison recorded everything she had to do on a list, including tasks that were months away. Time was a crucial factor in her success or demise. The medical school lectures were scheduled for one hour, but they often ran over. To preserve her energy, Madison left the classroom 15 minutes early because she needed a longer break than her peers did. "It meant that I missed the end of the lecture, but it also meant that I could focus again for the lecture coming next." Fortunately, her friends would tell her what she had missed. "I just knew my own limits and worked around them."

Besides developing compensatory techniques, Madison learned that she had more personal resources than she'd thought—"more of the capacity to put up with being exhausted and lonely and in culture shock." She also discovered that despite the emotional severity of the year, she was not prone to depression. Friendships helped her a lot. "Everyone in the program was pretty miserable that year," so the students supported each other. Madison was fortunate to have a support system both at school and at home.

Residency

After she finished medical school, Madison returned to the United States for a demanding pediatric residency and discovered new ADHD-related problems. "When I'm super stressed and when the wards are super busy, I can sense myself becoming more forgetful or becoming more absent-minded, which scares me more now," she said. Working with a university physician, she began taking long-acting Ritalin. "It's not always perfect. During my first month, I didn't do as well as I would have liked. However it provides a very good baseline control." By her second month, Madison's attending physicians had already commended her for her excellent work.

Finding Advantages in ADHD

Having learned to control her symptoms relatively well, Madison sometimes saw ADHD as a constructive tool in her residency. "When we do have those rare medical zebras, I don't have to remember to think outside the box. There's no box in here. I'm not sure my brain could draw a box on command." For day-to-day diagnoses, Madison had to rely on pattern recognition. But with unusual diagnoses, her non-linear thinking became a benefit. She approached problems from an atypical perspective and was good at finding answers.

Giftedness, Mastery, and Success

Madison's ultimate success in medicine and in life stemmed from her sense of purpose and from her use of "successful intelligence."[4] Her values and perspective drove her to overcome the enormous learning obstacles posed by ADHD so that she could help underprivileged people become healthy and empower them to make proactive decisions about their lives. She also found the resources and developed the skills necessary to shape her environment, a critical component of success.

Both Madison and her parents agreed that she was born with her intellectual gifts and purposeful spirit, and Carla and Henry nurtured these qualities in their daughter. Madison credited the far-reaching effects of her parents' childrearing. "They have never been to Africa, and yet they somehow raised a daughter who is willing to devote her whole life to a country they've never seen and to helping people who don't have the resources to help themselves." Carla and Henry supported Madison's goal of "being a foot soldier in the changing of the world scheme." As her parents applauded her principles, they also boosted her confidence and commitment.

Interestingly, Madison chose medicine as a vehicle for change because she felt that she was *not* gifted in it. She defined giftedness as natural talent that allows one to do things easily, which would not be fulfilling to her. Instead, Madison's real sense of satisfaction came from "mastering something that was hard and knowing that you can be wonderful at something that didn't come easily to you."[5]

Madison said that her life was driven by purpose, not by giftedness. Despite her relative weaknesses in math and science, she knew that her interpersonal skills would bolster her performance once she began working on the wards. Understanding medicine as both an art and a science, Madison envisioned her future work with people as the "art" that could help her persevere through the "science" of medical school. Prompted by a love of genetics, Madison fused her interests with her sense of purpose to determine her life's direction.

Madison's desire to help disadvantaged people was rooted in her personality and in her parents' moral example. Her philosophy was that individuals are responsible for imbuing life with meaning. "I don't think life in and of itself has some great objective meaning. I think it's something we find in and of ourselves," she said. Always having known that she wanted to lead others by serving them, she had a realistic grasp of her future: "residency and a lifetime of debt and poverty spent in tent hospitals and in relief efforts all across the world." Madison was willing to devote herself, both personally and professionally, to her goal. Driven by her purpose, she forged ahead, overcoming hurdles with courage.

Conclusions

Madison's life of dynamic growth came from creating challenging pathways, coping successfully with obstacles, making constructive choices, and shaping supportive environments. She was well on her way to fulfilling her desire to make a positive, lasting impact on the world through international medicine. Propelled by her deep intelligence and need for challenge, Madison entered college early, a decision that both thrilled and scared her. Drawn to medicine, she became a doctor despite her ADHD and relative weaknesses in math and science. Madison's future plans were also daunting—training in areas of poverty with great demands, spending years repaying her medical school loans, and working most of her life in underdeveloped countries. Because Madison had observed her parents' strong work ethic, she knew that it could take many years of commitment and perseverance for one person to substantially help another. She learned to get the support she needed and persist until she reached her goals. Her driving sense of purpose, creativity, courage, and common sense helped her to meet increasingly difficult challenges with considerable success.

Madison's personal progress was a testament to the outstanding parenting she received. Carla and Henry Kennedy demostrated that parents do not need to be biologically connected to their child to provide every kind of support and guidance necessary to ensure the healthy development of an exceptionally gifted young woman. They loved Madison unconditionally while insisting that she stay productive and improve her skills and inner resources. Every step they took was aimed at making Madison independent and self-reliant while always being trustworthy anchors of support.

CHAPTER 11

Jessica Holmes: Beyond Fame, Fortune, and Stereotypes

Jessica Holmes said that a true measure of a society lies in its treatment of its poorest citizens. Because of this belief, when she visited other countries, she went out of her way to explore neighborhoods that typical tourists do not wish to see. Before living abroad for several years as an African American doctoral student, Jessica traveled extensively in Thailand, China, and parts of Africa. She found the worst conditions in the South African townships. "That was the most heartbreaking poverty I've seen because you had a half million people using one clinic. They didn't have enough latex gloves. People were living in tin shacks." Jessica saw "so much self-hatred and self-loathing. You could see it in the way they drank and in the violence." In Thailand, Jessica also saw great poverty, "but it's not as desperate. People lived in shacks, but they had enough to eat. They had joy in their lives." Although she recognized Thailand's problems, including rampant sexual exploitation, Jessica still felt the hopefulness of its people, whereas in the South African townships, there was only hopelessness and misery.

Realizing how deprived people's lives could be, Jessica felt intense gratitude for her many gifts. Those depressing scenes stirred her compassion but also gave her greater optimism. Making a beneficial difference in the world seemed more achievable when she realized that her own obstacles as a gifted young Black woman would not be as severe as the ones she had witnessed in her travels.

A Brief Biography

Jessica was the oldest of three daughters to two strong, progressive, Christian parents. As an eighth grader looking ahead to high school, she was afraid that she would be under-challenged. After qualifying for a talent search program, Jessica received a PEG brochure in the mail. Since she had always wanted to attend boarding school, the early college entrance program looked attractive. Encouraged by her mother, Jessica applied and was accepted.

Following her graduation from PEG at 17 years of age, Jessica enrolled in an economics Ph.D. program at a prestigious university. Leaving the program with a Master's degree, she worked as a journalist at a well-known business magazine, and although business appealed to her, the magazine did not. She left it, and after spending a year teaching economics at a small college, Jessica finally decided that she wanted a Ph.D. in business. Eager for new experiences, she applied to a top international business school abroad and was accepted. Extremely happy with her life there, she was one of the school's top students.

Beyond Fame and Fortune

Values from Home: Responsibility and Service

Jessica grew up in a home where personal responsibility was paramount. During middle school, when she wanted to be in a play in addition to her already full schedule, her mother insisted that she find transportation to the rehearsals on her own. Jessica learned that "if I was going to take on another activity, it had to be a priority for me, and I had to work out my life to accommodate it." Her parents also stressed the importance of giving back to society. Mr. and Mrs. Holmes volunteered often while continuing their educations, raising their daughters, and working full time.

Their religious values and practices inspired Jessica's spirituality, self-discipline, and desire to help others.

Being raised as a Christian provided a moral framework. "What religion offers is a yardstick by which you can weigh your actions and your thoughts, but it also offers practicing religion as part of the community," she said. The church community welcomed the Holmes family with love and kindness, which they reciprocated.

Despite coming from poverty and "the working class," Jessica's parents both transcended their modest economic backgrounds to achieve higher education degrees. Mr. Holmes earned an MBA and was working on his Ph.D. Mrs. Holmes became an engineer with a Master's degree and then earned a second Master's. Although they were strict disciplinarians, they were also joyful people and modeled a real delight in life.

The PEG Experience

Grounded by a strong family, Jessica was only 13 years old when she entered PEG. She was enormously excited about the incredible choices for learning, the other smart girls she would meet, and the chance to live independently. In the beginning, Jessica dreamed of becoming rich and famous. "I was young. I was dumb. I didn't know any better," she said. "Now I realize there's much more to life than that, and there's something in between. I want something in the middle." Going to college when she was still formulating her personal values and identity meant that Jessica did not stay focused too long on external rewards. Instead, her experiences helped determine more important goals and a deeper sense of purpose

Attending MBC's early entrance program promoted Jessica's self-awareness through creative exploration. "It added an element of not just academic achievement, but also self-knowledge and being unconventional and creative about how you approach life that I think changed my life," she remarked. Jessica's optimistic belief that "there's always a way to get things done and that you don't have to do it like everyone else" came as a result of enrolling in PEG. That philosophy was liberating, Jessica explained, because it made her feel freer to "to do what I want to do and do it the way I want to do it."

As a student, Jessica couldn't wait to explore academics. She could barely contain her enthusiasm when handed a catalog with "hundreds of classes, not just the eight or 10 they let eighth graders take." College also offered 50 to 70 extracurricular activities to choose from instead of the limited number at her middle school.

Sports were a new area of exploration. Jessica had never thought of herself as an athlete "in terms of being rough and tough, but playing lacrosse well changed my perception of myself," she stated. Being at a women's college gave her confidence because women were encouraged to challenge themselves physically as well as intellectually. In high school, Jessica might have maintained her identity as an intellectual who did not play sports, but at PEG, she felt encouraged to explore other aspects of her identity.

PEG also broadened Jessica's exposure to the arts, "particularly because my friends were so wacky and creative." The freedom to explore all aspects of the self was invaluable, she said. "There was room to play, to goof off, to learn, and to express oneself and also to be creative with your life, how you live your life. I also learned that there's no one solution to any issue in life." PEG significantly opened up Jessica's world. Her increased self-exploration, independence, and self-reliance helped her move away from the simplistic "fame and fortune" dream.

Jessica was grateful that Mary Baldwin was not as highly ranked or competitive as some other colleges. If she had attended an Ivy League college, she said, she would not have been able to find out as much about herself and about areas in which she could excel. Having to maintain her highest achieving mode at such a college would have forced her to focus almost exclusively on her academic performance, others' expectations, and outward signs of success. At lower-key Mary Baldwin, she could discover much more about her character and abilities through a wider array of extracurricular activities without sacrificing her academic work.

Keys to Growth

Exposure and Discovery

Jessica saw herself as an explorer, a risk taker, and an experimenter. She began a doctoral economics program but realized that she was not interested in academic economics, predominantly because its mathematical focus precluded the social interaction that was important to her, and she left with only a Master's degree. Most of her four years in graduate school were spent growing up, she said. She took a year off and supported herself through multiple jobs, helped to produce and direct a play, and moved to a large city to work at a think tank. These activities made her feel more independent and self-reliant.

Coping with Obstacles

Jessica's unhappiness with the doctoral program also stemmed partly from prejudice and isolation. At such a competitive university, "you have to be in a study group in order to get your work done." None of the predominantly international male groups welcomed her. Being a young African American female made it harder to integrate into their tight-knit circles, and her coursework suffered. As she struggled, she looked to her advisors for support, but they were often away from campus. "In grad school, your advisor is essential," she said, "and if your advisor's not looking out for you, you're not going to go anywhere." Lacking a true mentor to guide and promote her, Jessica became more alienated from the doctoral program.

Paradoxically, while Jessica's academic work withered, her social life bloomed. "I developed an extensive social network—an international social network—which I think has changed my life and also changed my perspective about things," she commented. Exposure to "extraordinary people who had done things I'd never done before, never even heard of" proved to be an emotional antidote to her negative academic experience. Interacting with "brilliant" people from diverse backgrounds fueled Jessica's desire to expand her world. Her new primary goals became gaining "more international experience and developing more international contacts."

Enjoying the international crowd helped Jessica realize that her values were changing. Moving away from dreams of fame and fortune, she discovered that "status and all those things don't matter, which was a relief. It really freed me, took a lot off my shoulders," she said. A profound shift was happening. Although she had never had trouble making friends before, Jessica began to understand how much she depended on others for her well-being. She understood that accomplishing her goals meant drawing information, strength, and friendship from peers, as well as giving back to them. She also recognized that failure was a necessary part of life. She had to rebound from unsatisfying experiences and learn from her mistakes. The road to success was not necessarily straight.

Counseling helped Jessica cope when she got depressed in graduate school. "It saved my life because it helped me break a lot of habits that were making me unhappy. I used to be a perfectionist. Now I seek excellence." The shift away from perfectionism made Jessica less critical of herself and others. By not expecting too much from other people, her patience increased. Although it took time to relinquish old habits and to embrace better ones, she was moving in a healthier direction.

Solidifying Personal Values

Just as Jessica gamely took on the challenge of entering a doctoral program at age 17, she showed similar fearlessness when she became a writer at *Best Business* magazine at the age of 22. Impelled by her desire to be a journalist, she moved hundreds of miles away from her graduate program to a very large city.

Despite her realization that obtaining status was not a priority, Jessica admitted that two major motivations for taking the journalism job were money and status. It took repeated negative experiences to convince her that her true priorities lay elsewhere. She acknowledged that having access to famous and powerful people was intoxicating. "I do relish elite access to things—being able to go to places I want to go and talk to people I want to talk to." Yet access to the rich and powerful was a double-edged sword. While some of the people she met were fascinating, too many "insanely wealthy and powerful" ones were "not very nice people." She also realized that these individuals often were not any smarter than she was and that no matter how hard she worked or how good a person she was, she would probably not reach the same high-powered and moneyed pinnacles. Jessica concluded that reaching that kind of fame and fortune was not worth the personal cost.[1]

Politics and stereotypes contributed to Jessica's disenchantment. She was unwilling to play the workplace game to gain-advantage. "The politics killed me; there was definitely a lot of favoritism. Because I wasn't anyone's pet, it was really difficult," she said. Racial distancing also accounted for some of Jessica's disadvantages. "The older, white editors at *Best Business* wouldn't jump to be my friend because from just looking at me, they wouldn't think we had anything in common." Jessica felt stereotyped in other ways, too. "People create myths about you, and it's very difficult for them to deal with you when you don't fit their notion of who you are, or what you can do, or who you should be." The editors and other writers pigeonholed her as a reporter who could do only "techie or nerdy stories." Just as the lack of a Ph.D. mentor had hindered her development, so too did the lack of an editor's support. Jessica needed a mentor who would supply critical, tacit knowledge about achieving success. Without that kind of support, she was not going to progress adequately at *Best Business.*

Expectations about the quality of writing were so high at the magazine that it took Jessica a long time to trust that she did not "have to be a Nobel Prize or a Pulitzer Prize winner" to prove her competence. *Best Business* made Jessica feel that she had to be the "best of the best" right from the start. The unfairness of the demands helped her realize that she did not have to aspire to the hilt of achievement to feel worthwhile. She could tolerate a much slower development of her talent and focus on her journey of growth rather than on an idealized endpoint.

Taking Control

Jessica's qualities of resourcefulness, inner strength, and self-reliance formed the basis of her proactive choice to combat adversity, which often led to greater insight about her alternatives. When no one at the magazine would provide specific, constructive feedback on her articles, Jessica decided to take a freelance writing class. Not only did her skills improve, but she also gained the self-confidence "to start making plans to get the heck out of *Best Business.* I could see a life for myself where I would have a lot more say in what kind of work I did." The promise of autonomy and new directions appealed to Jessica, making her much more optimistic than before.

Another personal triumph occurred when Jessica decided to write her first feature story. She found an engaging question, formed a research project, and spent two months developing her concept. "That was one of the first times I've ever truly done independent research and actually felt like an economist," she said. The result was one of the magazine's most successful articles, which generated tremendous reader response. When others refused to give her opportunities, Jessica created her own and experienced the meaningful power of taking control of her life.

Bitter Lessons

The bitter lessons she learned at *Best Business* magazine helped Jessica focus on what she really wanted. Gaining so much insight about how she did not want to live her life gave her significant new perspectives about her choices. She liked challenges, even when they meant that she would suffer. Otherwise, achievement would be too easy. It was by doing things the hard way that she gained strength and self-awareness. "Struggling financially, struggling through grad school, struggling in the big city, trying to make friends who actually enrich my life were all the things adults go through—being lonely, being scared," but they also led to social and emotional growth. She might frequently mess things up, Jessica said, but "at least the gears are always grinding."

As a former "loner," Jessica found that too often, her friends and work colleagues thought that she did not need their help. Part of her growth was learning how to expose her vulnerabilities so that others could help or provide support. Even though Jessica felt that she was creating a unique path in life, she also recognized that "you need other people, and I needed to learn how to reach out."

Travel

Traveling fulfilled Jessica's desire to meet people of different nationalities and to learn deeply about their cultures. It also represented her need for challenge, excellence, novelty, and experimentation. By coping with obstacles during her trips, Jessica increased her ability to deal with all kinds of difficult situations, which greatly enhanced her personal growth.

During her time in Asia, Jessica traveled alone to a number of countries because she wanted challenge. "I went from scuba diving, to living in a hut in a village in the mountains, to climbing the Great Wall of China. All of this took a lot of time, a lot of money, and a lot of logistics." Recognizing that she did tend to "go to the extremes," Jessica was proud of her self-reliance. She liked to "shoot for the moon" because she wanted to grow resilient, resourceful, and skilled. The problem with the safe and predictable route, she said, is that "the answer is already there" and results in no growth. Jessica wanted to find answers to her questions and to forge her own life path.

Vacations are for exploration and experimentation, not for inner reflection. "In my daily life, I make the time to sit still and reflect every day," she remarked. "The point of traveling is to understand how people live." Jessica wanted depth and insight. During one trip, she traveled across the U.S. to help a friend run a bed and breakfast. "I was up at six in the morning scrubbing toilets, making omelets. It was great." She enjoyed taking time off from school or work "to do things that I wouldn't necessarily have time to do otherwise, or to have unconventional experiences, or to do something I always wanted to do." Jessica attributed this need to explore life to her parents. Because Mr. and Mrs. Holmes never constrained her with specific achievement expectations, they gave her the freedom to explore and experiment in the world.

Risk taking with purpose was important to Jessica. "One of the things I like to do whenever I go somewhere is to visit the slum, the ghetto, or the hood." She wanted to see how the poorest people survived. She took precautions to stay safe, but "I'm not afraid of poor people," she said. "That fear happens in the States particularly because Black people are so often demonized, and part of it is because of the economic differences." Although she and her companions were careful, "that didn't keep us from making friends who could take us places and do things and talk to us." Jessica's push to see beneath cultural surfaces provided her with greater meaning. Seeing life as it really was in the poorest places deepened her resolve to be more patient and compassionate.

Traveling in Asia jolted Jessica's system, but dealing with setbacks made her feel resilient. "I got lost. My luggage got lost. My wallet was stolen. I missed my flight. After all that, I said to myself, 'I can do anything. I can survive anything.'" Overcoming the difficulties increased Jessica's optimism, persistence, and empathy.

From Difficulties to Delight

When Jessica reached the International School of Business (ISB) campus for her Ph.D. program abroad, she "arrived" both physically and mentally. Despite her initial fears of being "around people who've had these big-time jobs and were very sophisticated," Jessica was psychologically healthy because of her self-awareness and self-reflection. At the same time, she knew that her arrival was, in a sense, temporary. Not only would she graduate from her Ph.D. program, but she would also progress in self-understanding. "I'm still working on this impatience and tolerance thing," she said. "It's a constant struggle, but it's a process, and I've gotten much better at it."

Jessica adjusted to being less competent in a foreign context. "You can't control it all. The things that used to be so easy at home are so hard here." But by using coping skills and the insight she gained from therapy, Jessica made peace with her shortcomings. "I've made so much progress in my emotional and spiritual life. I'm much more comfortable taking emotional risks, and I know that I will continue to grow in that way." Jessica realized that personal growth was a lifelong endeavor.

At ISB, Jessica felt transformed. "I'm joyful now. Even my parents would say that I'm a completely different person. I don't worry anymore. I get irritated and annoyed, but I don't lose sleep over anything." Jessica felt proactive about her career decisions and the way she was living her life. She also benefited from letting go of things that she could not control. "Once you let go, more things come to you. By not worrying so much, I'm a lot less self-involved, so I have more emotional energy to give to my family, to give to the people in my life." Protecting her positive energy was crucial for Jessica's well-being.

For Jessica, her PEG experience was a benchmark of intellectual nurturance and excellence. "My ideal would be to end in another PEG-like incubator where I have this tight circle of friends, and we all hatch ideas and nurture each other," she said. But Jessica doubted that she'd have that kind of experience again. "I don't think it will ever be quite as exciting or that tight, that intense again." She enrolled at ISB partly because she was "trying to get back to an environment where that might happen again." Although she did not find her ideal, Jessica experienced tremendous growth and satisfaction at ISB.

Conventional vs. Unconventional Definitions of Success

Jessica's unconventional definition of success partly accounted for her happiness. Being successful meant setting and reaching personally meaningful goals without regard to what others consider important. Successful individuals live their lives as they choose and become fulfilled on their own terms.[2] Some people thought that Jessica was successful because she attended two elite graduate schools, worked at a high-profile magazine, and taught college before the age of 27. But according to her values, those external achievements were not the true measure. "What I think makes me a successful person is that I regularly accomplish what I set out to do."

Although not well off financially, Jessica had "this sense of abundance that I feel in my life." She was not happy all of the time, but "I have a wonderful life. As bad as I feel some days, I'm doing exactly what I want to do, what I set out to do. I'm very grateful for that." By moving beyond her childhood goals, Jessica attained a different kind of fortune that was more deeply embedded in her values and spirit. She distinguished her desires from those of status-seekers she had met. "I want the best for me, so I disdain their arrogance because they just want the best. It's about status." Jessica clarified her position: "Don't get me wrong. I want the best for me. That is what motivates me, what makes me willing to play the game and willing to do all this graduate school work because I really want this Ph.D." However, that Ph.D. would help Jessica to live as she wanted, prioritizing her interests in business and her relationships with friends and family.

Failure is an essential part of success. "Sometimes what I thought I wanted to do wasn't really what I wanted to do," Jessica said. "You fail sometimes when you get there and it wasn't what you wanted. The conventional idea of success is that you don't fail," but Jessica's belief was that most successful people, "particularly the way I define it, definitely fail." Failure helped Jessica understand both what she did and did not want from life. It also made her smarter about reaching her goals.

Learning to transcend her failures ultimately helped Jessica thrive. By surviving tough times and being alone, she knew that "the pain is temporary and that some good does come from the hurt." Dealing with "the hard stuff" made Jessica "a little tougher than the typical young person." Not only did failures help her develop a thick skin, but they also made her more pragmatic. Instead of getting frustrated with the parts of projects that she could not control, Jessica faced reality and worked on the things that she could.

Managing Expectations

Just like everything else, achieving success has its price. Too often, people are unsympathetic to those who have succeeded. "They try to shoot you down. You can't take it personally. You can't take it in. You gotta just keep on truckin,'" Jessica stated. Persistence helps people survive, but survival was not enough for Jessica. She wanted to flourish.

As a pragmatist, Jessica knew that to thrive, she had to deal with other people's expectations, even when they had nothing to do with her values or goals. "In terms of what I decide to do about my goals, their expectations don't play a role. But because I need people's cooperation and help, I do tend to manage their expectations," she said. For example, when people focused on her radical acceleration and early college entrance, Jessica redirected the conversation to the more "normal" aspects of her life so that people did not expect her to be a wunderkind all of the time.

Some people painted extraordinary pictures of Jessica's future. Such expectations were impossible to meet. "Because I have managed to string together what you would call a career of accomplishments, people get this impression that I'm going to be a great leader or writer one day," she said. Others' expectations often exceeded hers. "People tend to blow things up in their minds, and I feel like I'm just an everyday schmo like everybody else." At ISB, Jessica wanted to be the best student possible so that she would have options when she graduated, but she did not feel the need to aim for a job teaching at a Top Twenty business school. She was more internally than externally motivated.

In contrast, Jessica's self-expectations were very high. "Intellectually, I expect to constantly learn, not to be lazy, and to think about the 'whys,'" she stated. Morally, she was rigorous in her self-assessment; she analyzed the rightness and wrongness of her actions. Emotionally, she wanted to act honestly and openly. "Am I caring for other people? Am I expressing my needs? Am I being vulnerable enough for people to engage with me?" Jessica focused on her present behavior, not on distant goals dictated by people who did not really know her.

Attending ISB helped Jessica attain another level of freedom. "Doing this is my final break with the 'shoulds'—you know, 'You have to live your life this way and do things that way.'" Enrolling at PEG had been Jessica's first step toward freedom because she chose a path very different from her peers, which meant not having to follow the crowd. Going so far away to ISB for so long was "the final step. I literally had to leave the country" to become fully liberated from other people's expectations. "I'm not bound anymore." With such a mindset, shaping a life of possibilities seemed natural.

Living the Life She Wanted

Jessica did not simply want to survive in life; she wanted to thrive. More obstacles will arise, she said, so resilience is adapting mentally to moving on, not just living through difficult things. Being resilient includes some of the promise of flourishing because "being resilient takes creativity. Being resilient takes optimism and a certain amount of smarts, be it intellectual or street smarts." A fundamental component of resilience is coping well with change; an individual has to be able to transcend bad experiences and refocus her direction and goals. Despite obstacles and difficult events and circumstances, Jessica concluded, "to still have joy, to still be blessed, and to have abundance, you need to be resilient."

At ISB, Jessica made choices that enhanced her experience and learning. She actively sought talented people to befriend "because I thrive around people who are so much better than I am because they have so much to tell me, and maybe I can get better from their influence." She didn't care as much about being the best as she did about learning from the best.

Jessica's advisor was a well-regarded professor, and she made the most of the academic relationship. She highly valued Dr. Wolfe's intelligence and experience and tried to be well-prepared at their meetings. Dr. Wolfe said that Jessica used her time with him well. He especially admired her refreshing questions. He commented, "I don't get the sense that she says, 'I want to do something because I want to facilitate my career.' I see her looking for intellectual problems to address, which is great." Besides finding Jessica to be very personable, Dr. Wolfe noted that "she's got drive, and she's looking for what's tough." He said two of Jessica's finest qualities were her mature outlook and her well-balanced life. That maturity allowed Jessica to shape her life on campus according to her principles.

Beyond Stereotypes

Not only did Jessica have to endure gender and age stereotypes, but she also had to contend with racial and national identity prejudices. She made sure to carefully scrutinize foreign cultures, but she wished that others would take a closer look to discover who she truly was.

Just as she had experienced at her former graduate university, when Jessica first arrived at ISB, most of the men in the study groups did not invite her to join them. Jessica was sure they did not think she was smart enough to contribute meaningfully. Those gender biases annoyed her. "But now, at the beginning of this second semester, everybody wanted to be in my group," she said. Her classmates asked to work with Jessica only after they discerned that she was a top student. Counteracting the female stereotypes required extra effort that Jessica could have used more productively.

At ISB, Jessica didn't discuss her early college entrance with classmates. It had been 15 years since she first attended PEG, and she didn't feel the need to explain her past. "As to whether or not I can do my job well, does it really matter that I went to college when I was 13?" she asked. "Not really." Telling people the truth about her life was often not worth it because some "people perceive radical acceleration very negatively." Some individuals reacted defensively. They would say, "Oh well, I could have done that, but I'm normal, and you're not."

Anti-Americanism was also apparent to Jessica. "People have preconceived notions. For example, at ISB, people say, 'Oh, you're American. You're smarter than we thought,' so there definitely is a lot of prejudice." The students' stereotypes rankled her. One friend said, "I want to meet some real Americans." Jessica asked what he meant. "He said, 'Well, blonde and blue-eyed.' And I said, 'My family's been in the United States a lot longer than most blond-haired, blue-eyed citizens, and I'm as American as it gets.'" Jessica fought against incorrect assumptions about Americans whenever she could.

Although she identified as an African American, Jessica was in reality one-eighth American Indian and one-eighth Caucasian. The Holmes daughters felt that "all we've ever known is being Black, but we are a mix of different races." Paradoxically, Jessica was sometimes mistreated based on people's ignorance of her racial background. She was often misperceived as a Latina and was even scolded for not using her "home" language in neighborhoods where Spanish was spoken. And the disrespect she experienced abroad happened mostly because people thought that she was an Arab.

Racial pride was very strong in Jessica's household, yet at the same time, Jessica said that she felt like "a stranger in a strange land" as a Black woman attending mostly white schools. By learning how to handle being culturally different from the majority, however, Jessica was better prepared to adjust to foreign cultures. Often, she was the only very young African American female in her environment. In the U.S., she was annoyed when people told her that she "didn't act Black." "I was raised that I don't have to 'act Black' because I am Black. I'm Black through what I do but not with a superficial meaning." Jessica felt that she did not have to have a certain accent or to wear certain clothes. Instead, being Black "shows in the cultural practices I've learned or the way I treat people."

Dr. Wolfe thought that Jessica fit in well at ISB's international, interracial campus. And despite some gender, age, and nationality biases she encountered, Jessica said that she was generally comfortable socially. She knew how to handle people's misperceptions and protected herself against unreasonable expectations. Coping with stereotypes and misperceptions was not going to prevent Jessica from succeeding on her own terms.[3]

A Sense of Purpose

Throughout her life, Jessica wanted to make a difference in the world. "To me, it's really important to not only be part of the community, but also to contribute to the community," she said. Jessica felt that "a lot of people don't think of anything outside themselves or even necessarily their family, so I always try to participate in community organizations." While she worked at *Best Business* magazine, Jessica also belonged to a group that produced "a teen online magazine that teen reporters wrote and edited. They designed the web page, did the photography, and even did streaming video." For three years, Jessica volunteered "to help them think of story ideas, report their stories and edit them, go places with them, and also help raise money for them." Jessica highly valued her involvement with urban teenagers.

While Jessica volunteered as much as she could, she felt that business had the potential to promote purpose. "If you have an idea that's good and that you could execute well, then you could build something that could give other people a livelihood. That's a great accomplishment," she stated. Jessica's goal of teaching in the business school, however, did not feel altruistic. "One of my current existential dilemmas," she said, "is how I'm going to reconcile being a business school professor with my desire to serve. I'm going to educate the next generation of capitalists—yeah, the world really needs that," she said self-mockingly. She wondered if she would be able to bring her values into her teaching "to be of service in a business school environment" or if she would have to fulfill her need to serve outside of her job.

Although she did not know exactly how to integrate her values into the classroom, Jessica wanted to treat her students decently and give of herself. She found a mentor who had graduated from ISB and who had previously studied Catholic theology. Jessica discovered that her mentor truly believed that his mission was to serve his students and that his values must pervade his interactions. She said, "If he can be a business school professor and incorporate his spiritual values into his everyday work, then that's something I want to emulate. Particularly given what we do in business, we need to learn how to use our powers for good." A strongly determined and self-reliant young woman, Jessica was facing her next challenge with strength of conviction and a focus on service to others.[4]

Conclusions

According to positive psychologist Nancy Cantor, traditional psychology emphasizes what a person achieves rather than the processes in which a person is engaged. Positive psychology focuses on the process.[5] Jessica moved from the goal of achievement to a personal commitment of "doing." Not only did she wish to serve others, but she also knew how to reflect on her life's journey. Her realization about the importance of interdependence contributed to her self-awareness and growth. She learned from her failures, created opportunities when they did not exist, and chose new settings and directions to reach her goals of purpose and to improve her well-being. As she developed more insight, Jessica's goal was growth, not attainment for its own sake. In having less, she experienced greater abundance because her "doing" led to discovery and joy.

CHAPTER 12

Claire Hagan: Coping with Chronic Illness and Building Community

An experienced biology professor at age 29, Claire Hagan was stricken with fibromyalgia, a disease that causes tremendous fatigue, disruption of sleep, and muscular pain throughout the body. As she learned to cope with the symptoms, Claire managed to regain some strength and resume some of her daily routine. Not content to focus solely on herself, she decided to volunteer as an English as a Second Language (ESL) tutor. At night, she worked with young men and women from Nicaragua, Puerto Rico, and Mexico.

Teaching English was rewarding for Claire because she knew that she was helping immigrants cope with living in their new country, the United States. She expressed great compassion for their situation. "Can you imagine? I haven't spent any extended period of time trying to live in a place where I didn't speak the language. It just boggles my mind what my students go through in trying to make it." Despite her exhausting college workdays, at the end of the two-hour ESL night sessions, Claire said, "I come out of there energized" and satisfied by making a difference.

A Brief Biography

Claire grew up in a rural area with an older sister and very supportive parents. Under-challenged educationally and teased mercilessly by schoolmates for her intelligence, she moved from her original elementary school to an urban one, hoping for greater academic challenge and social acceptance. Although some things improved, Claire was still afraid to demonstrate her love of learning in school. When she discovered PEG in eighth grade, she applied and was delighted to be accepted. Despite worries about handling the rigorous academic work, Claire performed very well, majoring in biology at Mary Baldwin College.

In addition to her parents' support, Claire credited her older sister, Daniella, with making her feel at home at Mary Baldwin. Daniella, a traditionally aged student who also attended MBC, welcomed Claire into her dorm room when she needed to get away from the teenage drama at the PEG residence hall. Daniella also introduced Claire to her friends so that when she graduated, there would be someone to watch after her younger sister. Another supporter and close confidante was Claire's mother's best friend, Sharon, who gave warmth, love, and encouragement that persisted into Claire's young adulthood.

After college, Claire's parents divorced; however, they both continued to support her dreams. Claire traveled to the Galapagos Islands to see that region's unique ecological environment, played her violin and gave lessons, and studied physics at a large university. At age 18, she started graduate school in biology. There, she met her future husband, Jeremy. "The experience of caring for someone more than life itself is definitely life altering," she said. Marriage gave her the support of an intimate relationship. It touched a profound sense of compassion in her and initiated new hopes, dreams, and responsibilities.

At 24, Claire got her first job at Sanfore College. Five years later, she took a position at Groppen College to enhance her career. She and Jeremy lived near the campus. At that point, she had already been diagnosed with fibromyalgia and was struggling to put the shattered image of her hopes and dreams for the future back together.

Intellectual and Personal Pursuits

Claire's parents raised her in an intellectual household with no television. In their home, reading and discussing ideas were paramount. Claire's father, a university mathematics professor, was very intelligent. However, it was her mother who influenced Claire's interest in biology as a child. "She raised wild birds (turkeys, quail, grouse, and pheasants) and imprinted them on herself so she could photograph them. I helped out with that," Claire said. In college, Claire loved her biology classes and the process of becoming a biologist. "I am a scientist—not just in my career, but in my approach to life. I like to figure things out." In science are countless "mysteries waiting to be deciphered," she remarked. "I have always had a love of learning, and it continues to be an important part of my life."

In adulthood, the parent-child intellectual pattern continued. "My mom is absolutely amazing in her ability to learn new things and excel at them very quickly," she stated warmly. "My parents were (and still are) always willing to listen to my questions and engage in serious discussions. I was always encouraged to pursue my interests wherever they took me." As models of continual growth and learning, Claire's parents nurtured their daughter's lifelong intellectual curiosity and excitement.

Despite her enthusiasm for academic and intellectual pursuits, Claire was a rather quiet person, and she had to work hard to act more gregarious than she felt. By making a strong effort at sociability, she learned that she was able to draw people out of their shells and bring them together through a sense of community. She described herself as "a friendly, thoughtful, compassionate person who feels things very deeply," and these qualities were apparent in her professional life as well. As a professor, she encouraged students to visit her during office hours and constantly worked on self-improvement. She responded positively to feedback, evaluated her teaching style, and fine-tuned it to make her students more comfortable and to show that she cared about how they felt.

Claire had learned to give deeply of herself when she was an undergraduate at PEG. Even though she had good friends in elementary school back home, "you couldn't do the same type of giving because you weren't faced with the same type of circumstances," she said. At college, Claire and other PEGs "had all sorts of things where we just thought the world was going to end, and what were we going to do?" When she consoled the other girls, a new kind of friendship emerged because "you really got a chance to learn how to give of yourself to somebody else." With girls whom she could trust, rely on, and share values, Claire learned how to establish deep, lasting friendships. It was this same ability to give of herself that she took into her classrooms and which made her such a conscientious educator.

At a relatively young age, Claire was a successful biology professor. But the biggest success of her personal life was "waiting long enough for Jeremy to be ready to get married!" After meeting in graduate school, she and Jeremy were separated by several hundred miles when Claire took her first job as a professor at Sanfore in the fall of 1997. They dated long distance, spoke on the phone often, and visited each other when possible. But by the spring of 2000, Claire and Jeremy were still not married. "I was pretty patient, though," Claire said. "I wanted it very badly, but I knew I couldn't push too hard." When she had practically given up on the idea of marriage, Jeremy finally popped the question. They wed in the summer of 2001. Claire's four-year wait culminated in her happy marriage, but her positive outlook was quickly tested.

Coping with Chronic Illness

A Life Transformed

Claire described the transformation of her life due to fibromyalgia as "radical." The illness affected her sense of self and almost every sphere of her experience. There were physical disabilities, emotional upheavals, professional limitations, intellectual repercussions, and difficulties managing her responsibilities. Not simply a matter of withstanding pain, losing sleep, or enduring diminished stamina, fibromyalgia fundamentally changed Claire's ways of being. Her identity, hopes, goals, family plans, and notions of success all had to be adjusted and revised.

Claire's fibromyalgia slowed her pace of life considerably. Before she became ill, she was an active, healthy athlete. Her weekly workout had consumed most of her spare hours. "When the pain started, I was running, lifting weights, and doing aerobics regularly. I was biking an average of 100 miles a week!" No longer able to exercise in the same fashion, Claire felt weaker. The unbearable pain restricted a woman who was used to moving at top speed and competing rigorously. The cost to her physical well-being was enormous.

Stamina was another major problem because Claire had a full teaching course load. "That first semester I was ill in Spring 2001, I missed a lot of classes. Early that summer, Jeremy and I got married, and I suffered through pain the whole time." Claire had a reduced teaching load in the Fall 2001 semester, but even so, "we put a bed in my office so I could lie down and use a laptop," she stated. Claire was in significant pain and had little strength.

By the summer of 2002, Claire's condition had improved, but her quality of life was still strongly affected. She took several medicines, including a slow-release narcotic, and her physical activity was limited. In an effort to regain some of her former stamina and strength, she said, "After the diagnosis, I started physical therapy because exercise is so important in dealing with the symptoms." That helped by "alleviating the symptoms and reducing flare-ups." To take care of herself, Claire had to be vigilant about eating well, exercising daily, reducing stress, and managing her emotional problems. "I have to be careful not to overdo it, or I pay for it later."

Everything took more time for Claire, and the slow tempo tested her patience. She learned that she could not push her recovery along. It had a pace of its own. Her professional tempo changed, too. At Groppen, Claire taught a number of field science courses but was dismayed at having to switch her research goals and techniques. "My health has kept me from being able to pursue the outdoor procedures because I can't work in the field all day long," she remarked. Although she hoped to return to field study one day, Claire now conducted and taught lab research, which was less exciting and meaningful to her.

Despite her slower pace, Claire was involved with an impressive array of activities and obligations. She volunteered in more than one venue, contended with family issues, spent time with her husband, took care of her pets, planned and taught courses, advised students, participated in campus events, and co-developed an ecology program in the biology department. However, she worried about not having enough time to do a good job with the tasks she had taken on, "so that's a source of a lot of angst and guilt," she said. Feeling knocked off-kilter, Claire wanted to find balance.

As might be expected for anyone, becoming ill was very difficult for Claire. She reassessed her identity and became disheartened from the enormous changes in her life. Experiencing so much pain was grueling and caused her to rethink her self-concept. "It has changed my identity. I am a person with a chronic disease. I have to accept that," she said. She went from seeing herself as a healthy person to someone with a permanent, debilitating condition. The change in self-understanding was especially hard because she knew that the transformation would last for the rest of her life.

The Coping Process: Five Components

Struggling to maintain her sense of purpose, Claire had to come to grips with her chronic illness. Getting well was her new, purposeful focus. Her coping process had five components, which helped her regain a balanced sense of self. These components were not strictly chronological or hierarchical. Some took place simultaneously; others repeated in an unpredictable order. But all of them occurred as she dealt with the repercussions of fibromyalgia. Initially, Claire had to understand her medical condition and develop a qualified acceptance of it. To heal, she had to let go of many previous ways of being but also take control of certain aspects of her life. Ultimately, she expanded in new directions, giving herself greater strength and the ability to refocus more fully on her career and personal goals. Not everyone who gets ill will go through the same processes that Claire did. However, her coping strategies illustrate one woman's way of grappling with adversity to maintain purpose and may help others learn ways to thrive despite obstacles.

Understanding the Medical Condition

Claire had to experience her illness for months to know its limitations, frustrations, and implications. For a long time, she was not sure what disease she had because fibromyalgia is so difficult to diagnose. Once properly diagnosed, though, Claire was able to grasp the enormity of her hardship. If she had not understood the true scope of the challenge, she might not have worked as hard to alleviate her pain, get better, and compensate for any lost capabilities. Before she could set off in a new life direction, she had to know her starting point.

Qualified Acceptance of the Illness

Despite being initially depressed, Claire was optimistic about a cure because she was a problem solver. She thought that by consulting experts, trying medicines, and monitoring her activities, her symptoms would gradually disappear. Accepting her diagnosis was especially tough when many physicians did not believe that fibromyalgia was an illness. Even Claire had trouble accepting the diagnosis at first. Her skepticism may have helped keep some of her condition's emotional impact at bay long enough for her to reframe the illness and thus lessen its traumatic effects. Eventually, Claire made a qualified acceptance of the disease. She said, "I am learning to accept that the symptoms are probably never going to go away."

Claire's acceptance, however, was not one of resignation. She was proactive in her search for ways to manage the symptoms of her illness. She sought information and guidance from a number of doctors, from medical literature on the Internet and elsewhere, from her fibromyalgia support group, and from the National Fibromyalgia Association. Her optimism lay in her ability to learn and grow despite her disappointments.

Letting Go and Rediscovering the Self

Letting go was a central theme in Claire's healing process. She let go of her striving self and the ways she used to control her life. She redefined success. Previous standards and expectations had to be modified so that she could manage to perform at her current levels of strength. The range and number of life choices that Claire once had were no longer available. To let go, Claire adjusted her dreams and goals and then adapted to them.

Prior to Claire's sickness, career success had meant significant achievement. She traced that belief back to PEG's emphasis on high-quality performance. In college, she had imagined that reaching a certain goal would fulfill her. But once she had achieved her goal, she would set the bar higher. As an adult, Claire was dissatisfied with what she already had accomplished. Living for the future meant that she could never fully get comfortable with the present. Fibromyalgia forced her to re-conceptualize success because "there were probably some things that I really, really wanted that I wasn't going to get."

As an adolescent, Claire imagined doing innovative, groundbreaking research. But once she reached graduate school, she decided that she "was not really cut out for the high-stakes competitive environment of a big research university with undergraduate teaching—something you have to do alongside of your more important research." As a professor, Claire wanted to publish original findings and insights on both educational techniques and research. She hoped to make a meaningful difference in biology by leaving a legacy of high-quality work.

After two years of illness, though, Claire had to forego the goal of reaching the heights of her profession, partly because of her personality and prior decisions but also because of her fibromyalgia. She developed a new understanding of her capabilities, and in the process, she became more patient about reaching goals and did not expect everything to come to her rapidly. She also no longer focused solely on traditional achievement because she had transformed from a person who could do certain things to one who could not. "I am learning to accept and be happy with who I am and separate that from what I can do," she said. Claire reframed her sense of achievement and took pride in accomplishing tasks that required new skills. She also stopped pushing and evaluating herself so severely and found that she became happier because she was deriving fulfillment and contentment more from "being" than from "doing."

To find inner tranquility, Claire learned healing techniques taught by her spiritual guide, a samyama therapist.[1] Claire viewed spirituality "as a path to self-discovery and acceptance—a way to be the best person I can be to myself and to others." Samyama gave Claire a calmness that previously had eluded her. Related to her samyama approach was the serenity prayer—*God, grant me the serenity to accept the things I cannot change, the courage to change the things I can, and the wisdom to know the difference*—which, Claire said, was something "that resonates with me when I think of how I want to live my life."[2] By changing the things she could, Claire took control of her life again. Concentrating on self-discovery, tranquility, and equilibrium allowed her to achieve the serenity she needed to be at peace with her lifelong condition. By learning when to sit back and when to move forward, Claire was growing in her wisdom.

Taking Control

Paradoxically, some of Claire's steps in letting go were also part of her taking control of life. Practicing samyama allowed her to shift her focus from anxiety toward peace. Meditation reduced her stress through relaxation and helped her cope with pain and anxiety, but it also entailed a conscious decision to seek spiritual help. In that sense, Claire was taking control of her emotional self-management. She said, "By looking inward, I feel more in charge of my life—like I'm in control of what's happening instead of everything just happening to me." Taking control became an important way to cope.

Instead of feeling victimized by her disease, Claire gained strength by deciding what she could do to improve her quality of life.

As Claire's spiritual healing progressed, she learned "to listen to my body very carefully and not be so hard on myself when I physically need to take a break. Not feeling guilty certainly makes it easier to enjoy time off." Claire did not want to use her illness as an excuse for laziness, but she enjoyed reducing the pressure of pushing too hard. She adjusted her self-perception, her goals, and her attitudes by emphasizing awareness of the present more than objectives for the future. She found ways to compensate for her limitations, thereby minimizing fibromyalgia's impact.

Throughout her life, Claire had demonstrated her independence by standing up for her beliefs, even when faced with powerful opposition. When she later became sick, that same strength of character bolstered her when she most needed it. During her ordeal, Claire took the highly addictive drug Oxycontin. When she wanted to stop her small dosage, her doctors suggested that she enter a month-long detoxification hospital program. Claire's response was swift and strong because she was unwilling to sacrifice her personal and professional life for what she considered to be over-treatment. She resolutely believed she could overcome her dependence. "I said to myself, 'Well, let me show you!'"

After trying a radical withdrawal protocol suggested by her rheumatologist, Claire got a different doctor's advice to withdraw much more gradually. When Claire was able to forego medicine for 27 hours at a time, she went cold turkey. It took her a summer to get off Oxycontin completely, but she was proud of her accomplishment. She had taken charge of her well-being, with strong support from her husband, extended family members, friends, colleagues, and the fibromyalgia patients' group. "I can be pretty determined to go after something I want," she said. Claire's determination counterbalanced the restrictive nature of her illness, helping her move forward when circumstances conspired to hold her back.

Expanding in New Directions

While many people would feel overwhelmed at managing an active personal and professional life while battling a chronic illness, Claire felt the need to do more. She began teaching ESL at night and also started volunteering for the Consortium for Peace, an organization that promotes peace and social justice. She admitted, "Volunteering used to be more about generic things that I was doing to make myself feel better about the issues." But her latest efforts affected Claire deeply. "Now, I feel like there are concrete things that I'm doing that help other people as opposed to just making me feel good." Now she was working at a different level. "Just by spending time teaching English to this person, you feel like you're making a difference in her life." The new dimension of Claire's feelings came from producing tangible results and focusing more on others than on herself.

According to psychologist Jonathan Haidt, growth may result from adversity "because it forces you to stop speeding along the road of life, allowing you to notice the paths that were branching off all along, and to think about where you really want to end up."[3] Claire's chronic disease helped her recognize the goodness of her life. With an uncertain future, a deep appreciation of the present was crucial for her satisfaction and happiness.

Claire also sought to change the way she lived. She and her husband learned about a new cooperative living venture organized by 13 families that were trying to build an intentional community for environmental sustainability. Claire and Jeremy liked the group's goals of living independently and interdependently. Plenty of space would separate the families so that they could live on their own, but the group would be tied by a common purpose: to act as responsible stewards of the land. Claire wanted to belong to a community of residents who were mutually concerned about the environment. By joining the cooperative living group, she was getting settled with an extended family of individuals who shared her concerns. She and Jeremy were putting down more roots and expanding their circle of social support.

Building Community

Although Claire wanted to have a fulfilled life and to help others, she did not believe that those desires converged into a single focus. "In some ways," she said, "I still feel like I'm plowing through life from one thing to the next without considering a larger meaning." However, Claire did not seem aware of her pervasive connection to community. Throughout her life, Claire needed community, looked for community, participated in community, contributed to community, and maintained community. This thematic recurrence points toward a unifying sense of purpose.

Claire's new cooperative living community reflected her highest values. These elements revealed the closeness, cooperation, interdependence, unity, and generativity (providing a better world for future generations) that Claire sought throughout her life. For Claire, *community* meant a group that supports each individual's growth and wellness. Being a part of a community, Claire said, should give people a sense of belonging, of welcome, comfort, and home. Public school had not been a kind place for Claire. Fortunately, PEG provided an early model of a caring community where she felt safe to reveal her true self. Her goodness, her intelligence, and her warmth could all be shared and appreciated. Growing up as a very young college student in an atmosphere of trust, support, and interdependence, Claire then sought those same community qualities as an adult. Building those types of communities became Claire's way of making the world safe and satisfying for her and for others; it was a way of repairing the world, and it became Claire's purpose, her way of giving back to society. By creating healthy communities where people could flourish, she was creating environments similar to the one where she had flourished.

As a community builder, Claire worked to repair fragmentation and discord in the world. She worked diligently toward establishing and maintaining unity and harmony in every group with which she associated. In addition to those two essential qualities, three others appeared repeatedly in her different communities: intentionality, democracy, and sustainability. These five qualities reflected not only

Claire's values and what she desired in a community, but also the ideal qualities of a better world.

Intentionality

An intentional community is formed when its members share values, goals, and purpose. PEG was Claire's first intentional community. Mary Baldwin formed the program to serve the needs of very smart girls who wanted to study at a college level several years before their age peers. Claire found other girls at MBC with similar interests and sensibilities. The majority of the girls were highly driven to learn, which positively affected the atmosphere in the residence hall and in the classrooms.

Teaming with people who held similar principles was meaningful to Claire. At the Consortium for Peace, she joined forces with individuals who wanted a more just and peaceful world. Similarly, cooperative living offered the promise of living and working with like-minded people. "I like having it be an intentional community where you meet these people and you agree to join the community, and everybody has the same values—in this case, about the environment," she said. From Claire's perspective, the people involved in the venture offered positive qualities that enhanced the well-being of everyone in the group. There is "a respect for people and a caring for people," she remarked. By associating with a group of individuals with similar principles and the same focus, Claire helped create a cohesive community that felt like home.

Democracy

In a democracy, according to Claire, people's rights must be upheld so that everyone's voice may be heard. At the Consortium for Peace, Claire demonstrated her love of democracy by working toward social justice, which empowered legions of people when the group's efforts were successful. In addition, Claire's cooperative living group epitomized democratic living. Decisions were made by consensus instead of the majority winning. She said, "You go through the step-by-step process of making sure that everyone is okay with what the final decision is." She explained that the goal was to "avoid the tyranny of the majority." Claire recognized that the process was often painstakingly slow and cumbersome, but she preferred the sacrifice to suppressing others' opinions. In the end, she said, all participants could come away satisfied from self-governance sessions because they had come to mutually agreed-upon resolutions to their problems. The cooperative living individuals could live their lives as they chose, knowing that 13 other families would be there to support them in times of need and that they all shared the same goals of protecting and nourishing the earth.

Sustainability

Claire wanted not only to give back to society, but also to ensure that important institutions and groups could sustain themselves into the future. As such, many of her behaviors promoted organizational sustainability. She became an ESL trainer, not just a tutor, so that she could help others learn how to tutor non-English speakers. Claire hoped that if a few of the tutors became trainers, then she would have helped to generate a self-perpetuating string of ESL teachers. At the Consortium for Peace, Claire became a board member, and she imagined becoming president of the board one day. By assuming leadership and shaping policy, she could help the Consortium stay strong and continue its mission of working toward social justice and peace. And of course Claire's new cooperative living situation not only afforded a warm sense of mutual caring and community, but also promoted the goal of environmental sustainability.

Not least among Claire's purposes was her life as a teacher. She supported Groppen College because she wanted it to survive as a place of learning. Not only could the college sustain scholarship and instruction, but it also could provide years of community leadership and service. For her part, she said, "I want to provide a high-quality educational experience for my students—to help them learn about and conduct solid scientific research in biology." By helping students to become proficient and competent in their fields of scientific study, she was ensuring that her diligence, dedication, and commitment to lifelong learning would be passed on to generations to come.

Conclusions

Why is the concept of building community so important to the discussion of purpose? Harmonic, unified, intentional, democratic, and sustainable communities have the potential to bring greater meaning to people's lives. They hold the promise of a greater sense of purpose for their members. As a highly educated woman, Claire lived in communities that could serve as a model for others. Perhaps Claire could not perceive her overarching purpose because she was too close to building overlapping circles of community to be able to get a broader view of what she was accomplishing. However, her efforts to bring people together in communities of interdependence and shared values contributed to one of the central, underlying purposes in her life.

Claire achieved good mental health despite daunting odds. By shifting her focus from future achievement to present contentment, she became more at peace with her lot in life. Although she did not believe that she would ever contribute groundbreaking work to her field, she still wanted to leave a legacy, and she felt satisfied with sharing her innovative educational techniques at conferences and in papers as opposed to making unique research discoveries. She could still be creative and innovative in the classroom while performing her favorite activity: teaching. Her dedication to self-improvement meant that she had a lifetime to become a master biology professor.

Claire's emotional, spiritual, and interpersonal growth was strongly influenced by her illness. By being realistically optimistic, persistent, patient, rebellious, vulnerable, and willing to change, she was able to cope effectively. She proactively transformed her striving self into a fulfilled self through therapy, spiritual guidance, meditation, moderate exercise, love, service, and building community. Over time, she discovered new reservoirs of strength, courage, and resilience. Instead of constantly looking ahead, Claire looked inward for self-understanding and self-acceptance, outward to serve people in need, and around to find people who shared her interests and values as they built communities. By reaching out to others for support and then using that energy to turn back to others as a helper and unifier, Claire achieved wisdom and established purpose in her life.

Lucy Jacobs: Grappling with Sexuality and Career Conflict

Lucy Jacobs was finishing her MFA in poetry and was far from home when her mother Barbara became extremely ill after experiencing a serious reaction to medicine. At 29, Lucy was the oldest of six children, and since her parents were divorced, the caretaking responsibility fell on Lucy's young shoulders. Through the process of handling doctors, switching Barbara to a different hospital, tending to legalities, and coping with many other difficult decisions, Lucy eventually managed to bring her mother home to recuperate.

Fortunately, Barbara recovered. But at the time when Lucy was trying to bring her mother home, she could not have predicted that, and she found herself facing the prospect of becoming her mother's long-term caregiver. Pondering that possibility, she walked alone on a nearby beach and found herself thinking of her surroundings. "I sat down for a minute, looking out at the waves—a gorgeous day, sun sparkling across the water—and pressed my hands deep into the sand. The warmth and the pleasure of this simple act overwhelmed me," she remembered. Lucy said that she had never noticed "how incredibly delicious warm sand can feel." She felt that it was a "spiritual moment, and I was recognizing something otherworldly: the gift we have to simply feel pleasure in being alive in our skins, perceiving our world." Lucy also learned about "the gift of being able to help one another to love." At that moment, she suddenly realized "my own ability to really appreciate simple pleasure. Not just note it, but feel it in my core, almost like what I imagine rapture to feel like."

Lucy developed a deeper appreciation for life as she experienced a heightened physical and spiritual awareness of the world. From that awareness, a keener sense of gratitude for life arose. The combination of awareness and gratitude sparked her desire to be more giving and nurturing. Lucy wanted to use her abilities to improve the lives of others.

A Brief Biography

Growing up on a farm with a free-spirited mother and a stern stepfather, Lucy learned the meaning of responsibility early. She not only tended to her five younger siblings, but she also completed numerous household and farm chores daily. Lucy loved learning and knew that she performed better at school than her peers. An avid athlete, she broke the gender barriers of Little League. However, constrained by a stepfather who derided her enjoyment of sports, disturbed by family turmoil, and bored in her freshman year of high school, Lucy jumped at the opportunity to attend PEG.

A college graduate at age 19, Lucy spent her first post-college year as a nanny for the son of her favorite English professor. The following year, she entered a graduate literature program at Simson University, where she earned her Master's degree. After that, she taught part-time at Simson as an adjunct professor and worked full-time at a bookstore. She quickly became manager of the bookstore, but after six years, she knew that she wanted to push further professionally. So Lucy enrolled in a Master of Fine Arts program at the highly selective Waite University in another state. After receiving her MFA in poetry, she began teaching at Waite full-time and then entered its Ph.D. program in English and Education, one of the best in the country. At the time of the study, Lucy was in the third year of her doctoral training and was living with her partner, Gabby.

Grappling with Sexuality

Sexual Awareness: Realization, Not Choice

Lucy realized that she was sexually different from other girls when she was 11 years old, but her attraction to girls began even earlier. "From a very young age, I knew there was something different about me, and I was just slowly getting the language for what that difference was," she said. "I always wanted to be a little boy and put my hair up and first started having feelings in fourth and fifth grade with my little friends." As she approached puberty, those feelings were "really heightened." When she lived with the other PEG students in the residence hall, she became "hyper-aware" of her sexual difference. While the other girls were constantly talking about boys, Lucy hid her true feelings.

Lucy did not choose homosexuality. Rather, she recognized how she felt before she could express it. Even after she did know how to explain her feelings, she felt that she could not. The result was the emergence of a false self that continued to develop throughout her childhood, becoming more entangled during adolescence.

Struggle with Sexuality

Getting Help

During her four years at PEG, Lucy did not speak about her sexuality with anyone. In her junior year, she became extremely depressed when a close friend became seriously involved with a boyfriend. Lucy was overcome with jealousy and sadness. She lost weight, and her grades slipped. These warning signs alerted the college administration that Lucy was in trouble, and they arranged for her to see a psychologist, which was a crucial step in her emotional growth.

Lucy said that she "had frequent suicidal thoughts" in her later PEG years, "despairing over not wanting to be gay." She knew that her depression was linked to her need to "find a way to live true to my heart, because otherwise I was not going to live, literally." As she started her sessions with the psychologist, Lucy was grateful to have the chance to talk about her sexuality with someone for the first time. "I remember that feeling of huge relief to actually say it out in the open, that it was something that I was worrying about."

Reflecting on that time, Lucy felt that the PEG staff could have done a better job of talking with the girls about sexuality and the emotions of romantic relationships. Although she understood why the administration might not have wanted to broach the subject, she thought that introducing it would have allowed her opportunities to discuss her anguish. However, despite the fact that she could have used more psychological support for her sexual self-discovery process, Lucy still felt indebted to PEG for all it taught her. "I think the program was awesome," she stated.

Society's Moral Message

Before meeting with her therapist, Lucy did not know how to judge the societal repercussions of her sexual feelings. With no confidante and with no media images of happy gay couples to reassure her at that time (the early 1990s), she felt that others judged her feelings as morally wrong. Her greatest fear was that people would reject her because of her sexuality. She was emotionally conflicted because she felt like a good person, but she had absorbed society's negative messages about being gay. She said, "I was constantly dealing with the question of 'How can it be that I feel totally fine and like a good person; I don't feel evil; I don't feel sick, and yet I'm getting this message that if I act on these other feelings, then that makes me morally reprehensible and just icky to people, and that people have this gut reaction against something that to me feels like a positive, beautiful, natural thing?'"

Lucy had to actively reconcile these contradictory ideas about her feelings so that she could attain self-acceptance. To be highly productive and purposeful, she had to learn how to share her true self with others.

Acceptance of Sexuality

As an 18-year-old in her third year of college, Lucy's therapist spoke to her "about what it would mean to be gay and moved me toward being able to 'come out' to certain trusted people a couple of years later." As Lucy approached graduation, understanding her sexuality became more important to her than figuring out her future. She grappled for two more years with the idea that homosexuality was a lifelong identity. When she finally accepted that identity, she was in her first Master's program at Simson University.

In addition to studying literature at Simson, Lucy took classes in feminist and queer theory.[1] Her discovery that the university was conducive to building sexual identity was very welcome and felt like a big change from her time at PEG. She recalled thinking, "Wow! There's an intellectual culture where I can search my identity and think about it." At the same time, discovering her identity took all of her "primary energy." Since her girlfriend had settled in a nearby city to maintain their romantic relationship, Lucy moved from her university town to the city during the summer months. "So that was my first big city experience, and we did a lot of gay-related cultural things," she said. Becoming part of the gay community helped Lucy "carve out an identity" and feel good about who she was.

Activism and Sexual Identity

During one urban summer, Lucy joined ACT UP, an activist group that supports gay rights, and she joined others in the organization to march in protest demonstrations. "When you're coming out as gay, you realize that there are these anti-gay prejudices," she explained. Huge numbers of homosexuals were still dying of AIDS, even though medicine had created new drugs to lengthen patients' lives. Lucy wanted to help bring about change, and she participated in the gay community's fight against "the injustices of the American Medical Association and decisions about privacy, blood tests, medicines, and all of that."

Lucy's concern about gay causes was genuine, but in retrospect, she felt that her involvement "was all about me and my identity and less about the causes." She adopted the prevalent attitudes and the then-current style of protest so that she could better identify with gay culture and its community. "I think of myself in my twenties.

I was so sure I was right about the issues, and the way to go about getting your message across was to just say it louder."

As an adult, Lucy realized that loudness did not always breed understanding, and her fight for social justice took a quieter turn. She came to understand that careful consideration and communication of issues were important to produce real solutions. Still, activism was necessary because "it makes conversations happen." When she became a college writing instructor, Lucy raised social justice issues in her class but tried not to impose her beliefs on her students. She was honest if asked a direct question, but she hated any form of proselytizing. Instead, she tried to induce her students to reflect carefully about varied perspectives and to come to their own conclusions.

"Coming Out" to Family

Lucy "came out" to her family in stages. Not everyone was ready to hear about her sexuality and lifestyle. Trusting her mother's open-mindedness, Lucy felt comfortable telling her mother about her sexual identity long before she told her father. She guessed that Barbara would accept her. "I give a lot of credit to my mother," she said. "She definitely raised me in a liberal household." Growing up, Lucy never heard any "derogatory remarks about gays, Blacks, or Jews," and she felt confident that her mother would respect her lifestyle. She knew that Barbara had hoped she would marry a man and give her grandchildren, but in time, Lucy saw her mother adjust more fully to her sexuality, her female partner, and her desire to bear a child in that union.

At about the same time that Lucy confided in her mother, she also told one of her sisters and one of her brothers about her sexuality. These two siblings then told the other brothers and sisters before they met Gabby in person. Despite their acceptance, Lucy was still reluctant to tell her father, Norman. In fact, the prospect of telling him the truth terrified her. Norman had left the household when Lucy was only four years old, so they were not close. She worried how he would react to her homosexuality because he was so conservative. Although he was a wonderful man in many ways, she said, he also had many prejudices. She could live without her father's blessing, but she wanted his approval.

Finally, Lucy sent Norman a letter, which took her months to write and rewrite. In an email, he responded, "What took you so long to tell me?" He had suspected for a while that Lucy was a lesbian. He wrote, "I'm old-fashioned, and I won't march in gay pride marches with you, but I'm glad you're happy." Lucy was surprised and greatly relieved that her father accepted her. Although she knew that her father and stepmother were not yet ready to host Gabby in their home, she had faith that the next step would probably come with time.

Awareness, Understanding, and Empathy

Through her struggle with sexual identity, Lucy said, "I learned that being gay and being a nice, perfectionist kid and a beloved daughter can be a terrible conflict." Yet Lucy also saw some benefits to her journey. She had transformed anger to happiness and poor psychological health to a new vitality. As she gained both self-acceptance and acceptance from her loved ones, she became a much more content, secure, and grateful person. "I often feel a kind of gratitude that I was born with this difference; it has been a challenge that makes me more conscious of myself and my world," she said.

Career Conflict

When she entered PEG at age 15, Lucy intended to go to medical school but felt too young as an undergraduate "to have any specific picture of my desired future. I remember having some vague image of myself as a doctor, financially secure, in a stable relationship, perhaps with children." But by the time she graduated from Mary Baldwin, "this image had disappeared completely." Instead, Lucy saw herself "as someone dynamically involved with others—either in research (as an anthropologist or archaeologist), or in education, or both, although really I had no specific idea what I wanted to do," she said.

Matching Interests with Enthusiasm

Trying to figure out a direction for study and work was not easy for Lucy. "I remember spending weeks after my graduation just sitting in my room, writing and writing, trying to determine what I wanted and what my next steps should be." Eventually, she thought more consciously about what was physically in front of her. She said, "I've got a volume of poetry, a dictionary, a journal, and a novel that I'm finishing." She realized that "obviously, these are activities that I enjoy. I knew that I had to do a job that felt meaningful to me, and I knew that something like business was not going to cut it." Lucy's choice of literature might seem self-evident, but she had taken a winding path to reach that realization herself.

Lucy's post-graduate year of being a nanny "was a big, huge soul-searching year. I kept thinking 'What do I do now?'" She applied to a variety of graduate school programs, but even though she was offered admission to a top university anthropology Ph.D. program, Lucy turned it down. When it came down to it, she just "didn't feel excited about" studying anthropology. Lucy next applied to an experiential education program at another university. She gained acceptance to the program but rejected that offer, too. She lacked enthusiasm for these fields and didn't know what direction to take. She finally decided upon a Master's of Literature at Simson University.

Professional Stalling

Earning a Master's degree in literature didn't immediately point Lucy toward enlightenment about her dream career, so she bided her time working at a bookstore. She described her years as a bookstore manager as "professional stalling because I took so long to complete what I have now completed. I see my six years spent at the bookstore as important personally but wasted professionally." On the other hand, Lucy believed that she might not have "felt as ready for doctoral studies as I feel now, had I stayed in school after my first Master's program rather than taking some time away from academia."

Lucy stayed on at the bookstore partly because she needed time away from school, partly because, fresh out of her Master's program, she needed the financial stability that the bookstore position provided, and partly because she was still struggling with what direction to take with her life. Having taught composition as an undergraduate and literature as a college instructor, she considered teaching as well as writing for her future. She wrestled with the "desire to be a writer first, and teacher second. I admit that I had grand visions of myself suddenly producing stellar poems, novels, and articles that would be in high demand and open many doors for me."

But her reality was much different from what she had imagined. Instead of finding time to write, Lucy ended up "completely spent at the ends of my days, without the energy to write. I had fallen into a grind, and it took me several years to find a way out."

The Conflict: Medicine vs. English and Education

The real career conflict in Lucy's life was not whether to teach or to write. The most profound dilemma was choosing between medicine and English and Education as a career. Even though Lucy said that she had relinquished the idea of being a doctor when she graduated from college, the medical profession continued to attract her for many years.

Medicine

Before she attended PEG, Lucy had been drawn to medicine and the prospect of healing sick minds and bodies. On her application to PEG, she had written, "Ever since fourth grade, my ambition has been to become a doctor." She wrote about her delight in hands-on experiences, which further kindled her desire to be a healer. "Living on a farm, I am familiar with many animal diseases and health problems. Treating and caring for animals have increased my curiosity about human illnesses and injuries. I am fascinated with the various systems of the human body and their functions." As she got older, she found herself more intrigued by the illnesses of the mind and the field of psychiatry.

Whether as a doctor of the body or the mind, Lucy particularly liked the idea of the good income that doctors earn. She had lived for several years working more than one job to pay her bills, and she did not want to have to struggle with money for her entire life. She already had experienced financial duress in childhood, so fiscal stability was a major life goal.

Certain aspects of medicine did not appeal to Lucy, however. The cost of medical school was a concern, but also the long hours of work. The profession was not conducive to having children, a high priority for her. There were academic deterrents as well. To be competitive for medical school, Lucy needed to excel in the sciences as an undergraduate. Instead, she labored through her initial chemistry and biochemistry classes at MBC. Although she earned B's, she was not as interested in those classes at a time when she knew she needed to be. A self-reported perfectionist, Lucy said, "I didn't know how to be interested in them because I just didn't get it. I was so lost."

But as Lucy got older, she continued to wonder whether she might have preferred medicine as a career. She sometimes wondered if she would have learned science concepts more quickly despite being bored if she'd stayed in high school. "Would I have been more likely to succeed in science as a freshman at age 18 and then seen myself as able to go on that path of medicine?" she asked. As a student in the earliest years of PEG, Lucy's science literacy gap hindered her ability to explore medicine as a possibility.

Philosophical by nature, Lucy loved to ask the big questions in life. She described herself as "self-reflective; I embrace ambiguities; I try to 'live the questions,' as the poet Rilke would advise. I do not think in black and white." When Lucy contemplated pursuing medicine, she worried that the daily grind would not afford her enough time to reflect, a habit that she considered essential to her being.

English and Education

Studying English literature and composition so that she could teach college students how to write well appealed to Lucy. Her love of literature began in childhood with her mother, who also loved it, and English was an area in which Lucy excelled. She said, "Writing and literary analysis have always been particular strengths of mine" and felt that "my early success in this field motivated me to continue in it." Because she understood literature so well, Lucy said that she "often had some image of myself as a writer/teacher."

As a young PEG student, the scholarly life attracted Lucy. "Because I was in an academic setting and I loved learning and I loved school, I thought the professors and the administrators that I saw around me had it good." Lucy pictured the academic life as "full of reading and thinking and just simple living." Sure enough, two years into her doctoral program in English and Education, Lucy was happy. "I love the work I do—the reading, the learning, the writing, the teaching. I love the flexibility in my schedule." She also appreciated the benefits of university life with its cultural events and intellectual rigor. "I love the minds and hearts of the people with whom I interact daily: my fellow graduate students, my professors, my own students." Having summers off to write was another advantage.

PEG played an important role in stimulating Lucy's intellect by encouraging "interests and habits of mind that I'm grateful to have had supported," she said. As a humanities student, her PEG education encouraged "her natural tendency to explore answers to the unanswerable questions: Why do we do the things we do? Why do we hurt each other? Is there one 'right' or 'wrong' way to behave? How do we learn?" She said that thinking deeply about human issues changed her from being "an absolutist" when she entered college to being much more open-minded to others' ideas, even when they directly opposed hers.

PEG also gave Lucy the freedom to explore language, which was her greatest love. "I love the texture of words and admire poets and others who can make a kind of music with them that is at once physical, emotional, and intellectual," she said. Her eventual career path as an educator and as an award-winning poet focused on the power of language. During her years at Waite's top-tier English department, Lucy wrote many articles and presented multiple sessions on composition and on pedagogy, her two research specialties.

Lucy had thought about education since attending MBC. As some of its earliest students, she and her classmates were especially aware of being "experiments" in education. "One of the beauties of PEG was that we did a lot of meta-engagement, thinking about our entire educational experience and reflecting on ourselves as learners," she explained. Lucy said that it made her "extra reflective" and prompted her thinking about teaching. Being a "well-treated educational guinea pig" made Lucy want to conduct her own educational experiments to determine how people consider questions and gain knowledge.

Although Lucy very much enjoyed teaching literature, her true love was teaching writing. "I think of writing as a mode of learning, and I care about sharing my enthusiasm for writing with young people," she said. Everything useful that she learned in her coursework and in her research Lucy translated into her classroom practice. She wanted to see which theories worked and which did not, so she constantly self-evaluated her teaching to ensure its improvement. Her hard work paid off in many teaching awards and accolades. Among them, she won a special teacher recognition award at Simson University and two other highly prestigious teaching awards at Waite.

Besides enjoying the daily interaction with her students, Lucy loved the challenge and creativity of teaching. It kept her sharp because of the minute-by-minute changes in the classroom. "It's creative in that you have to be so responsive. It's one of the hardest things about it for me, but I think also one of the wonderful things. You don't know what will happen at any point." Creativity also lay in the challenge "to accomplish something even just a little bit better than you did before."

Despite the many positives of her teaching career, Lucy also felt the impact of the negatives. Financially, college teacher pay and benefits were dismal. "Teachers work so hard for so little, and I feel pretty confident that I have the skills to have chosen a more lucrative career than English studies," Lucy said. She added, "My hesitation about entering higher education has been my distaste for the Ivory Tower culture and the politics of tenure." Also, English literature doctoral students who acted snobbishly about their work irritated her. Lucy felt the sting of their unstated but evident message—that literature study was "high brow" and pedagogy was "low brow." When she felt discouraged or depressed about her career, Lucy sometimes found herself unsure of her chosen path. "I have little glimmers of worry and ask myself, 'Was this the right choice of profession?'"

Qualified Resolution

Despite her occasional doubts, Lucy believed that she had made the right choice to become a professor of writing. When her thoughts turned to the more lucrative career she could have had in medicine, she countered that temptation by asking herself, "Would I be happy with more money doing something I enjoy less?" She said, "I sometimes envision my days as a doctor, and I know I would feel sad because I would not be asking the kinds of questions or investigating the subjects that fill my days now." Lucy's intellectual self needed daily nourishing. "While medicine and other professions certainly involve creativity, I don't think they would feed my spirit in the ways I feel fed today."

Lucy explained that she was always soul-searching because she wanted to do meaningful work. Longevity was another concern. She wanted to ensure long-lasting interest in her field so that she could retain her energy and commitment. She remarked that she felt satisfied "when I leave the classroom and the students were on and I feel like we pushed through somewhere, and it was challenging, and they're going home with their heads cracked open a little bit." She heard her inner voice say, "This is great! I just love this, and it's always different every day." The rewarding days sustained her.

Despite remaining somewhat unsure of having picked the "right" career, Lucy poured all of her energy into purposeful work. She was not simply a teacher of writing; she was a shaper of lives.

She derived great joy from her students, her studies, and her inquiring mind.

Becoming Whole

Achieving authenticity, or staying true to oneself, is of critical importance during middle adolescence. Psychologist Susan Harter explains that many teenagers struggle with their desire to act consistently with their beliefs and feelings. False-self behavior can be very disconcerting because it is self-alienating. In contrast, being authentic is psychologically beneficial for the developing child. Adolescents who are aware of their real selves and act accordingly "report much higher self-esteem, more positive affect, and more hope for the future."[2]

Lucy stated that authenticity was one of her highest goals in life. Two major aspects of her identity were her homosexuality and her intellectualism. Her adolescent and early adult struggle to recognize and accept her sexuality was a critical prerequisite to her being able to pursue meaning and purpose successfully. Being true to herself was the key to her well-being. She developed the courage and conviction to live a life that was consistent with who she really was and what she believed. She then turned her positive energies toward more fully helping others.

Lucy's need for authenticity was also a powerful key to her choice of career. As a girl, medicine had seemed attractive as a profession. However, the desire to spend time ruminating about philosophical questions that truly mattered to her, to express herself in poetry and fiction, and to persuade others of her opinions in writing and in speech swept her toward an intellectual and creative life. Until she found a career that authentically answered her greatest needs, she could not settle down.

Motivation

As a student, Lucy was often motivated to perform exceptionally so that she could impress teachers whom she greatly admired and respected. She felt challenged to win over the Mary Baldwin

College professor Samantha Collins because she valued the kind of feedback Collins gave. Collins "didn't withhold honest criticism." Like other gifted individuals, Lucy was "tired of hearing, 'Wow, you're so smart. You're such a great writer.'" Instead, Collins said, "I don't understand what you're saying here." That feedback made Lucy think more carefully about how she was expressing her ideas and stimulated her to work more exactingly. Lucy also cherished teachers who were genuine but serious, maintained high standards, and kept classes focused and students engaged. Because she paid close attention to educational methods, Lucy understood that the importance of professors transcends the content they teach. "Half of their effect is just who they are, and only half of it is how they present their subject matter," she said.

Teaching as Purpose

Lucy's professional purpose was to help college students, especially freshmen, grow into productive, fulfilled, and contributing members of society. She saw that many university freshmen had trouble adjusting to college, and she wanted to assist them in their transition. As she advised her students, she used her PEG experiences as a basis of comparison. "I can relate to them and understand how they're feeling the world right now, even though I know it's different for each of them," she said. The daily adult guidance at PEG had made a "huge difference" in Lucy's life as a young teen; she felt that even traditionally aged freshmen could use the consistent presence of a caring adult at college.

Just as Lucy had been inspired by teachers and professors with high standards and genuine interest in their students, so too did she want to become a professor whom students could respect. In doing so, she hoped to convey certain values and qualities that might influence them for the better. To be a good role model, she had to think carefully about how she conducted herself both in and out of the classroom. She also wanted to inspire her students' love of learning by sharing her joy and enthusiasm for writing. Her students' welfare was always on her mind. "I think about my students and what they need, what they know, and what they have to contribute." She continuously fine-tuned her teaching so that her students might investigate new ways of thinking and expressing themselves.

Lucy wanted her students "not only to become better readers and writers, but to develop as responsible and happy human beings." To achieve that outcome, she taught them how to think critically, write clearly, and communicate honestly. The measure of Lucy's impact lay in what she called her greatest achievements. They came in "the form of positive course evaluations, notes and letters from students, and evidence that a student's writing and/or thinking improved over the course of a semester." More than anything else, Lucy loved "the feeling that a student has gained some revelation about something important to him or her as a result of interactions with me or with other students in my classroom." In her generous desire to help people grow, Lucy did not need direct credit for her efforts.

Philosophy of Life

Lucy used the term *sustainability* to characterize her philosophy of life. She believed that people exist for no particular reason, which gives humans the "tremendous freedom to make our lives as wonderful as we can imagine them being." Explaining how such a system worked, Lucy warned that it did not mean "that we are entitled to be selfish. The achievement of a wonderful life requires awareness that actions are reciprocal or, to borrow a tired cliché, 'what goes around comes around.'" Engrained with a strong sense of responsibility, Lucy said that she interpreted "the best that can come around" as "support for one another."

Lucy's commitment to her philosophy of sustainability was attained through her contributions to society as a teacher. She defined making a difference in the world as making a social difference as opposed to becoming successful in conventional terms. She believed that since knowledge was socially constructed (i.e., humans interact socially to develop the meaning of concepts), the act of teaching—of facilitating academic knowledge and of guiding students toward self-knowledge—constituted a significant way to make a social difference. For Lucy, knowledge and wisdom were inextricably tied to purpose. By training her students to think critically and to respond sensitively to others, Lucy tried to instill in them a mindset of reflection and caring action. The import of her life's work was grounded in the concept of sustainability so that her students might similarly go on to inspire others.

Conclusions

Lucy's focus on authenticity helped her become a self-accepting, strong, happy, and purposeful individual, but the growth process was arduous. Even though she loved the way PEG enhanced her learning, she lagged behind in a critical area of her emotional development. Her initial inability to come to terms with her sexuality meant that too much of a false self was present during her early years at PEG, and it deeply affected her ability to progress productively. It took Lucy almost three years to get psychological support to explore her sexual identity, but once she found a good and wise therapist, she was on her way toward inner stability. Moving fully into that true sense of her new self took a few more years, but it was a process that Lucy kept refining because it yielded self-acceptance and long-lasting emotional health.

While Lucy was moving toward a truer understanding of her sexuality, she was on a parallel journey of discovery regarding her purpose in life. As someone who wanted to make a difference in others' lives, she found herself jockeying between practicing medicine and teaching as two different ways of using her talents to best serve others. For Lucy, being authentic vocationally was as important as being authentic emotionally. And just as her road to self-awareness and self-acceptance was not straightforward, neither was her route to a purposeful career.

Lucy's efforts to become a whole person were not restricted to the spheres of sexual identity and vocational choice, but those two areas represented crucial aspects of her intellectual, social, and emotional development. Becoming whole was the natural consequence of her search for authenticity. As she sought to find her true self, she engaged in the process of repairing the "broken" parts of her being. By restoring those components of her character to health, Lucy was better prepared to give kindly and generously to society. Her resultant "wholeness" produced positive energy that she then shared with others. Lucy's purpose was sustainability: the hope that authentic individuals, from their sense of satisfaction and fulfillment, would then help others to achieve those same goals of contentment and productivity.

Nina Carpenter: Creativity, Leadership, and the Struggle to Maintain Life Balance

As the 27-year-old director of a community art center, Nina Carpenter created powerful outreach programs that involved people who had not previously participated in the center's activities. One exhibit she designed focused on mental health. Patients from a psychiatric hospital and local artists with mental illness displayed their work. One contributor's growth moved Nina particularly deeply. A painter named Lily had sunk into a severe depression after her daughter had committed suicide. Lily had barely ventured out of her home that year and had not publicly shown her art. For this exhibition, she brought in portraits of her daughter. Inspired by the exhibition's healing effects and using the experience as a stepping stone to wellness, Lily was able to reemerge into society.

As she recovered, Lily became an advocate for people with mental illnesses; she appeared with Nina on a television special about mental health. "It was a really amazing experience for her to suddenly start talking about herself. After that, she had a lot of hopes," Nina said. "Once the art show was over, Lily was going to start taking art classes again, show her work, and talk more about her illness." Nina was grateful that her outreach efforts had stimulated Lily to want to help others with mental illness.

A Brief Biography

Always an imaginative child, Nina grew up in a loving home. With no television in the house, Nina and her younger sister, Ariel, spent their free time creating plays and inventing games with the neighborhood children. When Ariel expressed interest in skipping some years of high school, Nina went with her sister to tour PEG. Although Ariel decided to delay her decision, Nina applied to the program and was accepted. While at PEG, Nina displayed her leadership abilities when she co-founded and co-led a vibrant and influential organization for women.

After graduating from Mary Baldwin College at age 19, Nina moved to a small town, where she honed her woodworking skills for six years and then bought her own shop. Two years later, she got a full-time job as an art center director in her town, but she continued to work on her woodworking projects and to volunteer for social justice organizations. Between her job, her woodworking shop, and her huge time commitment to disparate worthy causes, Nina found herself pulled in several directions, which threatened to dissipate her effectiveness as an agent for change.

Nina's life story illustrates the power of creativity coupled with a compelling ethical core; she contributed enormously to her community. Yet her trajectory also demonstrates how her particular forms of giftedness ultimately required her to develop a clearer path, a more intentional way of functioning, and an integration and balance of her various roles to pursue purpose meaningfully.

Early Development of Creativity and Leadership

Entering college from a household where creativity flourished, Nina more fully developed her strengths at Mary Baldwin. The PEG faculty, including her advisor, Cynthia Lambert, supported and guided her in the development of her artistry. One professor said that Nina was the most remarkable and creative student he had taught in 30 years.

In addition to her artistic talent, many of Nina's key personal traits were nurtured in college. "PEG allowed me to strengthen my independence and be courageous, strong, and self-reliant in my endeavors to pursue a career (woodworking) dominated by men," she said. She applauded the faculty's "expectation of high work standards, methods, and results" because those principles translated into "a sense of determination, confidence, and ability." Not only would those qualities stand Nina in good stead for her woodworking career, but they also helped her to become a resourceful community leader.

Mary Baldwin College proved an excellent training ground for Nina's social activism. "PEG/MBC was helpful in encouraging my leadership and organizing abilities, which I used both in school and in the creation of a women's group, as well as running three summer women's conferences." Nina worked diligently to establish a cooperative group that promoted understanding and support for gay, heterosexual, bisexual, and transgender women.

As Nina became a campus leader, she discovered how much she had to learn about organizations and then quickly absorbed those lessons. Starting the women's group was "huge," she said, "because it involved finding advisors and figuring out how the organization was going to work and what its mission was." As a young teen, she learned about campus policies and regulations. "Putting on events, focusing on education, supporting women in need, and trying to balance all of those different things was quite a challenge." She learned "a lot about group dynamics and grassroots organizing within the MBC community and beyond"—skills that she continued to use throughout her life.

The PEG community encouraged Nina to explore her sense of purpose. "My friends and teachers at PEG/MBC were completely inspiring in helping me see the world and to discuss and be concerned about issues and how I might bring about some sort of change," she stated. They valued and promoted Nina's artistic and leadership abilities, which strengthened her confidence "to take big steps, risks, and feel unabashed about being seen as 'creative,' 'unusual,' 'different,' or 'odd.'" PEG gave Nina a potent foundation for venturing bravely into the world to create art and to pursue social justice.

Nina's ingenuity and leadership prompted her to initiate a number of original programs at MBC. "I connected very much with most of the faculty, not just as professors, but in a more intense way as mentors or role-models, and I wanted to hang out with them outside of the classroom." To deepen student relationships with favorite professors, Nina arranged lively events. "We had tea parties and dinners at our dorm rooms where our professors came and ate with us," she recalled. Nina also organized activities for PEGs outside of the residence hall. She helped produce "Open Mike" and "Dada Nights"[1] in the nearby town and coordinated many other cultural and artistic events. The more Nina combined her creative and organizational strengths, the greater were her positive effects on campus life.

With strong support and encouragement from her professors in a safe atmosphere for experimentation, Nina thrived. By taking full advantage of the opportunities to contribute to the health and liveliness of the Mary Baldwin community, she set the stage for her foray into the bigger world beyond the campus. As she entered the adult world, she continued to learn organizational skills and strove to fulfill her creative dreams while still feeling the urgent responsibility to repair the world in whatever ways she could.

Scott Lambert, her advisor's husband, gave Nina her first art-related job out of college by hiring her in his woodworking shop. After working for five and a half years as a paid apprentice, creating distinctive, artistic furniture pieces, Nina started her own wood-working business, where she created fine furniture and captivating sculptures—and where she developed a new sense of purpose. The shop afforded her a new independence. Having to plan, design, price pieces, buy material, and talk to clients gave her "a better understanding of woodworking as a business." As an entrepreneur, she wanted to maximize the efficiency of her operation while maintaining excellent craftsmanship and design.

The joy of owning her own shop and the love of her work buoyed Nina through many challenging tasks. There "were moments when it was thrilling to be working on a piece," she said. But in addition to being artistically creative, as a business owner, Nina had to apply her creative mind to solving practical problems as well. Maintaining her machinery was a challenge because she couldn't move it outside for repair. Learning how to fix large machines and handling almost any kind of woodworking challenge strengthened her self-efficacy.

Once established in her shop, one of Nina's first goals was to switch from doing clients' projects to designing original creations. She dreamed of selling her pieces in a gallery. "A solo exhibit would be an exhilarating accomplishment," she said. "It would be my first art show with woodworking." But before she could achieve her dream, Nina had a lot to learn.

Being free to make all of the business decisions was exciting, but Nina quickly discovered her weakness in time management, which diminished her ability to stay balanced with all of her commitments. Besides having clients' work to complete, Nina promised her parents that she would conclude the renovation work on their kitchen, a project that could take months. When too many obligations piled up, Nina had a hard time finishing everything that she had set out to do. With too much to do and too little time to do it, Nina ultimately abandoned her goal of mounting an exhibit of original work, which was source of great disappointment to her. She realized that she needed to prioritize her tasks.

Nina's sense of purpose had expanded with her new business. She wanted to teach women and children how to use tools so that they could take care of their needs and enjoy the craft of carpentry. "Teaching and empowering women to feel like they could use a saw and could make an accurate cut felt very important to me," she said. Although Nina did successfully teach women at her shop, she did not design the children's sessions with enough structure. By not planning ahead, Nina had further impeded her personal goals.

As she became more self-reliant in adulthood, Nina embraced knowledge and sought consistently to improve her business and design skills. She was a business owner, problem solver, designer, learner, and purposeful teacher. She applied her talents constructively, kept learning assiduously, and grew dramatically. Taking the risk of becoming an independent businesswoman required self-confidence and courage to face many challenges. Nina grappled successfully with many obstacles but was not as successful with her schedule. While her creativity and leadership furthered her purposeful goal to empower women and children, her failure to prioritize meant that she could not fully implement her plan. Similarly, she was unable to realize her personal artistic aspirations; she was somewhat haphazardly pursuing purpose. She unwittingly missed reaching some meaningful goals because she hadn't focused on her methods.

Outreach to Neglected Residents: The Mentally Ill

In addition to her woodworking business and her volunteer work, Nina had taken a full-time job as the director of the nonprofit regional Hanson Art Center in her hometown, Reistown. During her two-year tenure as director, Nina's purpose was to make all people feel welcomed and encouraged to participate. In that short time, she widened the outreach and increased the diversity of the populations that frequented the center by spearheading a number of innovative, collaborative exhibits. By teaming with others in the region, incorporating her hallmark creativity, and gaining the support of the center's board, she spread the benefits of art to Reistown communities that were formerly not involved.

During Mental Health month, Nina collaborated with a local art therapist at a psychiatric hospital, and the Hanson Art Center held an art show to give patients with mental illness the opportunity to display their work. The show was highly successful. Nina described the community's enthusiastic reaction: "People thought, like we did, that an art show was a great place to talk about things that are difficult, such as mental illness." Many psychiatrists and psychologists attended the exhibition. "Other state hospital patients came, and the patients who had artwork in the show visited it frequently," she said.

The most powerful aspects of the programming for Nina were the effects that continued after the show ended. The patients returned to the art center to view other art exhibitions and submitted their work for the outdoor art festival. Nina and her office manager went to see the patients' shows at the hospital. "They started hanging their work at the hospital." Nina said. Her innovative idea for the exhibit had broadened the art center's audience by inducing a new segment of the community to participate.

To strengthen the experience even further, Nina extended the programming. She invited a renowned author to speak about creativity and mental health at the art center. According to Nina, the event was "standing room only, and it was wonderful." Nina's collaborator, Carol, then offered a workshop on creativity and the mind, which got excellent reviews. Through their dual efforts, Nina and Carol maximized the impact of the initial art exhibition by expanding the community discussion about mental health.

Outreach to Neglected Residents: African American Artists

Nina knew that the African American community had never been targeted for representation at the Hanson Art Center, so she invited Ruben Taylor, a local African American artist who had been painting for more than 30 years, to mount a substantial solo show. "Taylor took high school art classes, but he didn't have any formal training beyond that," Nina explained. An excellent representative of Reistown, Taylor painted portraits of local community members. By incorporating his life experience into his art, he provided insights into local history. He was a valuable resource, and Nina was able to spotlight his talent for the community.

Wooing the African American community to the art center was Nina's next step. She wrote letters to all of the African American congregations in the area, encouraging them to come. "It was definitely the most racially diverse opening reception we've ever had, and the most diverse audience for a show, also," she stated.

Paring Back

The Hanson Art Center programs were highly effective. The enthusiastic response of the community and the huge turnouts for art shows and lectures increased overall attendance at the center. Instigating discussions about mental health and African American cultural participation were just as important to Nina as creating well-attended exhibitions and programs. She hoped that the discussions would expand people's thinking about the artistic needs and the well-being of the community's different populations.

As soon as Nina began devoting long hours to the art center, however, she struggled to find time for her woodworking; she didn't know how to balance the two jobs. And as if those weren't enough, she was also a Big Sister, a volunteer role that was very time-consuming, as well as a volunteer for Habitat for Humanity. Eventually, Nina realized that she had spread herself too thin. Although she felt responsible to help others, she did not reserve enough private time to decide on the direction she wanted to take.

Ultimately, Nina decided to quit her position at the art center. She had worked hard to encourage African American artists to advocate for themselves there, and she hoped that after her departure, there would be an annual show featuring African American artists so that talented individuals could showcase their work. Since the artists could advocate for themselves, their program seemed sustainable. However, she was worried that the Mental Health collaboration would not continue when she left Hanson. "I would have loved for this exhibit to happen every other year, and probably it won't," she said. She knew she would not be in a position to guarantee its sustainability once a new director arrived.

Nina understood that her life was "not very balanced, but I think my time spent with work and income, my time at home with Ted [her boyfriend] and with other friends, and my time with the other nonprofit feels really good to me." Still, she knew she needed to pare back, which meant that she would be able to better devote herself to the things that really mattered to her.

A Hybrid Approach to Social Activism

While Nina made inclusion and education her dual art center purposes, she also served her town, region, and state through social activism. Before she entered PEG, she had seen poverty first-hand in her travels abroad with her parents. Mr. and Mrs. Carpenter made their children aware of the vast disparity between the "haves" and "have nots," and in doing so, they emphasized empathy, caring, and responsibility for the betterment of society. Although her family lived simply, Nina's parents always underscored how fortunate they were. They did not want their children to take their advantages for granted.

In response to the inequities they saw, Nina's mother and father modeled two distinct ways of serving others. Her mother tutored children and volunteered locally at several organizations. Her father tried to bring about international reform by writing letters to powerful officials. While Nina admired her parents' efforts, she adopted a hybrid of her mother's local and her father's global perspectives. Her approach was grassroots organizing, and it had less of a focus on one individual working alone for change and more on working with a small group, "building coalitions with other organizations so that we can build a movement toward a specific goal like providing education on issues affecting our community." Nina wanted to corral people's energy to be "united on something so that we have a larger voice that may have an impact at a large level."

As an activist, Nina assumed responsibilities in the National Association for the Advancement of Colored People (NAACP), the local Democratic Party, and the State Coordinating Project (SCP). From these experiences, she saw the pressing need for greater collaboration among groups.

To accomplish that goal, Nina and her boyfriend Ted co-founded the Collaborative Regional Association of Fairness and

Global Harmony (CRAFGH), an organization that brought various communities together to produce significant social action results. Just as she had done as a business owner and an art center director, Nina strove to increase the power of the disenfranchised. As she expanded her repertoire of skills, strategies, and understandings through her various activities, her primary goals were to make the groups efficient and effective so that they could have the most powerful influence possible.

Collaborative Regional Association of Fairness and Global Harmony (CRAFGH)

The mission of Nina's group was to "locally promote a more peaceful and just society" and to create "sustainable relationships with people and organizations." Maintaining healthy mutual relationships was crucial: "We will have much more of an effect if we take the power of established organizations and work on projects together." CRAFGH teamed with the State Coordinating Project (SCP) to promote living wages for employees and tax reform for all citizens. That collaboration was useful, Nina said, but CRAFGH also originated significant projects.

CRAFGH began as a result of various local groups individually protesting the imminent participation of the U.S. in the Iraq War in 2003. Inspired by speakers at a national protest, Nina and other CRAFGH members united to initiate conversations in Reistown about the war. At first, their demonstrations were small and attracted little attention. As they grew larger, however, they triggered a counter-protest. The anti-war activists were standing on a downtown corner near the courthouse when the counter-protestors arrived. "There was not a lot of standing space, so we were intermixed almost alternately: pro, con, pro, con, around the corner." The President Bush supporters then brought "a tank with kids in it, and they came piling out. The people in the tank ran over the sidewalk when they parked in the parking lot. It was really intense," Nina said. A great deal of arguing ensued between the two opposing groups.

A lawyer from Nina's group tried to build consensus by investigating which statements both sides could agree on. "That is when I realized that her approach was really where we had the most effect," Nina remarked. "It was in people thinking and not being so emotional and not relying on gut reactions." Nina concluded that CRAFGH's goal was to stimulate true dialogue about the war. CRAFGH members thought more strategically about how they could best influence people. They staged another demonstration, but this time, they marched from the downtown location to a new gathering place in the park. The local residents drove through the park slowly, stopped, and talked with the protestors. Through those conversations, CRAFGH had a greater impact on people's consideration of the war. Distributing information, Nina hoped, would prompt people to think more deeply about the issues. "We've decided that we're going to be working in ways that are more integrated with the culture of the community," she said. Switching to tactics that touched the values and held the attention of individuals long enough to engage in dialogue made the group more effective in achieving its goals.

As delighted as Nina was to promote her anti-war message and to get people thinking, she still experienced an enormous personal impact. "In January 2003, with the start of the war coming in March, I was really overwhelmed with the CRAFGH work. It really ate into my income earning time, so I got deeply into debt because I lived on my credit card for a few months, and that was really bad." Driven by a profound sense of world responsibility, Nina continued to sacrifice her personal welfare.

CRAFGH decided to tie the past to the present. Reistown annually sponsored the Nineteenth Century History Festival. Women would promenade in large, hooped skirts, wear white gloves, and carry parasols, which were costumes of the upper class in that historical time. CRAFGH decided to address issues of the Victorian era "that weren't glamorous and pretty and fluffy and fun" by dressing as the working class, wearing "lots of raggedy clothes." The group presented a startling contrast to the typical participants.

CRAFGH members held up signs that said, "Ask us about Irish immigration, Chinese immigration, the Mexican American War, Civil Rights, slavery, etc." Nina and others distributed flyers that were fact sheets about each issue. On one side were points about problems in the 19th century, but on the flip side, there were facts about recent issues like child labor, racism, and immigrant discrimination.

Although the CRAFGH members were worried about negative reactions to their message, "the parents loved it because it was information that their kids were studying in school," Nina explained. The strategy was a hit. Despite its success, however, the local police were afraid that if the CRAFGH group participated in the July 4th parade, there would be a riot. Through reasoned conversation that respected the police officers' viewpoints, Nina persuaded those who opposed her social activism to find a place for the group's positive involvement in the community. CRAFGH was allowed to march in the parade.

By using clever techniques, Nina and CRAFGH gave the citizens of her community information about social injustice. Being recognized and heard as a group with a mission, CRAFGH gained greater power to effect change. Nina was creative, strategic, and had fun while dealing with serious topics and goals.

Social Activist as Social Entrepreneur

As an activist dedicated to social justice and a businesswoman with strong organizational skills, Nina possessed the qualities of a social entrepreneur. Social entrepreneurs are individuals who create "innovative solutions to society's most pressing social problems. They offer new ideas for wide-scale change…. They have implemented their ideas across cities, countries, and in some cases, the world."[2]

Business entrepreneurs want outcomes that increase profit and wealth. "Social entrepreneurs have only one ultimate bottom line by which they measure their success, i.e., their intended social impact, whether that is housing for the homeless, a cleaner environment, reduced poverty or some other social improvement."[3] Given that any significant societal change tends to be met by resistance, new ideas "need champions—obsessive people who have the skill, motivation, energy, and bullheadedness to do whatever is necessary to move them forward and artfully maneuver them through systems."[4] Exceptional social entrepreneurs are people "with vision, drive, integrity of purpose, great persuasive powers, and remarkable stamina."[5]

Nina had the makings of a social entrepreneur. Through her organizational and business skills, her personal qualities and values, and her sense of purpose, she wanted to make a constructive impact on the world, and she used her creativity and leadership to move toward that goal. With no mentor to guide her, she made her way idiosyncratically, yet every undertaking led to growth. Each experience put her one step closer toward a greater integration of her roles.

In Pursuit of Balance

Although her woodworking shop clearly showed her entrepreneurial spirit as a businesswoman, Nina was at heart a social entrepreneur. To fulfill that role, she needed to achieve a unified vision that would prompt her to prioritize her efforts. As she grappled with multiple commitments, she had to cope with the imbalance that pervaded her life. She knew that she needed to integrate her professional work, volunteer service work, and personal life in order to live in better alignment with her sense of purpose.

Part of Nina's imbalance came from her job at the art center. Although it helped to satisfy her need to reach out to others, the position also came with serious restrictions. "This is a wonderful job, and it suits me really well in many ways," she said, "but I can't be political here at all." Nina found it difficult to be so involved with politics and social activism while maintaining a neutral stance at the art museum, especially because political conservatives predominated in Reistown.

From the outset, the issue of Nina's activism flared because she was naïve about the media. A local reporter interviewed her as the new art center director. Nina expected it to be an innocuous story about her job responsibilities and why she chose to become director. When the saw the headline, "War Protester Becomes Director of Art Center," she was shocked. "Within the first few weeks of being there, I had to defend all of this in front of the board. They were very upset and said that I shouldn't be involved in a political party," she stated. From then on, Nina had to monitor her language with the media, the board, and the art center's visitors. As her involvement with the Democratic Party and social activism increased, the internal tension mounted. Although she found ways to cope with the political constraints that the board imposed on her, she wanted to be more fully herself while at work.

Despite its restrictions, the directorship at the art center was an opportunity that Nina felt lucky to have. Ultimately, she saw it "as a stepping stone for going to other organizations that might be more suited to me." The art center "doesn't bring about much change," Nina said, "because it's mostly about pleasure and aesthetics." Although "art can be political and change minds," Nina felt that the Hanson Art Center sponsored only one exhibit a year "that sparks a conversation or educates someone." The focus of the art center was usually "about something completely different from what I think I might want to go into."

It was always Nina's intention to have as great an impact on society as she could. She felt that she was wasting her time, effort, and energy on relatively inconsequential tasks like editing the art center newsletter. "If it were a newsletter for Amnesty International or for a big organization, that would be different," she said. At the same time, she realized that if she switched her job to a larger organization, then "one of the drawbacks would be that I potentially could be far removed from the change that's happening." Nina weighed both perspectives and considered her options for the future. She hoped to find "another small organization where I could be directly connected to the potential change, where hopefully the organization is having the kinds of impact that would be more satisfying for the amount of work I was doing."

Nina's personal life had suffered as a result of her multiple involvements. "I don't eat very well, I don't exercise, and I don't feel in touch with the natural world as much as I used to," she lamented. She also regretted not having enough "quiet or alone time or just reading time." Her life lacked a focus on self-development. Nina wanted to relax, write in her journals, and reflect, and she didn't have time for any of it. She wanted a "more balanced personal life and to spend a healthy amount of time with Ted, with myself, and with friends." Work was still important in that equation, Nina explained, but she wanted to fit it in better with her other needs. Leaving her art center job would give her more time to create a well-rounded life and to retrieve some of the original flexibility that she'd had before working there.

As Nina transitioned to a newly balanced and refocused life, she became more realistic about her capacity to handle so many involvements at once. She felt as if she "should be able to do everything, but I can't." She decided to de-clutter her schedule of the excess responsibilities that she had assumed. She became more selective in her volunteer tasks, concentrating increasingly on being even more efficient and effective in her choices. In addition to pulling back from her CRAFGH meetings, "I intentionally missed the last NAACP meeting. I fully had intended to go, but I ended up not going," she said. As her priorities shifted, Nina was beginning to put her home life ahead of her social activism.

As she slowed down the pace of her activities, Nina reflected more. She recognized that her previous life choices had been spontaneous; she decided she wanted to become more intentional about them so that her path would be clearer. "I'm really getting in a phase of trying to plan more carefully," she explained. She realized that if she combined her full-time work with her sense of purpose, she would have more time for her personal life.

Integrating Work and Purpose

Nina envisioned a few possible paths for her future. They all held the common goal of melding her social action and her professional work. For years, Nina and Ted had dreamed of moving out West. They had traveled there together and both liked the outdoors. They also liked the feeling of freedom that the West conveyed. Nina knew of a peace center in the region. "There's a wonderful peace and justice group there called the Organization for Peace, and that's the kind of job I would love to have," she said, "working either as a director or assistant director or even working in their library." Not a "city person," Nina said that she would most likely forego the greater social action opportunities that large cities afford.

The State Coordinating Project (SCP) was another organization that Nina admired and thought might be a good match for her professional needs and her sense of purpose. SCP seemed to be making wide-ranging social change efficiently, which was a motivating force in Nina's decision making. "It's a statewide organization, and I would be interested in a career with them, too," she said. The group also was trying to create smaller SCP groups throughout the state. "They're not leaving out a single county or hill or mountain. It's really good coverage, which I think gives them a lot more political leverage." Joining the SCP as an employee would satisfy Nina's desire to have a larger impact on society, if she stayed in the Reistown area.

SCP would also provide Nina with the opportunity to work with an effective group. "It's non-partisan, and I think that's part of its effectiveness." She admired SCP's focus on two issues a year, which they picked by consensus across the state. "They pick goals that they think can really make a difference so that the goals (such as legislative bills) that they propose will hopefully get passed." By focusing her attention and effort on a single organization that embodied so many of her goals, Nina would have a better chance of bringing flexibility and balance back into her life.

A political career was another way to achieve social change professionally. Nina anticipated the need for more schooling in political science and history if she made such a choice. She already had taken a few graduate-level conflict mediation courses, which she both enjoyed and found very useful in her organizational work.

"A lot of organizing is mediating," she said, knowing that a political life would entail the same kind of skills.

Throughout her struggle to make a decision, Nina felt grateful to have someone like Ted standing beside her. She admired Ted's way of being in the world. "Ted is a very good balance because he doesn't feel that obligation to help everybody and to say 'yes' and obligate himself with lots of time commitments," she commented. "He's a much more Zen-type, quiet, reflective person, so I am definitely influenced by that."

As the complexities of Nina's life fostered imbalance, she increasingly sought a better equilibrium. She needed to address three issues of growing importance: her split self, her desire to impact society more fully, and her need for a healthier life. With the aim of pursuing purpose meaningfully, efficiently, and effectively, she realized that it would be necessary to fuse her professional and volunteer goals. Integrating her roles offered the promise of not only a balanced life, but also of a more powerful directedness for the pursuit of purpose. With the extra energy and focus, Nina could more readily become a social entrepreneur of significant influence.

Conclusions

"In the popular imagination, creative individuals are often seen as oblivious to the ties of responsibility that hobble lesser mortals," write researchers Csikszentmihalyi and Nakamura.[6] They counter, however, that "the culture has much to learn from the distinctive ethical sense that directs most creative individuals." Creative people believe in the possibilities of the future and are "curious about how to make things better." The values of responsibility, high-quality work, and social concerns combine to thrust some innovators "beyond the boundaries of their discipline." Such individuals take courageous stands in support of peace and against social injustice; they want to create a better world.

Nina Carpenter exemplified the creative and responsible person that the researchers described. A gifted artist and an innovative leader, she infused a sense of purpose into everything she did, and her giftedness allowed her to contribute enormously to her communities. Using her gifts indiscriminately, however, affected her adversely. It was only when she could no longer sustain her level of involvements successfully that she embraced the idea of personal change. She withdrew from some service commitments and realized that she could lighten her schedule by combining work and purpose. At that point, it was not clear what road she would take, but she seemed to have learned enough about herself to design a more integrated and balanced life. Nina had learned that focus and planning were critical to personal well-being and the successful pursuit of purpose.

Epilogue

One of this book's findings counters the prevalent societal view that acceleration is ill-advised for gifted children. Just like any other educational choice, acceleration is not perfect, but parents and teachers must ask: *Is it substantially better for the individual child? Does it remove certain debilitating or fatal toxins from the child's environment so that she can flourish and continue to build her strength?* Resistance to using acceleration may impair some gifted students' dynamic growth.

These 14 exceptional young women's lives have shown us that a sense of purpose often begins in childhood. The girls were independent, empathetic, and concerned with justice. Most of the families' philosophies and actions about caring for others, being socially obligated to help others, and being grateful for their gifts helped nurture these positive qualities. The children whose parents were not as supportive had other significant people or experiences to boost them.

Negative school experiences threatened to wither the girls' optimism and courage. Fortunately, the girls found the Program for the Exceptionally Gifted at Mary Baldwin College just in time. It was a safe place to grow and continue to develop their purposeful directions. Our research suggests that the program enhanced their courage, helped them to become what they wanted to be, and successfully inoculated them against many harsh aspects of the working world, which was critical to their well-being and to their continued pursuit of purpose.

Enrolling in PEG took the young girls out of potentially toxic situations, but they still had to cope with some daunting and painful academic, social, and emotional challenges as early college entrants. Fortunately, the PEG environment provided them with a good balance of support. The girls were finally in an appropriate educational setting for healthy growth and reaching their maximum potential.

The PEG study women's lives were not smooth sailing when they graduated, but they usually had friends and family to help them get back on a purposeful track, or they found additional mentors to help them envision their way. The young women were able to maintain their empathy for others into adulthood and retain a sense of service as a paramount value.

Pursuing purpose requires a heartening of the self. Without the stabilizing anchor of emotional health, an individual can veer out of control, make bad decisions, career onto unproductive paths, and ultimately lose a sense of personal meaning. Feeling firmly rooted and comfortable with oneself can help the individual plan her course, see clearly where she wants to go, and feel in control of her destiny while still remaining flexible enough to respond creatively to unpredictable circumstances.

This book explored not only the young women's childhood influences, but also their time at PEG and afterwards in the adult world. While at Mary Baldwin, the faculty, staff, and peers gave them a caring, nurturing environment and acted as role models and mentors. The girls no longer felt out of place; they felt celebrated.[1] PEG encouraged them to be their true selves and to follow their passionate interests in its safe environment. They illustrated some of the fundamental aspects and concerns of positive psychology. Instead of capitulating to pressures and losing hope, the girls became stronger, more courageous, and more successful at reaching goals based on their ideals.

What has become of the five young women we profiled in detail? We know that they, like the other women in the study, graduated from PEG at 17, 18, and 19 years old to pursue graduate studies, get good jobs, be productive, be active citizens, and have families, friends, and fun in their lives. But six years later, have they maintained their sense of purpose? Here is what they wrote:

Dr. Madison Kennedy

After completing my pediatrics residency in 2007, I specialized in pediatric infectious disease. I also earned a Master's in Public Health on the global health track. After completing my fellowship, I remained at the medical school as a faculty member to complete a joint research project with UNICEF in Peru. I also participated in several international healthcare projects, including work in Haiti right after the earthquake, and in Mozambique and Liberia. This August, I was commissioned as a captain in the U.S. Army. I'll be working as a general pediatrician and as a clinical investigator on one or more infectious disease projects. I'm still writing an article for peer review publication. I'm not married and have no kids, but I still have my dog and my cat.

Before PEG, I had always dreamed of doing amazing things. I wanted to speak other languages, see a giraffe, and scuba dive. I wanted to walk a mile in everyone else's shoes. They say you can't miss what you don't know. For me, that was definitely not true. I knew that all these amazing experiences were out there, but they seemed like things that happened to other people. Coming to PEG changed all of that. It gave me the strength to do the unexpected. I learned not just to weather change, but to love it. While change and uncertainty can be incredibly intimidating and even frightening, through PEG I learned that change is just another word for opportunity, and I wasn't going to let any of the good ones pass me by. Life is not something that is happening to me; I'm the one living it.

Dr. Jessica Holmes

I'm now a research fellow at a major university in the U.K. I live with my husband, whom I met when I was doing my Ph.D. I think that PEG's long-term effect on my professional choices is that it allowed me to pursue my intellectual interests intensely at an age when there is considerable social pressure for girls to pay more attention to their social development, but I think that attending PEG creates a catch-22 for women. If I hadn't attended PEG, I might not have maximized my potential due to intellectual discouragement as a teenaged girl. Certainly, sexism is still common in the professions. But since I didn't face it in high school, I was not prepared for it when I encountered it later and in more subtle forms, even though I have done well since. Also, being the only woman of African descent sometimes takes a toll.

On the other hand, I can't say that I would have been able to tough it out in high school. The experience for boys and girls is probably different. My husband learned how to camouflage his intelligence (he was an underachiever in high school and blossomed in college), but his incentives were different, and it was a short-term solution because he doesn't face any barriers to expressing his intelligence now as an adult professional. [It is dispiriting that] a high-achieving high school girl will face lifelong obstacles, and camouflaging her intelligence, even in the short term, won't address the issue (or open any professional doors). I will be eternally grateful for the lifelong friendships that I made at PEG.

Dr. Claire Hagen

Jeremy and I built our house at the farm in 2007 and moved in that summer. We absolutely love living "in community," as they say. I have joined the facilitation team and have been to some conflict resolution workshops, which have strengthened my group process skills. I also became a certified mediator through our local mediation services organization.

Health-wise I am doing pretty well. I am not taking any medications for fibromyalgia. I still experience back pain if I overexert myself, but I bounce back pretty quickly. Fatigue is occasionally a problem. I'm not doing anything in particular to manage the condition, so I feel pretty lucky! Jeremy and I are doing well together—no kids yet, though.

My job has changed somewhat, at my request. My teaching load is a little heavier, but I devote a lot more time to my volunteer work, which I find more fulfilling. While it's been a bit difficult to let go of that long-time dream of being a tenured professor, I am much happier now!

Lately, my volunteer work has focused on anti-racism work. Last spring, I helped organize a discussion session on fighting racism as part of a local peace conference. At the college, I have incorporated my interests in social justice in the freshman seminar course I've been teaching. I continue to co-lead the Literacy Council's ESL tutor training workshop and am still on the board of the Consortium for Peace. After the KKK came to a nearby city a while ago, I helped organize a local unity coalition. We consist of 15 local organizations, and we're getting ready to expand. By working together, we can demonstrate our community's shared commitment to peace, justice, and equality.

Lucy Jacobs

Our daughter just turned three in June and is doing great. Gabby and I have not had more children, and there are none on the way. I still direct the college writing center, which is now the writing and speaking center (I have expanded the services to provide students with feedback on oral presentations as well as papers). In terms of volunteerism, last year I served as chair of the advisory board for a creative writing summer day camp for local kids entering grades 6-10. I wrote grants and applied for other funding so that underprivileged kids in the area could attend the camp on full scholarship. I stayed on the advisory board this year but was less involved, as I've decided to devote serious attention to finishing my Ph.D.

Nina Carpenter

I've been an extension agent with 4-H in a western state for just over two years. I oversee my county's 4-H youth development program of more than 500 youth and their families and work with about 135 volunteers. I've been learning about everything from how to de-lice chickens to how to program a robot, teach art and woodworking classes, and inspire teens to be the best counselors they can be for younger kids at our 4-H camp. I enjoy the diversity and challenges of my daily work experiences!

I get my "volunteer fix" through this work with Extension, partly because I am working with so many people in a role that has some impact on their lives, and partly because our 4-H program is very involved in community service and in partnering with nonprofits and other community groups. I spend my non-work time studying for classes toward a Master's degree in Sustainable Food Systems, hiking and camping with my partner, Ted, and exploring the lectures, festivals, and films our university town has to offer.

Ted and I are coming up on our tenth anniversary of being together, and we've decided to celebrate the occasion by getting married. We're also expecting our first child, which we are (excitedly) certain will significantly enhance our lives. My dreams for the future include setting up a hobby woodworking shop so I can finally make some furniture for our house, planting a vegetable garden, and working on a series of paintings.

The five women now range in age from 32 to 41 years old and have maintained their local, regional, national, and international civic involvement either through their professions or as volunteers. Their lives of purpose have taught lessons that are useful not only to gifted girls, but also to boys and girls of all backgrounds and abilities. Children and youth who share certain qualities that were displayed by the young women, and who have families and schools that support them, may be our next innovative leaders. If they find their way to an interest with passion and commitment, if they discover it to be their *raison d'etre* (even for a segment of their lives), if they get enough inoculation, and if they want to make a difference, then they will have created lives of purpose.

Endnotes

Introduction

1   For more information about PEG, go to www.mbc.edu/early_college/peg.

2   The term "PEGs" is used in the book to refer to the young women who attended the program. There is a distinction made between the PEGs and those who participated in the research study.

3   Psychologist Howard Gruber (1982) recommends the strategy of studying gifted people's lives to learn how individuals become creatively productive. Specifically, the study of highly creative females may psychologically strengthen and help other women to work innovatively. Models of productivity and interdependence, the PEG graduates chosen for this study show us how to nurture caring, concerned, compassionate, committed individuals who develop and use their giftedness for society's benefit, as well as for self-fulfillment (Rhodes, 1994).

4   In the 2011-2012 academic year, Mary Baldwin initiated a new Early College Entrance program that is broader in scope than the PEG program. PEG accepts girls ages 13-15, as well as some young 16-year-olds. Now, 16-year-old students who wish to start college only one to two years early can decide with program staff whether they would prefer the relative independence of the new program or the greater support of the PEG program.

5   The Spencer Center, developed at Mary Baldwin in the last four to five years for all its students, promotes community and global engagement.

6   Retrieved from www.mbc.edu/vwil

7   Seligman & Csikszentmihalyi, 2000. "A science of positive subjective experience, positive individual traits, and positive institutions promises to improve quality of life and prevent the pathologies that arise when life is barren and meaningless. The exclusive focus on

pathology that has dominated so much of our discipline results in a model of the human being lacking the positive features that make life worth living. Hope, wisdom, creativity, future mindedness, courage, spirituality, responsibility, and perseverance are ignored or explained as transformations of more authentic negative impulses. [Positive psychology discusses] such issues as what enables happiness, the effects of autonomy and self-regulation, how optimism and hope affect health, what constitutes wisdom, and how talent and creativity come to fruition.... [A] framework for a science of positive psychology [points] to gaps in our knowledge [and predicts] that the next century will see a science and profession that will come to understand and build the factors that allow individuals, communities, and societies to flourish" (p. 5).

Chapter 1

1   Noble & Drummond, 1992

2   Gross, 1998

3   Noble, Arndt, Nicholson, Sletten, & Zamora, 1999

4   Noble & Smyth, 1995

5   Gross & Van Vliet, 2005. "Research also documents positive outcomes for social and emotional development, with radically accelerated students adjusting well to their new learning context, making friends easily, being accepted by older students, and enjoying increased levels of self-esteem and self-confidence (Gross, 2003; Janos et al., 1988; Pollins, 1983)" (p. 168).

6   Noble, Arndt, et al., 1999, p. 79

7   Gross & Van Vliet, 2005, p. 164

8   Winner, 2003, p. 92. Winner cites Csikszentmihalyi's "Big-C" vs. "little-c" creativity distinctions. Winner distinguishes between individuals with "Big-C" creativity (meaning domain-altering innovation) and those who have "little-c" creativity (e.g., coming up with innovative approaches to problems but who don't become major creators): "That is, they neither created a new domain nor did they revolutionize an old domain. Yet expertise as an endpoint should not be lightly dismissed. Society needs experts, and we can neither expect nor hope that all prodigies will become creators. Many gifted children grow up to become happy and well-adjusted experts in their fields" (p. 91).

9   Miraca Gross, one of the world's leading researchers in radical acceleration, implies that a fair assessment of exceptionally gifted children's possible accomplishments and occupational status should be made only over the course of a lifespan (Gross, 2003). To best predict what the highly gifted children in her longitudinal study might achieve professionally, Gross suggested that one should look to the "current occupational status of the grandparents, who are nearing or have reached the end of their working lives," as opposed to the parents of these children who "may not yet have attained their full potential" (p. 85). These grandparents, along with those of earlier gifted studies, showed a "tendency…to achieve unusual professional success and rise to positions of considerable eminence in their chosen fields" (p. 84). The arc of the grandparents' careers may hint at the timeframe for socially recognized success by the grandchildren.

10 Colangelo, Assouline, & Gross, 2004

11 Arnold, 1995, p. 60

12 Reis, 1998

13 Gross, 1994

14 Ford, Grantham, & Milner, 2004

15 Reis, Callahan, & Goldsmith, 1996

16 Mendez & Crawford, 2002

17 Reis, 2002

18 Mason, 2007

19 Eagly & Carli, 2007

20 Amran, cited in Damon & Gregory, 2003, p. 409

21 Winner, 2003, p. 93

22 Gifted education expert Joseph Renzulli defines social capital as "a set of intangible assets that address the collective needs and problems of other individuals and our communities at large" (Renzulli, 2003, p. 77). Renzulli points to the great need for stimulating social capital because it "generally enhances community life and the network of obligations we have to one another" and benefits "society as a whole because [it helps] to create the values, norms, networks, and social trust that facilitate…cooperation geared toward the greater public good" (p. 77).

In his research, Renzulli discovered that other factors are as important as intelligence in children who might become our "social capital." Optimism, courage, romance with a topic, mental and physical energy, sensitivity to human concerns, and vision (or a sense of destiny) are characteristics of students who most likely will contribute meaningfully to the betterment of society (Renzulli, 2003). In recent years, Renzulli has applied the idea of social capital to gifted students who get involved in social action and hope to become change agents. "Once a school is able to establish an environment that fosters social action projects, students will begin to recognize that they are capable of being agents of societal change" (Fogarty, Koehler, & Renzulli, 2006, p. 22). Renzulli's Operation Houndstooth (Renzulli, 2003) and the Northwestern University Center for Talent Development service-learning curriculum (Lee, Olszewski-Kublius, Donahue, & Weimholt, 2007) are programs that show great promise in enhancing young people's service ethos.

23   Frankl, 1984, p. 162. First published in 1946 in Vienna, Austria.

24   Frankl, 1984, p. xxx. The positive psychologist William Damon defined purpose as "a stable and generalized intention to accomplish something that is at once meaningful to the self and of consequence to the world beyond the self." Purpose must be outer-directed; it refers to actions that promote the betterment of society. In this book, "purpose" is defined in Damon's terms.

25   Chickering & Reisser, 1993. Researchers Chickering and Reisser said that purposeful students are "well motivated and working for their own satisfaction" (p. 232). In their study, the students persevered in reaching their goals despite obstacles and mistakes.

26   Chickering & Reisser, 1993, p. 233

27   Chickering & Reisser, 1993, p. 233

Chapter 2
1   Gross, 2003

Chapter 3
1   Rhodes, 1994, p. 20

2   Kegan, cited in Rhodes, 1994, p. 20

3   Rhodes, 1994, p. 20

4   Rhodes, 1994, p. 21

5   Rhodes, 1994, p. 21

6   Arnold, 1995

7   Ford, Moore, & Milner, 2005. "The magnitude of this problem cannot be overstated nor overestimated. For at least seven decades, Black students, for example, have been under-represented in gifted education (Ford, 1998; Jenkins, 1943; Witty & Jenkins, 1935). Hispanic and American Indian students are also under-represented by 30% to 70% (U.S. Department of Education, 1993, 1998)" (p. 97).

8   Rhodes, 1994, p. 21

9   Rhodes, 1994, p. 21

Chapter 4

1   Goertzel, Goertzel, Goertzel, & Hansen, 2004

2   Lovecky, 1997

3   Clark, 2008, p. 76

4   Schulman, 2002

5   Schulman, 2002, p. 505

6   Schulman, 2002, p. 502

7   Schulman, 2002, p. 506

Chapter 5

1   Lovecky, 2004

2   Peterson & Ray, 2006a, 2006bb

3   Rimm, quoted in Boodman, 2006. "Sylvia Rimm, a clinical professor of psychiatry and pediatrics at Case School of Medicine in Cleveland, said Peterson's findings echo what she hears in her practice: 'Regular kids get bullied, too, but gifted kids are bullied based on their school performance, which makes the child's strength into a weakness and a potential source of shame.'"

4   Boodman, 2006

5   Gross, 1994, p. 29. Miraca Gross has noted the emotional cost of feeling different as a gifted child, especially in early adolescence: "Junior high school can be a critical period for extremely gifted students. The onset of adolescence involves the formulation of a personal identity, and this is facilitated by the development of a group of supportive and intimate peers (Steinberg, 1985). This can be problematic for gifted adolescents who differ...from the majority of students in their chronological age cohort. The adolescent peer culture is noted

for its intolerance of deviance from its standards and conventions (Coleman, 1960; Tannenbaum, 1983).... Janos, Fung, & Robinson (1985) found decreased self-esteem in gifted students who perceive themselves as 'different'" (p. 29).

6   Willis, 2009

7   Reis, 2002

8   Kindlon, 2006

9   Pace, Witucki, & Blumreich, 2008. "...[T]he number and retention of women in the sciences at all educational levels is still an issue. Although the number of women in science, engineering, and mathematics fields has slowly increased at all stages of the educational pipeline over the past several decades, percentages vary greatly across the different scientific disciplines. For example, today women earn 50% of the bachelor degrees in chemistry, but only 20% of the bachelor degrees in engineering and 23% in physics (Heylin, 2007). Retention remains a problem as well, with higher percentages of female students dropping out of science, math, and engineering areas of study when compared to their male counterparts (Seymour & Hewitt, 1997). The retention problem continues along many science-related career paths; for example, fewer than 10% of the full professors in science and engineering fields are women (Nelson & Rogers, 2005)" (p. 374).

See also Drury, 2010: "Many factors have been identified in the literature as influencing the under-representation of women in technology leadership positions. Fox (2006) and Wright (1996) discuss the masculine nature of information technology, leading to perceptions of an alien, undesirable culture. Bartol and Aspray (2006) and Eagly and Carli (2007) stress the lack of mentors and role models for women. Many, including Chliwniak (1997), Kanter (1977), and Rosene (2006) point to the dominance of male hegemony in social structures and socialization processes leading to occupational jurisdiction and authority favoring males (Abbott, 1988; Bechky, 2003). All of these factors contribute to the lack of women earning college degrees in technical fields (National Center for Women and Information Technology, 2007) and the lack of representative numbers of women in technology-related positions, including leadership positions (Bartol & Aspruy, 2006)" (p. 60).

10   VanTassel-Baska, 2004. Marginality may be a positive aspect of being different. Living on the outskirts of society may provide distinctive

perspectives on the dominant culture. This outsider viewpoint often contributes to creativity itself, as VanTassel-Baska noted in the enormous creative contributions of women and minorities—two marginal groups—in the past 25 years. "While being an outsider may be psychologically difficult, it can provide the material necessary to advance the thinking in a field and to keep traditions at bay."

11   Silverman, cited in Rivero, n.d. See also Silverman, 1999: "Up to this point we have been addressing primarily the issue of socialization. According to the dictionary, socialization is the ability to adapt to the needs of the group. Gifted children are very adaptable, particularly girls. But at what price? If one works very hard at fitting in with others, especially when one feels very different from others, self-alienation can result. And this is exactly what we find in so many 'well adjusted' gifted youth and adults. In their desperation to belong, they have given up or lost touch with vital parts of themselves. Social development, on the other hand, is not the pressure to adapt, but a deep, comfortable level of self-acceptance that leads to true friendships with others. Lasting friendships are based on mutual interests and values, not on age. Individuals with good social development like themselves, like other people, demonstrate concern for humanity, and develop mutually rewarding friendships with a few kindred spirits. Social development goes hand in hand with self-actualization, whereas socialization is merely the desire to conform—often the opposite of self-actualization. The research indicates that special provisions for the gifted foster good social development (Silverman, 1993); this, rather than fitting in, should be our aim for them."

12   VanTassel-Baska, 2004

13   National Association for Gifted Children, n.d. "Well-trained professionals are indispensable to the identification and education of gifted learners. Without trained teachers, even significant investments in other resources and services may fail to attain meaningful and sustained results. Despite this need, most college teacher preparation programs do not include coursework on gifted learners in their curriculum. Additionally, training in gifted education identification and teaching methods is not widely required through in-service professional development courses, even for teachers working in specialized programs for gifted students. As a result, most gifted and talented children, who spend the majority of their time in the regular education classroom, are taught by teachers who are not trained to meet their special needs"(p. 3).

14   Torrance, 1981, pp. 55-56

15   Csikszentmihalyi, Rathunde, & Whalen, 1993, pp. 187-188

16   Csikszentmihalyi, Rathunde, & Whalen, 1993, pp. 188

17   Csikszentmihalyi, Rathunde, & Whalen, 1993, pp. 190

18   Csikszentmihalyi, Rathunde, & Whalen, 1993, pp. 185

19   Csikszentmihalyi, Rathunde, & Whalen, 1993, pp. 185

20   Werner, cited in Benard, 2004. People may choose personally meaningful goals, but to move beyond the self and focus on service requires empathy. Resilience researcher Emily Werner defined empathy as both "the ability to know how another feels and to understand another's perspective."(p. 109) She says that it is fundamental to the development of specific qualities like compassion and caring and of moral development in general. Thus, empathy provides the impetus to act on behalf of others.

21   Snyder, Rand, & Sigmon, 2002

22   Snyder, Rand, & Sigmon, 2002, p. 263

23   Snyder, Rand, & Sigmon, 2002, p. 263

24   Snyder, Rand, & Sigmon, 2002, p. 265

25   Snyder, Rand, & Sigmon, 2002, p. 259

Chapter 6

1   Two studies emphasize the different dimensions that must be considered when determining the significance of an initially lowered, and eventually raised, academic self-concept for gifted students who enter a gifted program for the first time. The first is from Preckel and Brull (2010), who studied gifted students who had been placed in a full-time ability group of similarly bright students: "The impact of placement on future academic careers remains to be investigated, but research findings for similar educational measures showed positive effects on academic development.... Thus, belonging to this high-status group can be assumed to strengthen academic self-concept due to a basking-in-reflected-glory effect (BIRGE). However...gifted and regular classes differ in many ways, and a BIRGE is not the only possible explanation for positive assimilation effects. If attending special gifted classes influences self-concept positively, this could have multiple reasons, for example that students gain greater esteem from better teaching and more challenging curricula, or from having

high pride and efficacy in their own work, thus not necessarily from basking in reflected glory….

"For a sample of gifted students, we found that negative consequences of ability grouping on academic self-concept were cushioned by positive assimilation effects of class type. This finding supports special classrooms for the gifted as a fostering option. There is ample empirical evidence that ability grouping of the gifted is beneficial for their achievement…, and our study shows that full-time ability grouping of the gifted in special classrooms does not necessarily have detrimental effects on academic self-concept….

"This finding is of high practical concern because academic self-concept is a powerful predictor for a variety of variables related to achievement and learning, and this also applies to gifted students. Studies looking at the interplay between academic self-concept and achievement document reciprocal effects between the two variables (e.g., Marsh et al., 2005). Especially for younger children, there is evidence for a self-enhancement model—that is, stronger influences of academic self-concept on achievement than vice versa (Guay, Marsh, & Boivin, 2003). For students aged 14 to 15 years, Ireson and Hallam (2009) documented that math academic self-concept had a greater impact on learning intentions in mathematics than achievement or gender—which also applied to the most able students. The students in the present study were in their first year of secondary education. Decreases in academic self-concept at this point of time—that is, more negative self-evaluations of one's own confidence, effectiveness, and ability, which, in turn, are likely to have negative consequences for achievement, motivational and emotional variables, academic aspirations, or choices—should be taken seriously" (pp. 524-9).

The second study is from Rinn, Plucker, and Stocking (2010): "Self-concept should not be viewed as a means to its own end. There is little credible evidence that boosting self-concept with praise and a lowered level of challenge provides lasting change in a student's intellectual achievement. Indeed, challenge may have a short-term, negative effect on self-concept but a positive long-term effect as a student's confidence slowly increases. In this way, even failure during a challenging task can lead to an enhanced and healthy self-concept within a specific academic area. Emphasizing a student's unique, realistic contribution, rather than praising a hollow intellectual success, can boost self-confidence in a challenging program. Although an unrealistically high academic self-concept is not healthy for gifted students' development, teachers should be aware of opportunities to provide reasonable feedback that will encourage students' positive academic self-concepts and perhaps lead to increased achievement."

2   In any given year, there were about 70 to 80 PEG students. The Mary Baldwin College student population, including the PEGS, was about 800.

3   Bruner, 1960, p. 33

4   Bruner, 1960, p. 13

Chapter 7

1   Noble, Arndt, et al., 1999, p. 77

2   Tannenbaum, 1983

3   Many researchers who study gifted girls have highlighted the importance of mentors, including Fisher, Stafford, Maynard-Reid, and Parkerson (2005), Kerr (1994, 1997), Noble (1987), and Reis (1998).

4   Csikszentmihalyi, Rathunde, and Whalen (1993) discuss the behaviors of teachers whom talented teenagers most appreciate: "What appears to set some teachers apart as motivators—and makes them memorable to their students—is their ability to transcend institutional roles in favor of a more personal approach to teaching" (p. 181).

5   Noble & Drummond, 1992

6   Markus & Nurius, 1986, p. 954

7   Csikszentmihalyi, Rathunde, & Whalen, 1993, p. 247

8   Solomon, 2004, p. x

9   Clark, 2008

10   www.amnesty.org/en/who-we-are

11   Kerr, 1994, p. 231

Chapter 8

1   Noble, Subotnik, & Arnold, 1999

Chapter 9

Chapter 10

1 Excellent resources on gifted children with ADHD include Baum and Owen (2004), Kalbfleisch and Banasiak (2008), Lovecky (2004), and Webb, Amend, Webb, Goerss, Beljan, and Olenchak (2005).

2 Webb, Gore, Amend, & DeVries, 2007, p. xv

3 For further suggestions about compensatory strategies for twice-exceptional college students, see Reis, McGuire, & Neu (2000).

4 Sternberg & Grigorenko, 2002; Sternberg, 2010. Sternberg describes his "augmented theory of successful intelligence," or WICS (wisdom, intelligence, creativity, synthesized).

5 Some people have the same conception as Madison—that giftedness is a "gift" that requires little effort. When children find too many academic tasks too easy in school for too long, they may come to believe this notion. However, most theorists and researchers in the field of gifted education disagree with her viewpoint. Instead, they say that gifted individuals must work hard at tasks that are challenging for them, even in their areas of strength.

Chapter 11

1 Positive psychologist R.A. Emmons has written about the dynamic among personal goals, meaning, and virtue, which he said form the foundation of a positive life. However, it is not enough for an individual to strive for just any goal. Emmons cites researchers who have shown that extrinsic goals, like monetary success, social prestige, and physical beauty are "negatively related to several measures of well-being." In addition, people who focus on such goals display greater amounts of psychological and physical illness. On the other hand, people who "possessed the intrinsic goals of personal growth and community contribution reported higher levels of SWB (subjective well being)" (Emmons, 2003, p. 113). Jessica's social, emotional, and intellectual growth transformed her initial goals of fame and fortune to a focus on others, which led her to a happier, more positive life. She took control of her life and infused it with meaning.

2 Sternberg & Grigorenko, 2002. Sternberg and Grigorenko defined successful intelligence as goal-directed, adaptive behavior. The goals are set by the individual, not by society.

3 Conventional definitions of human strength include the "ways that humans overcome daunting obstacles, triumph over adversity,

and emerge successfully" (Carver & Scheier, 2002, p. 87). Current researchers recognize that "strength is not entirely about victory. It is partly about being overcome, about defeat and what follows from defeat. Strength is partly about holding on, but is also partly about letting go." It encompasses "changes that take place within the self. Strength is inherent in the processes of psychological growth" (Carver & Scheier, 2002, p. 87-88). Jessica did not simply overcome barriers such as stereotypes and misperceptions. She managed and contained them by adapting her behavior to minimize frustration.

4   Deeply grateful for her talents, gifts, opportunities, support, and self-reliance, Jessica expressed a tremendous optimism about her ability to help others. In *The Psychology of Gratitude*, C.M. Shelton discusses a "depth model of gratitude." He writes, "The deepest form of gratitude is an interior depth we experience, which orients us to an acknowledged dependence, out of which flows a profound sense of being gifted" (Shelton, 2004, p. 273). Feeling gifted in that way, therefore, is not the sole province of intellectually gifted individuals because it is a state of mind stemming from gratitude and interdependence. Deep gratitude leads to humility, Shelton said, "just as it nourishes our goodness." As a result, when we feel truly gifted, we become open and engaged "with the world through purposeful actions, to share and increase the very good we have received." With that sensibility, Jessica wanted to give back to society some of the goodness that she had experienced. She wanted to make other people's lives better.

5   Cantor, 2002

Chapter 12

1   "Samyama refers to the flowing of attention, awareness, and energy in meditation that occurs so spontaneously and effortlessly as to be said to be nearly simultaneous. Meditators are not born with the ability to perform samyama (unless they had fortunate past lives), but must coax it gradually like knots out of tangled hair" (Boyd, 1990).

2   Robert Sternberg's theory of wisdom explains how the serenity prayer can give people wisdom from suffering. One component of Sternberg's theory is to balance three responses to situations: 1. adaptation, when a person changes something about herself to fit the environment, 2. shaping, which is changing the environment to

better suit the individual's needs, and 3. selection, when someone leaves her environment because neither adaptation nor shaping will work as a solution anymore. Claire demonstrated wisdom by her ability to adapt, shape, and select her environments. When Claire became unhappy at Sanfore, she took a risk and applied for a new teaching position. She selected Groppen College as a better environment and was happier. Once she became ill, her work accommodations allowed Claire to function as a professor, even if her responsibilities were diminished for a while. Perhaps most importantly, Claire shaped her internal environment to deal with the devastation incurred by illness. She created a more peaceful inner world so that she could enjoy life rather than suffer through greater mental anguish.

3   Haidt, 2006, p. 144. Haidt wrote that although adversity can be debilitating, there are hidden benefits for those who cope with it successfully. The first is that "rising to a challenge reveals your hidden abilities, and seeing these abilities changes your self-concept" (p. 138). Surmounting serious difficulties helps people recognize their inner strength, which strengthens them for the next challenge. "They recover more quickly, in part because they know they can cope" (p. 139). In addition, relationships can deepen as a result of hardship, which is a second benefit. "Adversity strengthens relationships, and it opens people's hearts to one another. We usually feel love and gratitude toward those who cared for us in a time of need" (p. 139). A third benefit is the way adversity "changes priorities and philosophies toward the present and toward other people" (p. 140). Serious illness can be a "wake-up call, a reality check, or a turning point" (p. 141) because sick individuals can no longer take certain aspects of their lives for granted. Haidt contended that suffering is not always only bad: "There is usually some good with the bad, and those who find it have found something precious: a key to moral and spiritual development" (p. 141).

Chapter 13

1   According to http://en.wikipedia.org/wiki/Queer_theory: "Whereas gay/lesbian studies focused its inquiries into 'natural' and 'unnatural' behaviour with respect to homosexual behaviour, queer theory expands its focus to encompass any kind of sexual activity or identity that falls into normative and deviant categories."

2   Harter, 2002, p. 389

Chapter 14

1   "Dada Nights" refers to Dadaism: "Dadaism or Dada is a post-World War I cultural movement in visual art as well as literature (mainly poetry), theatre and graphic design. The movement was, among other things, a protest against the barbarism of the War and what Dadaists believed was an oppressive intellectual rigidity in both art and everyday society; its works were characterized by a deliberate irrationality and the rejection of the prevailing standards of art. It influenced later movements including Surrealism" (www.artinthepicture.com/styles/Dadaism).

2   Bornstein, 2007, p. 1

3   Dees, 2003

4   Bornstein, 2007, p. 94

5   Bornstein, 2007, p. 95

6   Csikszentmihalyi & Nakamura, 2007, p. 64

Epilogue

1   Noble, Childers, & Vaughan, 2008. Researchers of the University of Washington's Early Entrance Program (EEP) found that students and parents also called their program "a place to be celebrated and understood."

References

Arnold, K. (1995). *Lives of promise: What becomes of high school valedictorians*. San Francisco: Jossey-Bass.

Baum, S. M., & Owen, S. V. (2004). *To be gifted and learning disabled*. Mansfield Center, CT: Creative Learning Press.

Benard, B. (2004). *Resiliency: What we have learned*. San Francisco: West Ed.

Boodman, S. G. (2006, May 16). Gifted and tormented. *The Washington Post*. Retrieved from www.washingtonpost.com/wp-dyn/content/article/2006/05/15/AR2006051501103.html

Bornstein, D. (2007). *How to change the world: Social entrepreneurs and the power of new ideas*. New York: Oxford University Press.

Boyd, G. A. (1990). *Samyama: The three foci in the practice of meditation*. Retrieved from www.mudrashram.com/samyama1.html

Bruner, J. (1960). *The process of education*. Cambridge, MA: Harvard University Press.

Cantor, N. (2002). Constructive cognition, personal goals, and the social embedding of personality. In L. Aspinall & U. M. Staudinger (Eds.), *A psychology of human strengths: Fundamental questions and future directions for positive psychology* (pp. 49-60). Washington, DC: American Psychological Association.

Carver, C. S., & Scheier, M. F. (2002). Three human strengths. In L. Aspinall & U. M. Staudinger (Eds.), *A psychology of human strengths: Fundamental questions and future directions for positive psychology* (pp. 87-102). Washington, DC: American Psychological Association.

Chickering, A. W., & Reisser, L. (1993). *Education and identity* (2nd ed.). San Francisco: Jossey-Bass.

Clark, B. (2008). *Growing up gifted* (7th ed.). Upper Saddle River, NJ: Pearson.

Colangelo, N., Assouline, S. G., & Gross, M. U. M. (2004). A nation deceived: How schools hold back America's students. *The Templeton national report on acceleration.* Iowa City, IA: Belin-Blank Center.

Csikszentmihalyi, M., & Nakamura, J. (2007). Creativity and responsibility. In H. Gardner (Ed.), *Responsibility at work: How leading professionals act (or don't act) responsibly* (pp. 64-80). San Francisco: Jossey-Bass.

Csikszentmihalyi, M., Rathunde, K., & Whalen, S. (1993). *Talented teenagers: The roots of success and failure.* New York: Cambridge University Press.

Damon, W., & Gregory, A. (2003). Bringing in a new era in the field of youth development. In R. M. Lerner, F. Jacobs, & D. Wertlieb (Eds.), *Handbook of applied developmental science* (Vol. 1, pp. 407-420). Thousand Oaks, CA: Sage.

Dees, J. G. (2003). *Social entrepreneurship is about innovation and impact, not income.* Retrieved from www.caseatduke.org/articles/1004/corner.htm

Drury, M. (2010). You gotta be determined to get in there: Voices of women higher education technology leaders. *Journal of Women in Educational Leadership, 8*(2), 59-80.

Eagly, A. H., & Carli, L. L. (2007, Sept.). Women and the labyrinth of leadership. *Harvard Business Review.* Retrieved from www.hbsp.harvard.edu/hbsp/hbr/articles/article.jsp?articleID=R0709C&ml_action=get-article&print=true

Emmons, R. A. (2003). Personal goals, life meaning, and virtue: Wellsprings of a positive life. In C. L. M. Keyes & J. Haidt (Eds.), *Flourishing: Positive psychology and the life well lived* (pp. 105-128). Washington, DC: American Psychological Association.

Fisher, T. A., Stafford, M. E., Maynard-Reid, N., & Parkerson, A. (2005). Protective factors for talented and resilient girls. In S. Kurpius, B. Kerr, & A. Harkins (Eds.), *Handbook for counseling girls and women:*

Ten years of gender equity research at Arizona State University (Vol. 1, pp. 351-370). Mesa, AZ: Nueva Science.

Fogarty, E. A., Koehler, J. L., & Renzulli, J. S. (2006). Operation Houndstooth Intervention Theory: Social capital in today's schools. *Gifted Child Today, 29*(1), 14-24.

Ford, D. Y., Grantham, T. C., & Milner, H. R. (2004). Underachievement among gifted African American students: Cultural, social, and psychological considerations. In D. Boothe & J. C. Stanley (Eds.), *In the eyes of the beholder: Critical issues for diversity in gifted education* (pp. 15-31). Waco, TX: Prufrock Press.

Ford, D. Y., Moore, III, J. L., & Milner, R. (2005). Beyond cultureblindness: A model of culture with implications for gifted education. *Roeper Review, 27*(2), 97-103.

Frankl, V. (1984). *Man's search for meaning: An introduction to logotherapy.* Boston: Beacon.

Goertzel, V., Goertzel, M. G., Goertzel, T. G., & Hansen, A. M. W. (2004). *Cradles of eminence: Childhoods of more than four hundred famous men and women* (2nd ed.). Scottsdale, AZ: Great Potential Press.

Gross, M. U. M. (1994). Radical acceleration: Responding to academic and social needs of extremely gifted adolescents. *Journal of Secondary Gifted Education, 5*(4), 27-34.

Gross, M. U. M. (1998). *The "me" behind the mask: Intellectually gifted students and the search for identity.* Retrieved from www.sengifted. org/articles_social/Gross_TheMeBehindTheMask.shtml

Gross, M. U. M. (2003). *Exceptionally gifted children* (2nd ed.). London: Routledge Falmer.

Gross, M. U. M., & Van Vliet, H. E. (2005). Radical acceleration and early entry to college: A review of the research. *Gifted Child Quarterly, 49*(2), 154-171.

Gruber, H. E. (1982). On the hypothesized relation between giftedness and creativity. In D. H. Feldman (Ed.), *Developmental approaches to giftedness and creativity* (pp. 7-29). San Francisco: Jossey-Bass.

Haidt, J. (2006). *The happiness hypothesis: Finding modern truth in ancient wisdom.* New York: Basic Books.

Harter, S. (2002). Authenticity. In C. R. Snyder & S. J. Lopez (Eds.), *Handbook of positive psychology* (pp. 382-394). New York: Oxford University Press.

Kalbfleisch, M. L., & Banasiak, M. (2008). ADHD. In J. A. Plucker & C. M. Callahan (Eds.), *Critical issues and practices in gifted education: What the research says* (pp. 15-30). Waco, TX: Prufrock Press.

Kerr, B. A. (1994). *Smart girls two: A new psychology of girls, women and giftedness.* Scottsdale, AZ: Great Potential Press.

Kerr, B. A. (1997). *Smart girls: A new psychology of girls, women, and giftedness.* Scottsdale, AZ: Great Potential Press.

Kindlon, D. (2006). *Alpha girls: Understanding the new American girl and how she is changing the world.* New York: Rodale.

Lee, S-Y., Olszewski-Kublius, P., Donahue, R., & Weimholt, K. (2007). The effects of a service-learning program on the development of civic attitudes and behaviors among academically talented adolescents. *Journal for the Education of the Gifted, 31*(2), 165-197.

Lovecky, D. V. (1997). Identity development in gifted children: Moral sensitivity and self-concepts of gifted children. *Roeper Review, 20*(2), 90-94.

Lovecky, D. V. (2004). *Different minds: Gifted children with AD/HD, Asperger Syndrome, and other learning deficits.* Philadelphia, PA: Jessica Kingsley.

Markus, H., & Nurius, P. (1986). Possible selves. *American Psychologist, 41*(9), 854-969.

Mason, M. A. (2007, May). *Do babies matter? Closing the baby gap.* Retrieved from www.aps.org/programs/women/workshops/upload/Mason_Mary_Ann_APS_Gender_Equity_Conference.pdf

Mendez, L. M. R., & Crawford, K. M. (2002). Gender-role stereotyping and career aspirations: A comparison of gifted early adolescent boys and girls. *Journal of Secondary Gifted Education, 13*(3), 96-107.

National Association for Gifted Children. (n.d.). *State of the nation in gifted education (2008-2009)*. Washington, DC: Author.

Noble, K. D., Arndt, T., Nicholson, T., Sletten, T., & Zamora, A. (1999). Different strokes: Perceptions of social and emotional development among early college entrants. *Journal of Secondary Gifted Education, 10*(2), 77-84.

Noble, K. D., Childers, S. A., & Vaughan, R. C. (2008). A place to be celebrated and understood: The impact of early university entrance from parents' points of view. *Gifted Child Quarterly, 52*(3), 256-268.

Noble, K. D., & Drummond, J. (1992). But what about the prom? Students' perceptions of early college entrance. *Gifted Child Quarterly, 36*(2), 106-111.

Noble, K. D., & Smyth, R. K. (1995). Keeping their talents alive: Young women's assessment of radical, post-secondary acceleration, *Roeper Review, 18*(1), 49-55.

Noble, K. D., Subotnik, R. F., & Arnold, K. D. (1999). "To thine own self be true": A new model of female talent development. *Gifted Child Quarterly, 43*(4), 140-149.

Pace, D., Witucki, L., & Blumreich, K. (2008). Benefiting female students in science, math, and engineering: The nuts and bolts of establishing a WISE (Women in Science and Engineering) learning community. *NASPA Journal, 45*(3), 373-383.

Peterson, J. S., & Ray, K. E. (2006a). Bullying among the gifted: The subjective experience. *Gifted Child Quarterly, 50*(3), 252-266.

Peterson, J. S., & Ray, K. E. (2006b). Bullying and the gifted: Victims, perpetrators, prevalence, and effects. *Gifted Child Quarterly, 50*(2), 148-164.

Preckel, F., & Brull, M. (2010). The benefit of being a big fish in a big pond: Contrast and assimilation effects on academic self-concept. *Learning and Individual Differences, 20*(5), 522-531.

Reis, S. M. (1998). *Work left undone*. Mansfield Center, CT: Creative Learning Press.

Reis, S. M. (2002). Gifted females in elementary and secondary school. In M. Neihart, S. M. Reis, N. M. Robinson, & S. M. Moon (Eds.), *The social and emotional development of gifted children: What do we know?* (pp. 125-136). Waco, TX: Prufrock Press.

Reis, S. M., Callahan, C. M., & Goldsmith, D. (1996). Attitudes of adolescent gifted girls and boys toward education, achievement, and the future. In K. Arnold, K. D. Noble, & R. F. Subotnik (Eds.), *Remarkable women: Perspectives on female talent development* (pp. 209-224). Cresskill, NJ: Hampton Press.

Reis, S. M., McGuire, J. M., & Neu, T. (2000). Compensation strategies used by high-ability students with learning disabilities who succeed in college. *Gifted Child Quarterly, 44*(2), 123-134.

Renzulli, J. S. (2003). Conception of giftedness and its relationship to the development of social capital. In N. Colangelo & G. A. Davis (Eds.), *Handbook of gifted education* (3rd ed.). Boston: Allyn & Bacon.

Rhodes, C. (1994). Modeling interdependence: Productive parenting for gifted adolescents. *Journal of Secondary Gifted Education, 5*(4), 19-26.

Rinn, A. N., Plucker, J. A., & Stocking, V. B. (2010). *Fostering gifted students' affective development: A look at the impact of academic self-concept.* Retrieved from http: //escholarship.bc.edu/education/tecplus/vol6/iss4/art1

Rivero, L. (n.d.). *Home room: Debunking the myths of home schooling.* Retrieved from www.giftedbooks.com/authorarticles.asp?id=4

Schulman, M. (2002). How we become moral: The sources of moral motivation. In C. R. Snyder & S. J. Lopez (Eds.), *Handbook of positive psychology* (pp. 499-512). New York: Oxford University Press.

Seligman, M. E. P., & Csikszentmihalyi, M. (2000). Positive psychology: An introduction. *American Psychologist, 55*(1), 5-14.

Shelton, C. M. (2004). Gratitude: Considerations from a moral perspective. In R. A. Emmons & M. E. McCullough (Eds.), *The psychology of gratitude* (pp. 259-281). New York: Oxford University Press.

Silverman, L. K. (1999). *Social development or socialization?* Retrieved from www.terra.es/personal/asstib/articulos/social/social3.htm

Snyder, C. R., Rand, K. L., & Sigmon, D. R. (2002). Hope theory: A member of the positive psychology family. In C. R. Snyder & S. J. Lopez (Eds.), *Handbook of positive psychology* (pp. 257-276). New York: Oxford University Press.

Solomon, R. C. (2004). Foreword. In R. A. Emmons & M. E. McCullough (Eds.), *The psychology of gratitude* (pp. v-xi). New York: Oxford University Press.

Sternberg, R. J. (2010). *Assessment of gifted students for identification purposes: New techniques for a new millennium.* Orlando, FL: Elsevier.

Sternberg, R. J., & Grigorenko, E. L. (2002). The theory of successful intelligence as a basis for gifted education. *Gifted Child Quarterly, 46*(4), 265-277.

Tannenbaum, A. (1983). *Gifted children: Psychological and educational perspectives.* New York: MacMillan.

Torrance, P. (1981). Predicting the creativity of elementary school children (1958-80) and the teacher who "made a difference." *Gifted Child Quarterly, 25*(2), 55-62.

VanTassel-Baska, J. (2004, April). Creativity as an elusive factor in giftedness. *Update* (electronic magazine of the School of Education at the College of William and Mary). Retrieved from http://cfge.wm.edu/Gifted%20Educ%20Artices/Creativity.html

Webb, J. T., Amend, E. R., Webb, N. E., Goerss, J., Beljan, P., & Olenchak, F. R. (2005). *Misdiagnosis and dual diagnoses of gifted children and adults: ADHD, bipolar, OCD, Asperger's, depression, and other disorders.* Scottsdale, AZ: Great Potential Press.

Webb, J. T., Gore, J. L., Amend, E. R., & DeVries, A. R. (2007). *A parent's guide to gifted children.* Scottsdale, AZ: Great Potential Press.

Willis, J. A. (2009). *Inspiring middle school minds: Gifted, creative, and challenging.* Scottsdale, AZ: Great Potential Press.

Winner, E. (2003). The origins and ends of giftedness. In R. M. Lerner, F. Jacobs, & D. Wertlieb (Eds.), *Handbook of applied developmental science* (Vol. 1, pp. 81-99). Thousand Oaks, CA: Sage.

About the Authors

Dr. Razel Solow has been the Director of the Center for Gifted Studies and Education at Hunter College, City University of New York (CUNY) since July 2008. She is Program Coordinator for the graduate program in Gifted Education, teaches the Advanced Certificate courses, and partners with the Hunter College Campus Schools (grades K-12) in professional development. She established the Summer Institute for Gifted Education at Hunter in 2009.

The founder and president of School-Wise: Educational Counseling for Schools and Families from 2001 to 2007, Dr. Solow also taught undergraduate and graduate education courses at Mary Baldwin College. From 2004 to 2008, Dr. Solow served as Director of Research, Program for the Exceptionally Gifted (PEG) at the college. She received a grant from the Malone Family Foundation to write this book.

In 1976, Dr. Solow earned her B.A. in English, Magna Cum Laude, from Brandeis University, where she was elected valedictorian. Awarded Phi Beta Kappa in her junior year, she also received the Sachar Scholarship for her studies at the University of Sussex in England. As a Teaching Fellow at Cornell University, Dr. Solow received her M.A.T. in English in 1978. The University of Virginia

Curry School of Education awarded her the Doctoral (Merit) Scholarship in 1995. That same year, she received the John C. Gowan Doctoral Student Award at the National Association for Gifted Children (NAGC) and later served on the founding editorial board of the NAGC parent magazine *Parenting for High Potential.* Her 1995 Roeper Review research article won the President's Award at the Eastern Educational Research Association (EERA) conference.

While completing her doctorate, Dr. Solow taught elementary school at the Peabody School for Intellectually Advanced Students in Charlottesville, Virginia. In 1999, she earned her Ph.D. in Educational Psychology (Gifted) from the University of Virginia. After graduate school, Dr. Solow was Division Coordinator of Gifted and Talented Education in Greene County, Virginia, from 1999 to 2001. Many years earlier, she taught English at Horace Greeley High School in Chappaqua, New York.

 **Dr. Celeste Rhodes** was the Director of Research for the Program for the Exceptionally Gifted (PEG) at Mary Baldwin College in Staunton, Virginia, from 2001 to 2003. Previously, Dr. Rhodes was the Assistant, Associate, Director, and Executive Director of PEG over a 16-year span from 1985 to 2001. She was also Associate Professor of Education at Mary Baldwin from 1996 to 2002 and an adjunct faculty member from 1986 to 1996. Earlier, she was a founding board member and coordinator of the Lock Haven University Summer Enrichment Experience (SEE) in 1984. The residential program was for gifted, creative, and talented teens.

While at Mary Baldwin College, Dr. Rhodes received a grant of almost $200,000 from the Malone Family Foundation, which supported the research for this book. In Spring 2011, the foundation gave PEG a two million dollar scholarship endowment grant for full tuition scholarships for PEG students with serious financial need. Dr. Rhodes co-wrote the grant proposal with Dr. Lydia Petersson, Director of Sponsored Programs and Undergraduate Research. Dr. Rhodes was also instrumentally involved in implementing the 1.25 million dollar PEG development Jessie Ball duPont Foundation grant from 1986 to 1990.

In addition to publishing academic articles in major gifted education journals such as *Roeper Review, Journal for the Education of the Gifted*, and *Journal of Secondary Gifted Education*, Dr. Rhodes published a book chapter and many other articles. In 20 years, she presented more than 100 workshops and papers on creativity, leadership strategies and organization, parenting the gifted, radical acceleration, and gifted education advocacy strategies at numerous national, regional, state, and local conferences across the United States and in Canada.

Educated at the City College of New York, CUNY in art in the early 1960s, Dr. Rhodes earned her B.S., Magna Cum Laude, in Dance Education at the University of Maryland in 1966. In 1972, she got her Master's in Dance Education at Teachers College, Columbia University and received her Ph.D. in Educational Psychology (Gifted) at the University of Virginia in 1996.

The textbook *Exceptional Learners, Introduction to Special Education* (7th ed., 1997), by D. Hallahan and J. Kauffman, one of the most frequently used texts for graduate-level introductory courses in special education, featured Dr. Rhodes in "Success Stories: Special Educators at Work." In 1993, she received the John C. Gowan Graduate Student Award from the National Association for Gifted Children (NAGC). The American Association of University Women (Lock Haven Branch) named her the "Outstanding Woman of 1982."

Parenting/Education

What is it like to be 13 and going to college? Is such radical acceleration helpful or harmful? This book describes 14 highly gifted young women, now in their 30s, who left home to attend college at age 13 to 16, skipping ~~~~~~~~~~~~~~~~~~~~. authors describe what the women were like as young college ~~~~~~~~~~~~~~~ and sense of purposefulness they developed; and their lives 10 ~~~~~~~~~~~~~~~~ book will help educators and parents understand that gifted kids need academic challenge, that there are colleges with specific programs for such students, that it doesn't harm them to leave home early, and that keeping them interested in learning is vitally important.

This book gives a "face" to the robust research on acceleration and the extensive benefits of acceleration for students who are ready and motivated.... For those who are ready, it is not so much a radical acceleration as a radical fit.

Nicholas Colangelo, Ph.D.
Myron and Jacqueline Blank Professor of Gifted Education and Director of the Belin-Blank Center, co-author of *A Nation Deceived: How Schools Hold Back America's Brightest Students*

Razel Solow and Celeste Rhodes spent nearly a decade studying 14 remarkable young women to provide readers with a three-dimensional understanding of what it's like to grow through adolescence with a hunger for academic challenge and for peers who can join them in exploring complex issues—and in giggling and eating pizza.

Carol Ann Tomlinson, Ed.D.
William Clay Parrish, Jr., Professor, University of Virginia

This compelling and beautifully written book provides insight into the power of an early college experience in contributing to the talent development of an amazing group of young women.... [It] will help readers evaluate whether early college entrance is the right choice for the gifted students in their lives.

Linda Brody, Ed.D.
Director, Study of Exceptional Talent, Center for Talented Youth, Johns Hopkins University

Great Potential Press, Inc.
Guiding Gifted Learners
www.giftedbooks.com

ISBN: 978-0-910707-10-7

9 0 0 0 0

9 780910 707107

Cover design: Hutchison-Frey